growing
the church
in the power of the
holy spirit

growing
the church
in the power of the
holy spirit

seven principles of dynamic cooperation

brad long
paul stokes
cindy strickler

ZONDERVAN®

ZONDERVAN.com/
AUTHORTRACKER
follow your favorite authors

ZONDERVAN

Growing the Church in the Power of the Holy Spirit
Copyright © 2009 by Zeb Bradford Long, Paul Stokes, and Cindy Strickler

Requests for information should be addressed to:
Zondervan, *Grand Rapids, Michigan 49530*

Library of Congress Cataloging-in-Publication Data
   Long, Z. Bradford
    Growing the church in the power of the Holy Spirit : seven principles of dynamic
   cooperation /Brad Long, Paul Stokes, and Cindy Strickler.
     p. cm.
   ISBN 978-0-310-29209-8 (softcover)
   1. Church growth—Presbyterian Church. 2. Church growth—Reformed Church. 3. Holy
   Spirit. I. Stokes, Paul, 1964- II. Strickler, Cindy. III. Title
   BV652.25.L66 2009
   254'.5—dc22   2009026491

Interior design by Ben Fetterley

Printed in the United States of America

09 10 11 12 13 14 15 • 25 24 23 22 21 20 19 18 17 16 15 14 13 12 11 10 9 8 7 6 5 4 3 2 1

To the members of the PRMI Dunamis Fellowship International who have served as the "laboratory" in which these dynamic principles of growing the church in the power of the Holy Spirit have been articulated, refined, and implemented.

We thank you, Father, Son, and Holy Spirit, for calling us together into your Dance.

Contents

growing
the church
in the power of the
holy spirit

Chapter 1

The Holy Spirit Growing the Church

Early in 2008 I (Paul) returned home from attending one of the largest annual Christian festivals in Europe, conscious again that we make assumptions about Christian leaders. One of the seminar streams was specifically for those involved with church leadership, and as we considered crucial questions about teamwork and change, we received several reminders of the need to pray and seek the Lord's guidance and wisdom in our decision making—to keep in step with the Spirit. We heard examples of how such guidance had proved vital in particular situations, and yet something was still missing. Nobody addressed the practicalities of "how." We were urged and encouraged but not equipped or enabled. Hidden beneath the words lay the unspoken assumption that we all knew *how* to discern and then cooperate with the Spirit's guidance.

This book is born out of our belief that this assumption is wrong. From our personal experience in a variety of leadership settings, we believe there is a real need for the leaders of Jesus' church to discover more about how we may obey the Bible's instruction to "keep in step with the Spirit" (Gal. 5:25). Our purpose in writing is to help you explore the steps that we can take in that great "dance" of cooperation with the Father, Son, and Holy Spirit. Through this dynamic of cooperation, the Holy Spirit grows the church and expresses the reality of the kingdom of God on earth.

When you became a disciple of Jesus Christ, which took place because of the working of the Holy Spirit, you entered into the new reality of the kingdom of God. You are no longer fully of this earth; you are the beginnings of a new heaven and a new earth. In this new reality, each one of us is called and is given a role and a commission. We are called and enabled to become Jesus' friends and cocreators with God. Our effectiveness in this task depends on us understanding the dance of cooperation with the Father, Son, and Holy Spirit.

Led by the Holy Spirit

In the dark of the night, a light came on. After speculatively feeling their way forward through uncertain territory, groping to find the right route, the way ahead was brilliantly illuminated. At last they could see where they were going!

The small party of travelers had been journeying westward across Galatia and Phrygia, eagerly seeking fresh opportunities to tell people about Jesus. They had looked toward the virgin mission field of Asia, but the route had been clearly blocked off, frustrating their efforts. Persistent in their endeavors, they had turned northward toward Bithynia but again had met with the same "closed door" experience. Shortly afterward a doorway was flung open, the way ahead became clear, and they embarked on a two-day voyage across the Aegean to plant the first church on European soil, in the Roman colony of Philippi.

As Luke recounts this episode, he makes it abundantly clear that the entire venture was overseen and directed by the Holy Spirit. These disciples were first "kept by the Holy Spirit from preaching the word in the province of Asia.... [Then] they tried to enter Bithynia, but the Spirit of Jesus would not allow them to.... [Finally] during the night Paul had a vision...." Luke writes that the following morning, in faith-filled response to this, "after Paul had seen the vision, we got ready at once to leave for Macedonia, concluding that God had called us to preach the gospel to them" (Acts 16:6–10). Their evangelistic travel arrangements were being organized by the Holy Spirit!

Revelation and Cooperation

In the book of Acts, having set the scene with a description of the events of Pentecost, Luke paints a vivid portrayal of the church of Jesus living in dynamic cooperation with the guidance of the Holy Spirit. Similarly, when Paul teaches that Christ "is the head of the body, the church" (Col. 1:18), he is speaking of a reality experienced in his own life, one in which the members (or limbs) of the body receive revelation and instruction from the head and then act in obedient cooperation. These are fundamental principles underlying the activities of the church, and they are the same principles that Jesus himself employed. In his own words: "I tell you the truth, the Son can do nothing by himself; he can do only what he sees his Father doing, because whatever the Father does the Son also does. For the Father loves the Son and shows him all he does" (John 5:19–20). These two principles—revelation and cooperation—are critical components of the reign (or the kingdom) of God. They are made possible by the working of the Holy Spirit.

Henry Blackaby defines the role of leaders in one concise statement: "Spiritual leadership is moving people on to God's agenda." He adds that "only the Holy Spirit can ultimately accomplish the task."[1] In Luke's description of the early church, this is precisely what we see happening. The disciples discern God's agenda as revealed through the Holy Spirit, and then in cooperation with the Spirit, they pour their energies into the task.

Bill Hybels explores these core principles in the arena of personal evangelism as he encourages Christians to "just walk across the room"[2] without depending on a formula or script but simply relying instead on the leading of the Holy Spirit. This is revelation plus cooperation, expressed in the life of an individual. It also needs to be expressed in the context of congregational life and leadership.

All of us who are involved in the leadership of Jesus' church want to see it growing and fulfilling its mission in the world. To achieve this it is often tempting simply to look at some new plan or program, a method that we can apply in the hope that it will enable the church to become vital and growing. Such plans, programs, and initiatives do indeed have a valuable place and have been used greatly by God to accomplish his purposes. Their success, however, rests not in the programs themselves, but in the dynamic of cooperating with the Holy Spirit that happens both in selecting the program initially and then in implementing it. The Holy Spirit is the one who grows the fruit of disciples of Jesus Christ.

In the worldwide church, spanning the centuries and embracing an extraordinary diversity of cultural settings, the dynamics of revelation and cooperation have taken on an astonishing variety of forms and expressions. A persecuted band of Christians gathered as an underground house church in China appears very different from a traditional Anglican congregation in England, a crowded megachurch in Texas, or a rural congregation in Africa. But if each of these is truly Jesus' church, then we can look beyond all the different activities and outward forms and observe some common threads that make each one of these diverse expressions part of the same spiritual reality—the "body of Jesus Christ" on earth.

In each context we discover Jesus Christ working among his people as Prophet, Priest, and King.[3] As Prophet Jesus speaks the Word of God in

---

1. Henry T. Blackaby and Richard Blackaby, *Spiritual Leadership: Moving People on to God's Agenda* (Nashville: Broadman & Holman, 2001), 20–21.

2. Bill Hybels, *Just Walk across the Room* (Grand Rapids: Zondervan, 2006).

3. John Calvin drew attention to this threefold nature of Jesus' work in his *Institutes*. John Calvin, *Institutes of the Christian Religion*, ed. John T. McNeill (Philadelphia: Westminster, 1960), 2.15.1.

power and authority. As Priest he brings forgiveness, healing, cleansing, and reconciliation to his people. As King he advances the kingdom of God, calling men, women, and children to enter it; and he also overturns the kingdom of Satan. It is through the dynamic working of the Holy Spirit that these three aspects of Jesus' ministry become more than simply statements of true doctrine. They become experiential reality in the corporate life of the church.

The Metaphor: Dance of Cooperation

To describe this working of the Holy Spirit that gives our programs their vitality and effectiveness, we will use various images. Here we struggle with language and the limits of our symbols and metaphors when it comes to describing our human relationship with transcendent spiritual reality. We shall talk about this reality and our relationship with it as "the dynamic of cooperation." This phrase captures the personal and dynamic character of this reality.

From the opening of Genesis to the culmination of Revelation, Scripture portrays the Lord's relentless—almost reckless—desire to include people as his coworkers, giving us a genuinely responsible part in the great drama of redemption and transformation. For some this may seem to be a shocking statement. In cultures or Christian traditions that are rigidly hierarchical, or where the church has focused so strongly on the sovereignty of God that our human initiative has been lost or denied, the idea of a dynamic cooperation between God and his people may sound like an alien concept. It may be viewed as offensive or impossible. But in truth it is profoundly biblical and Christian.

Jesus our King calls us to work with him as colleagues. We are made his sons and daughters and are coheirs alongside him (Rom. 8:17). Jesus, the Lord of the whole universe, the eternal Logos made flesh, describes us as friends (John 15:14–15) and is himself our elder brother (Rom. 8:29). Together we are brothers and sisters. All of these terms of endearment point to a profound spiritual reality: we are called as coworkers sharing in dynamic friendship and dominion with the King of the universe as he implements his will among us.

Another way we will talk about this dynamic of cooperation is to use the metaphor of a "dance of cooperation." In the Bible we have images of Miriam leading the Israelites in joyful celebration, of David dancing before the ark of the covenant, and of the Israelites exhorted to worship with dance as well as music (Ex. 15:20; 2 Sam. 6:14; Ps. 149:3). Here is the joyful movement of people toward God and of God toward his people. In speaking of a dance of cooperation, we have in mind particularly the image of ballroom dancing with steps that flow wonderfully together creating the synergy of common movement.

Some years ago I (Paul) began taking ballroom and Latin American dance lessons with my wife, Cynthia. We smile now when we see other beginners taking their first tentative steps in a flat-footed waltz, recognizing that we used to look like that too. But the truth is that we have learned two things over the years. First, we have learned a variety of dance steps that can be linked together, not as a fixed routine, but as a flexible resource. And second, Cynthia has learned to read my nudges so that most of the time she knows what steps to take next. The enjoyable result is that we can manage to dance together for a song, moving in step with one another, avoiding collisions with other dancers, and making good use of the available floor space.

Scripture instructs us to "keep in step with the Spirit" (Gal. 5:25). This is a dynamic process that requires us first of all to be alert to the ways in which the Holy Spirit is moving and then to take steps of our own that are a faith-filled response. In our dance of cooperation with the Spirit, he is the director of the whole process: he calls us into the dance, leads the steps, and directs our movement toward his purposes. At the same time he leaves room for our full, responsive, joyful participation.

If we place too great an emphasis on human freedom and initiative and thereby minimize God's sovereign leadership, we are liable to forget that the Holy Spirit directs the whole dynamic. It would be like the woman trying to lead the dance partnership. Conversely, if we place too great an emphasis on divine sovereignty and therefore minimize the genuine need for cooperative steps on our part, we are liable to forget our own responsibility or to become fatalistic. It would be like the music hall comedy routines where a dancer has a mannequin attached to his shoes and performs the dance while the puppet "partner" plays no active role.

The purpose of this book is to welcome all leaders into a greater knowledge and experiential understanding of the dance steps in this cooperation with the Father, Son, and Holy Spirit. We will look afresh at the basics of working with the Holy Spirit that are portrayed vividly in the book of Acts. In the experience and teaching of the early church recorded there, we find a demonstration of the human steps in this dance of cooperation. These are steps that transcend our different cultures and context. These dance steps provide the foundations for growing the church as the body of Christ in all times and places.

The Two Foundations for
the Dance of Cooperation

In Acts we find that the ability to cooperate with the Spirit requires first of all that certain spiritual foundations are in place. People need to be converted and committed to Jesus Christ, be growing in the fruit of the Spirit and in knowing God, and be welcoming the Spirit's empowering presence and activity. This is true for those in leadership, and it is also true for the congregation as a whole. Without these foundations all of our programs and administrative structures might still point to Jesus Christ, but they will fail to provide the context in which he can work. When these foundations are in place, however, the great dance of cooperating with the Holy Spirit to do the work of Jesus as Prophet, Priest, and King can begin. We refer to this fundamental spiritual necessity for leaders and for congregations as the Two Foundations. Together they create a church culture in which the dance of cooperation with the Father, Son, and Holy Spirit can take place.

We will give special attention to the First Foundation: Leadership which embodies the kingdom of God. This form of spiritual leadership is modeled in Jesus Christ, the Word become flesh, who is the head of his body, the church. Through his teaching and example, we discover how to prepare people for this incarnational role. This foundation must be put in place if the church is to be the fusion of the human and divine that God intends for his work on earth. The Second Foundation is a congregation which likewise embodies the reality of the kingdom of God. We will use the concept of growing to fullness in Christ, reflecting Paul's teaching in Ephesians 4:13. The responsibility for nurturing such a congregation rests in the hands of those in leadership, who need to be able to say to the people: "Follow my example, as I follow the example of Christ" (1 Cor. 11:1).

The Seven Dynamics of Cooperating
with the Holy Spirit

After introducing the Two Foundations, we will then consider in detail what we have identified as the Seven Dynamics of cooperating with the Holy Spirit. These are like dance steps that may be learned and implemented, in which we work with the Holy Spirit and through which Jesus' headship of the church becomes an experienced reality.

Dynamic 1: Divine love drawing us into participation.
This was the starting motivation of Jesus' own ministry, and it opens the door for us to engage in ministry too.

Dynamic 2: Intercessory prayer: inviting God's engagement.
The Holy Spirit prompts us to pray, which opens the door for God to work in our situations, but he then guides and directs us in cooperating with him.

Dynamic 3: Faith clothed in obedience: opening the door to God's activity.
The gift of mountain moving faith opens the door for God to act in our midst.

Dynamic 4: Receiving divine guidance for cooperating with the Holy Spirit.
Individuals and the community engage in the discipline of listening to the leading of the Holy Spirit to learn how to take part in the dance of cooperation.

Dynamic 5: Spiritual discernment: making listening and obedience safe.
Discernment is a theological safety net that enables us to avoid both gullibility and skepticism and, instead, to identify and affirm what is truly from God so that we can step out in obedience.

Dynamic 6: Welcoming the gifts and manifestations of the Holy Spirit.
Since the gifts of the Spirit are the power tools for building the kingdom of God, we need to affirm and clarify their normality, purpose, and practice in the congregation.

Dynamic 7: Seeing and responding to *kairos* moments.
This dynamic involves learning to identify and cooperate with the activity of the Spirit in spiritually pregnant moments and thus go deeper into engagement with the work of God.

These dynamics are simply descriptive of our ways of working with the Holy Spirit. We will explore each in turn and make practical suggestions of how they may be cultivated in the local congregation. We will also explore briefly the ways in which the dance may be blocked, for obstacles to the dance of cooperation do exist in our churches, and we need to take them seriously if we want to see our churches growing in the power of the Holy Spirit.

The Synergy of the Dance

Of course, these dynamics do not normally occur in isolation or in a sequence. Instead, there is a fluid interplay with a tremendous synergy as they combine together, facilitated by the congregation's leadership but made reality by the activity of the Holy Spirit. Human and divine dimensions are intermingled, woven together under the direction of the Holy Spirit and the cooperation of God's people. This is a complex reality, one that evidences Jesus' presence and reign as head of his body, the church, and is expressed through concrete activities and ministries.

Through these dynamics the church as the body of Christ is formed, not as a spiritual ideal, but as an actuality. In this place Jesus Christ is actually experienced as present and at work on earth and in the lives of ordinary human beings as Prophet, Priest, and King.

Implementation in the Congregation

Throughout the book we will consider the practicalities of introducing these dynamics into the life of local congregations, illustrating it from case studies. There are unique advantages when planting new churches, but we will focus especially on the task of transforming the attitudes, understanding, ethos, and practices of existing congregations, for this is the probable context for the majority of the readership. Significant obstacles emerge as one seeks to keep in step with the Spirit, and we will identify some of these so that they may more readily be avoided.

The fresh approach advocated in this book is not about styles of worship or activities. Instead, it is concerned with the practicalities of the more fundamental matter of allowing the Lord to direct the life of his people and his church. As leaders enable their congregations to actively cooperate with the Holy Spirit, the church rightly serves as the vanguard and agent of the kingdom of God.

Our aim, therefore, is to help equip leaders and churches in the practicalities of seeking, discerning, and then acting on the guidance of the Holy Spirit. It is intended as a hands-on road map for intentionally working in cooperation with the Holy Spirit, whose purpose is growing congregations that are effective in advancing the kingdom of God in the world today.

Chapter 2

The Divine-Human Dance of Cooperation

The kingdom of God grows numerically and in its transforming impact when churches learn to join in a divine-human dance of cooperation with the activity of the Holy Spirit. In contrast with this, the fatal mistake is to concentrate merely on the "machinery" of the church while neglecting the vitally essential work of the Holy Spirit. This neglect may happen for a variety of reasons, ranging from misplaced priorities to misinformation, and leaders need to rediscover the fundamental need and genuine joy of living and leading in step with the Spirit.

Congregations Advancing the Kingdom of God

What does it look like when congregations cooperate with the Holy Spirit, allowing the Lord himself to direct the life of his people and his church? The stories of two very different congregations, one in Uganda and the other in England, help us see what the dance of cooperation may look like. And as we reflect on some of the factors that shape our thinking and leadership, we will begin to see how easily we may find ourselves relying on our human wisdom and insight rather than on the guidance and wisdom of the Holy Spirit.

The Church with No Roof (Uganda)

When I (Brad) was guest speaker at an Anglican church in the bush in Uganda, I saw how the dynamic of cooperating with the Holy Spirit is growing the church. Perhaps it was because the lack of humanly built structures made it easier to see clearly the work of God.

The mud bricks were half completed when the money ran out. Banana leaves tied to poles kept the tropical sun from burning our heads but were useless when the rains came. People crammed themselves into the building and spilled out around the edges, a ragged group of men and (mostly) women in their "Sunday best." A good number of unwashed children in rags—mostly AIDS orphans—hovered around the edges. The priest, Kezlon Semanda, a godly man with pastoral charge of this and several other congregations, was on fire with a love for Jesus and for these poor people. As I looked over the crowd, I found a similar love welling up from deep within me too, coming right from the heart of Jesus. I was overwhelmed, feeling a weight for their souls as well as for their desperate physical condition. This love for people and for the Lord is what sets the context for the dance.

The service, while traditional in format, was bursting with joy and power. Great joy and enthusiasm abounded as people declared (in the Bugandan tongue), "With angels and archangels and all the company of heaven, we praise and glorify your holy name...." These were heartfelt confessions of deep vital faith in Jesus Christ. Through Kezlon's ministry I sensed the powerful presence of Jesus speaking and ministering to these people. The Holy Spirit was welcome there, and the priest himself was anointed with the Spirit for that dance of cooperation within a traditional Anglican liturgy.

With Kezlon translating, I preached about the love of Jesus and how he truly is the way of salvation. Unexpectedly, an image flashed into my mind of the places on the floors of their mud-brick huts that had been made empty by children or parents who had died. I knew that I was being invited into the dance of cooperation, that this was a "*kairos* moment"[1] in which the Spirit was preparing to work, but I hesitated on the edge of the dance floor, struggling with my own inability and unworthiness. I was well clothed, wealthy, and healthy from America. What could I possibly say that would have meaning in this context of desperate poverty? In truth there was nothing I could say, but Jesus had a lot to say, and he wanted to say it through me! The image persisted, and I asked, "Lord, is that from you?" "Yes!" He said, "Speak it out and let me work."

As a step of obedient faith, I said that I thought Jesus wanted to tell us something. Kezlon's immediate response was, "Of course Jesus wants to speak to us! He is here! What does he want to say?" So I described the image I had seen, and Kezlon had hardly finished translating before there arose a wailing from the group, and the Holy Spirit fell upon the people in power and in love. For several hours Jesus Christ worked in our midst as Prophet, speaking words of life to the people; as King, calling them to follow him; and as Priest, offering healing from their hurts. We laid hands on people, speaking words from Scripture about Jesus being the resurrection and the

---

1. *Kairos* moments will be described later in the book as the seventh dynamic.

life. We received "words of knowledge" and "words of prophecy," speaking right into their individual circumstances. And as these things took place, the tears of sorrow and despair turned into tears of joy. Through the ministry of the Holy Spirit, and mediated through two ordinary men, Jesus was at work comforting his people with hope and life.

We spent all day with that congregation. The local Anglican lay reader took us to visit the people in their mud-brick homes roofed with banana leaves. Some showed us the places where a child or parent had once slept but now slept with Jesus. It was evident that Jesus was still working among these people, and I was profoundly uplifted by their vital faith and the depth of their love and care for one another amid their wretched existence.

In this roofless Anglican church in the Ugandan bush, the dance of cooperating with the Holy Spirit was taking place and the body of Jesus Christ was growing. The reign of God was noticeably real; the kingdom of God was in their midst. This was evidenced not just in the powerful, Christ-exalting worship, but also in the school supplying basic education for hundreds of children, in the orphanage providing a home to AIDS orphans, in the literacy programs teaching adults how to read, in the sexual morality that was growing among the people and reducing the spread of AIDS, and in the improving sanitation and the health care being offered in the clinic. The prosperity of the village was growing because people were working hard and taking care of one another in Christian love.

This is the kingdom of God, shaping and transforming every dimension of reality. At the heart of it all is the dance with the Holy Spirit making Jesus real in people's hearts and guiding them as they participate in the work he calls them to do.

The Church Bucking the Trend (England)

Since the early 1990s, I (Paul) have been minister of a small United Reformed Church congregation in Plymouth. Like many traditional denominations in England, the URC is struggling with general decline. Yet this congregation, made up of people from every generation and based in a housing suburb of the city, is bucking the trend, and the Holy Spirit has been steadily growing the church over the past decade.

My own call into the gospel ministry came in the midst of a vision of people wandering aimlessly and falling into a burning oblivion over the edge of a cliff. As Jesus gave me a glimpse of their peril, my heart was broken with a love for the lost, and I was burdened with a deep desire to reach out to them with the saving news about Jesus. It is a passion that has motivated my own ministry and has shaped the church I serve. The task of evangelism has been given a high profile in the church's life through the Alpha course,[2] which has become an integral part of the program. Through this a large proportion of the congregation has been introduced to the Holy Spirit in a personal way, and yet the program alone was not enough, as Deborah's story clearly shows.

Deborah had been attending a church for many years before she took part in Alpha, and as the course progressed, she found herself more and more drawn to Jesus. The Holy Spirit was at work in her, nurturing in her a desire for the new life that Jesus gives. Yet she was afraid of being disappointed, and she could not bring herself to take that step of faith by inviting him to enter her life as Lord and Savior. What if "nothing happened"? She could not face the prospect of finding herself rejected by him or perhaps discovering that the Christian faith was unreal. I could have pressed her to make a decision, emphasizing the urgency of acting before it was too late. But pressure might have made her resistant, so I chose to wait patiently, holding her in prayer and allowing time and space for the Lord to continue working. It simply was not yet God's time.

A few months later, one of Deborah's sons declared that he wanted to become a Christian. As I spoke with them both, explaining how we would pray and ask Jesus to come and sit on the throne of his life, I saw tears begin to trickle down Deborah's face. I realized that the Holy Spirit was stirring her heart. This was God's kairos moment as he prepared to bring about a new spiritual birth! This was my invitation to join in with the dance of cooperation with the Spirit, and as a step of obedience, I said, "It's time for you as well, isn't it?" She nodded, and so, gently and simply, I led both of them in the same prayer of commitment to Christ, inviting him to enter their lives as sovereign Lord and as Savior of their souls. Mother and son shared the same spiritual birthday, and over the days that followed, both of them testified to the sense of newness in their lives. For me this was a wonderfully privileged moment, not only because of their salvation, but also because I knew I had been sensitive to the timing and prompting of the Spirit.

On another occasion a small group had gathered as part of our regular prayer meetings. We had no humanly prepared agenda but simply desired that the Lord would guide our praying and show us the issues about which he wanted us to pray. I began the meeting by giving a few guidelines about

2. The Alpha course is a fifteen-session introduction to the Christian faith developed by the Reverend Nicky Gumbel who was then curate of Holy Trinity, Brompton, an Anglican Church in central London. The course is available on DVD, together with full support resources. The website for this ministry is www.alpha.org.

listening to the Spirit and to each other, and then we brought our praises, prayers, and petitions before the throne of God. After a while the prayers ignited in a powerful way, as if someone had put a match to touchpaper![3] We found an intense unity in the focus of our praying, centering on work among children and young families, and on our links with junior schools. One after another the prayers poured forth, each one building on what had just been spoken, or moving on to another facet of the same overall theme. Teachers from the local schools were prayed for by name and with unexpected clarity and authority. Woven through it all was an earnest desire that people should come to faith in Christ. The Holy Spirit was active in our midst, choreographing our prayers in a dynamic dance, and we were joining in!

At various times the Spirit has provided the guidance that has led people to establish a new area of ministry in the life of the church. Hospitality is offered to lonely elderly people on Christmas Day; a holiday club for the elderly provides them with both social and spiritual refreshment. A young mother was prompted to start a group for babies and parents. In each case the Lord placed a loving burden in someone's heart for a particular group of people, provided them with the vision, and invited the church to join in with the work that he was waiting to do. As the church responded in obedient faith, the result has been that a small, suburban English congregation has grown in depth of faith, in fellowship, in numbers, and in effectiveness of outreach to those around us.

What Is the Common Denominator?

These churches look superficially different. One has a long history, material resources, good buildings in the suburbs, and an academically trained minister. The other worships with the richness of ancient Anglican liturgy amid mud bricks and banana leaves, people of poverty whose lives are ravaged by AIDS. But in both cases, separated by different cultures, traditions, and material resources, the same dance of cooperation with the Holy Spirit is taking place. Each is growing in numbers, in depth of Christian fellowship, and in their impact on the world for the sake of the kingdom of God. Jesus Christ is at work in their midst as Prophet, Priest, and King.

This dynamic of cooperating with the Holy Spirit is the common denominator for all churches that are growing in expressing the reality of the kingdom of God. But this is not always the situation in our congregations or in our own leadership roles, and it is important that we ask why not.

---

3. Touchpaper is paper soaked in saltpeter that is lit to set off gunpowder, especially used for the part of a firework that is lit (*Encarta Dictionary,* http://encarta.msn.com/).

The Fatal Error: Neglecting "the Wheel within the Wheel"

Regarding the Church as Being Only a Human Organization

At the end of the 1970s, Richard Hutcheson, a retired navy admiral, was commissioned to conduct an appraisal of the life and structures of the Presbyterian Church in the United States. He observed the following:

> Management techniques are God-given tools, available for the church's use. But far more basic are the God-given characteristics of the church itself—its unique nature as the people of God and its unique gift, the Holy Spirit. The fatal error for the church is to employ management techniques as if it were just another human organization in pursuit of human goals. The fatal error is to focus on oiling the organizational wheel, without attention to the wheel within the wheel, [the Holy Spirit who] is the basic power source.[4]

When this fatal error is committed—as it often seems to be—the organization and program of the church lack genuine spiritual vitality. The church ceases to be the means through which people experience the presence and authority of Jesus Christ as the living, resurrected Lord. As a social organization, it may provide many useful services to humanity. It may contain in its founding documents, creeds, doctrines, and liturgies statements about biblical truth and the saving gospel of Jesus Christ. Its various ministries and work may all be directed toward great goals that are consistent with God's stated purpose for the church. But it is no longer an expression of the kingdom of God on earth. It ceases to be a dynamic, living, growing spiritual entity, an organic fusion of the divine and human that is the body of Jesus Christ. Instead, it becomes merely a human organization, functionally indistinguishable from any other human organization. While it may be full of very busy human beings, it no longer experiences God busily working through them. Lest this sound like critical condemnation, we have to confess that each of us three authors has succumbed to this fatal error in our own leadership in church life and has participated in organizations that were guilty of the mistake.

Early in the new millennium, the United Reformed Church in the United Kingdom faced up to a stark reality of decline. In thirty years its

---

4. Richard G. Hutcheson, *Wheel within the Wheel: Confronting the Management Crisis of the Pluralistic Church* (Atlanta: John Knox, 1979), 155.

membership had fallen by 55 percent. Clearly *something* needed to be done, but it was far less clear *what* needed to be done. A denominational task group was given the commission "urgently and radically to re-think the church's priorities, programs and processes,"[5] but attention focused initially on structural reorganization. The network of committees and councils that had served a much larger denomination was deemed unhelpful and unsustainable for a church that was less than half its original size. Proposals for change were greeted with some very strong reactions as people argued about the usefulness of any specific change. The organizational wheels were being well oiled through the process of structural reorganization. To some it seemed that a process entitled "Catch the Vision" had, in fact, precious little vision to catch hold of.

Yet there was real hope beneath the surface. The task group acknowledged that "God's people are disciples, called to participate in God's mission in their own particular space and time. We detect a yearning for a renewal of spirituality and discipleship at the heart of the church."[6] In turn, this recognition has given birth to a fresh initiative of "Vision for Life," which is "about moving beyond structures to the nitty-gritty of renewing the spiritual life of the United Reformed Church"[7] through a fresh focus on the Bible, prayer, and evangelism. While there is no explicit focus on the person and work of the Holy Spirit in this initiative, nevertheless, prayer and Scripture do provide opportunity for the Spirit to speak into the lives of churches and individuals, and Hutcheson's "fatal error" may actually be avoided.

The United Reformed Church stands at a crossroads, in danger of mere human reorganization yet with the exciting prospect of allowing the Holy Spirit to transform faith and discipleship. In the context of Christian leadership, we face these same issues in almost every area of our ministry: will we focus on human strength and structures, or will we cooperate with the Spirit?

The "Fatal Error": Due to Human Self-Sufficiency

Human sinfulness is a significant factor. Like Adam and Eve, we proudly succumb to the temptation of thinking that we know best. We place our confidence in "self"—in our own wisdom, understanding, experience, and

---

5. Catch the Vision Report to United Reformed Church General Assembly, 2004, http://web.archive.org/web/20070817200548/http://www.urc.org.uk/catch_vision/catch_the_vision_report.html.

6. Ibid.

7. http://vision4life.terapad.com

strength—rather than trusting the Lord's wisdom, guidance, and power. The disciples woke Jesus in a panic, demanding, "Teacher, don't you care if we drown?" and found themselves rebuked for their lack of faith (Mark 4:38–40). We, too, struggle with difficult situations and, then, out of fear and a lack of faith, turn from trusting Jesus Christ and begin trusting what we do know and can control. We place our confidence in our own human management methods and decision-making processes.

This overriding tendency to trust in "self" was something that I (Brad) experienced during a time of extreme financial need. Presbyterian Reformed Ministries International (PRMI) was near the end of a capital campaign, needing to raise $600,000 to purchase twenty-four acres of beautiful mountain land that would be a home for the Community of the Cross.[8] Just a few weeks before the deadline we still lacked $450,000, and I was terrified that the money would not be found. But I also had a long-standing commitment, a mission trip to Uganda that would cost us $25,000 and would also take me out of the final push to raise the funds. I was struggling in the middle of a crisis of faith and obedience, uncertain whether I should go on the mission trip or stay home and call major donors.

The day before I was due to fly, I sat on a bench on a high ridge on the land, filled with despair and fear, bereft of all faith. As I prayed in desperation, my mobile phone rang—I happened to be at the only place on the land where it could pick up a signal. The caller, Reid Henson, was a longstanding friend of PRMI's ministry, and as I shared with him my sense of despair, Reid abruptly asked, "Does Jesus want that land?" "Yes," I replied, "I am convinced that he does." Then Reid, full of mountain-moving faith, said, "Good, I know he does too! So I am praying right now that Jesus will give you the faith to receive all that he will be giving you to obtain it for his kingdom work." As he spoke these words, I felt the Holy Spirit birthing in me the gift of faith to trust that Jesus would provide all that money.

Next came the challenge to act in obedient cooperation. "Are you supposed to go to Uganda in the morning?" he asked. Immediately I felt a fear-filled temptation to step out of the dynamic of cooperation and confessed, "Reid, I am seriously thinking of not going and staying home to call all of our donors over these next two weeks and ask for that money we need to

---

8. Community of the Cross: A Place of Encounter with Jesus Christ for Prayer, Equipping, and Sending. This equipping center is located in the mountains of western North Carolina and is the base for the national and international ministries of Presbyterian Reformed Ministries International. Founded in 2003, we are in the process of building the program and the facilities to enable the program.

buy the land." This was the human way, based on our own wisdom, understanding, experience, and strength, and several people were urging me to do precisely this, convinced that my visit to Uganda would jeopardize the campaign and condemn the project to failure. But then Reid spoke again, moved by the Holy Spirit, and in his words the Lord spoke with clarity and authority to me: "No! You are not called to stay home and raise money for the land. I am calling you to be faithful to me and go to Uganda as my witness. I will raise the money in my own way. Your job is to obey and take my name to the nations." This word came with such power and authority that I knew I had to accept it and cooperate. Obediently I journeyed to Uganda.

The mission trip was an exhilarating experience, with many hundreds of young people coming to faith in Jesus Christ and a powerful outpouring of the Holy Spirit bringing signs, wonders, and healings in our midst. But when I returned to the United States just a week before the deadline, we still lacked $450,000. As we considered writing one last letter, we experienced the miracle of provision. A woman with terminal cancer was settling her estate and wished to make a gift of $250,000. She had heard through someone in her church about the conversions in Uganda and wanted to help purchase the land as a place where people could continue to know Jesus Christ. We had never had contact with this woman before; she had received none of the capital campaign materials. I was stunned! During the remainder of that final week, an avalanche of gifts both large and small flooded our office. Not only were we able to pay the $600,000 in cash, but we also had a significant amount left over for initial improvement work. God had worked in his own way and on his own terms as we acted in obedience. We were partners in the dynamic dance of cooperating with the Holy Spirit.

Whenever I walk on the prayer trails of this land, I know that I am walking on a miracle of provision. If I had disobeyed and stayed at home to raise money, which was the rational human thing to do, this miracle would not have happened. Perhaps the Lord would have shown mercy and graciously provided the money through my efforts because he really wanted to build this place of prayer. But then I would have faced the powerful temptation of pride in my own hardworking wisdom, stealing the glory from God.

In times of extreme need, we are often most tempted to fall back on our own strength rather than submit to God in obedience. Yet this temptation is constantly present within our fallen nature. When praying for healing, the temptation is to fall back on some method or technique rather than cooperating with God and trusting him to work. When preaching, the temptation may be to trust in our own oratorical skills and fail to seek the inspiration, anointing, and guidance of the Holy Spirit. Church councils may be tempted simply to depend on a particular program without first seeking the Lord's guidance. All this is subtle. Before we are even aware of it, our fear or lack of trust that Jesus will work dominates our approach. Instead of working in partnership with God, we become spiritually self-employed, working for ourselves and depending on all of our own human gifts, talents, and resources. We head toward burnout and exhaustion, and over time our efforts do not result in fruit that gives glory to God.

The "Fatal Error": Due to Loving the Bride More Than the Bridegroom

Jesus spoke hard words to the Pharisees on many occasions, including rebuking them for their tendency to "nullify the word of God for the sake of [their] tradition" (Matt. 15:6) by elevating human customs and concerns above the commands of Scripture. It is dangerously easy for leaders of God's people to become more attached to Jesus' church than to Jesus himself, falling in love with the bride rather than with the Bridegroom.

The temptation is not difficult to understand. This human community has been a significant means through which we discovered a living relationship with Jesus Christ. The church's life, people, and activities have become precious to us. We are moved by the majestic words of liturgy; the dynamism of praise songs; and the sense of celebration, intimacy, and adoration in worship. This is the atmosphere and the place in which faith was birthed and nurtured and has grown. We love those saints who have taught us the Scriptures, ministered to our needs, led us in worship, and celebrated the tapestry of life with us. In the graveyards rest our parents and ancestors, family names engraved in stone and rooting us to these sacred places. The committees, councils, and processes of running the church gave concrete expression of our commitment to Christ and of doing his work in the world.

As we look back into the pages of history, our love for the church is strengthened by those saints of old whose leadership and inspiration embodied and ignited the stream or denomination to which we belong. We honor John Calvin's institution of the Reformed tradition, John Knox's leadership for Presbyterians, John Wesley's founding of Methodism. We treasure the heritage of our churches' historic faithfulness to Jesus Christ, recounting the stories of missionaries who were pioneers of the gospel, sacrificing their lives for the sake of reaching the lost.

All these are visible, tangible expressions of Jesus' presence and his sovereignty. Through them the kingdom of God is made manifest. Despite all the heartache and pain that the church sometimes causes, is it any wonder that we nevertheless love this bride of Christ?

But a dangerous transition can subtly shift our understanding and attitude. Gradually these memories, traditions, and activities become the focus of our attention. We worship for worship's sake, organize activities for the sake of busyness, meet together only for the sake of human fellowship, cherish the past, and maintain the status quo. We focus on the activities of the church rather than on the authority of Christ. The church's life becomes nothing more than our human effort and work. Imperceptibly the "fatal error" is committed, and we are left with a wonderful human organization that needs constant oiling and repair but that has lost its vitality and its transcendent kingdom nature.

The love of Jesus Christ is no longer the preeminent love. Instead, we fall in love with the bride of Christ in the institutional form that we have experienced it, and as we do so, the denomination, congregation, or mission organization that we love so much ceases to be the body of Jesus Christ.[9]

The "Fatal Error": Due to Ignorance of the Holy Spirit

A final major reason why pastors and leaders fall into the fatal error of neglecting the "wheel within the wheel" is straightforward ignorance. Perhaps it is even the main reason. We frequently encounter men and women of God involved in leadership as pastors and elders who truly love the church and are committed to Jesus Christ but who simply have not been given any practical understanding of how to cooperate with the Holy Spirit in doing the work of Jesus Christ. In our training and equipping programs for various forms of leadership within the church, this is a topic that seems to receive scant attention. There are hints that this has to do with being faithful to the Word of God and with spending time in prayer, but often we are abandoned to our own devices in working out the practicalities of seeking, discerning, and responding to the Holy Spirit's guidance.

Of course, this has its own trickle-down effect. It is difficult, perhaps impossible, to lead people where we ourselves have not gone. So we find not only church leaders, but entire congregations who have not discovered the Christian life as a dynamic dance in partnership with the Spirit.

In the 1970s I (Brad) trained at Union Seminary in Virginia. At that time this academically excellent evangelical seminary provided me with

---

9. The history of how this has happened to the Presbyterian Church, USA, is well documented by Parker Williamson in *Broken Covenant: Signs of a Shattered Communion* (Lenoir, NC: Reformation Press, 2007).

rigorous teaching in Reformed theology and the works of John Calvin. My Bible professors trained me in exegesis and homiletics; the courses on polity and pastoral care were excellent; and the course on evangelism provided great clarity about the gospel. But at no point did anyone teach us about cooperating with the Holy Spirit. He was mentioned briefly in theology classes as the third person of the Trinity, but we were given no practical instruction regarding him. There was no mention at all about Jesus' promise that the Holy Spirit's gifts and power could equip us for ministry and help us practically in the task of growing the church. No wonder when I got to the parish and later to the mission field, I spent all my time oiling the organizational machinery and seeking to develop the best programs. I knew nothing about the Holy Spirit. It was not long until I burned out and, in despair of my own strength, cried out to God for help.

I (Paul) had a similar experience when I was at Cambridge training for ministry. Classes dealt with pastoral visitation, biblical exegesis, preaching, leading liturgical worship, management skills, and leadership but completely overlooked the role of the Spirit in directing the affairs of the church. During a study module about worship, I wrote an essay discussing the Holy Spirit's role, noting that this subject "appears to be a minority concern" and that the college's "course on the history and theology of Christian worship offers no consideration of this issue."[10] It was a very comprehensive criticism and elicited a revealing response from the examiner: "Were you there for the lectures on the epiclesis?"[11] Here was an implicit acknowledgment that the only teaching we had received about the Spirit's role in worship was focused on the mysteries surrounding the celebration of Holy Communion. If the Spirit had any other role to play, we would have to discover that for ourselves.

Others in leadership will have similar experiences. Many areas of our training received excellent attention in order to prepare us for the crucial task of leading Jesus' church. But with no practical teaching on how to cooperate with the Holy Spirit, we have been underequipped for our role. We have a significant sphere of ignorance, a "spiritual blind spot," because no one has shown us what life in step with the Spirit can look like. Consequently, we avoid or resist the Spirit's activity.

---

10. P. K. Stokes, "Discuss the Role of the Holy Spirit in the Church's Acts of Worship" (unpublished essay, 1992).

11. Epiclesis is that part of the prayer of consecration of the Eucharistic elements (bread and wine) by which the priest invokes the Holy Spirit (http://en.wikipedia.org/wiki/Epiklesis).

I (Cindy) began to see what life in step with the Spirit could look like after a time of physical and spiritual burnout. After graduating from Princeton Theological Seminary, I was called into hospital chaplaincy and worked hard to obtain certification as a Clinical Pastoral Education (CPE) supervisor. Every day I was busy caring for sick and dying people and their families. Several times a year I was also offering CPE classes to groups of seminary students and community clergy working under my direction at the hospital. In addition, my husband, Steve, was consumed with pastoring a Hungarian Reformed congregation, preaching and teaching in both English and Hungarian, while I carried out all the unspoken responsibilities of being the "pastor's wife." On top of all this, I was also a new mother with a young son, David, who refused to sleep through the night. I was a constant caregiver, relentlessly working to keep everything going at the hospital, with my students, and at home with my family. I knew that all this was for God, but somehow he just did not seem to be very present, and he certainly was not much help. I knew nothing about the Holy Spirit except as a part of the creed, which I believed with all my heart. I knew nothing of the dance of cooperation or the power and gifts of the Spirit, only that I was supposed to be busy serving God. Those things were just not part of my education or tradition. I became exhausted emotionally, physically, and spiritually. I was worn down, burned out, and resentful, and I knew I could not do any more. I had reached the end of my rope.

At this time, in February of 1991, my parents offered to send Steve and me to a five-day retreat titled "Gateways to Empowered Ministry," offered by Presbyterian Reformed Ministries International as part of the Dunamis Project.[12] For us, the selling point was that they would keep David. It was only when we were on the highway driving to the event that we read the brochure they had sent us and with horror realized that it was about the Holy Spirit. We nearly turned around straightaway, but the prospect of having time away from the pressures of work as well as from our sleep-resistant toddler proved too attractive. We also figured that we could skip the meetings and just enjoy being together at the beautiful conference center on the shore of Lake George in New York.

---

12. Presbyterian Reformed Ministries International is the ministry founded in 1966 during the Charismatic renewal, which we all have been involved with in various leadership positions. The Dunamis Project is PRMI's equipping course on the person and work of the Holy Spirit. This course consists of six units, each taking place over a five-day intensive equipping workshop. It was founded and the materials written by Brad Long in 1991 and is now offered in multiple locations around the world. For more information, go to www. prmi.org.

God had other plans. In the teaching sessions, we found ourselves in previously undiscovered country, learning about the work of the third person of the Trinity. In Jesus' words, I was "baptized in the Holy Spirit," and a whole new vista of reality opened up to me. I discovered that it was possible for me to cooperate with the Holy Spirit, that I did not have to do all this work on my own. He was present to provide power, authority, guidance, and support. Most of all, while I myself was a loving and caring person by nature, I discovered that Jesus wanted to show his own love and care for people through me, made possible by the Spirit. He was the one who would do the work, and my job was to dance in step with the Spirit, doing this alongside others who were called to share in the fellowship of the Holy Spirit. I was no longer alone in this ministry.

During that Dunamis Project retreat I did not have any special experiences, such as speaking in tongues (though I have since received that particular gift of the Spirit), but when I got back to the hospital, I noticed a freshness in my work. Alongside my human labors there was now a supernatural and spiritual working of God that had not been there before. On one occasion I was ministering to a woman who had a lump on her leg, and she was terrified that it would prove to be cancer. As I was praying for her, I was surprised to have a sense that the Holy Spirit was whispering to me, "Tell her that this is not cancer." I had a tremendous struggle within myself about this. It went against all my CPE training, and I was fearful of giving her false hope born out of my spiritual enthusiasm. But the sense of guidance was persistent, and so I took what felt like a terrible risk and spoke out what I thought the Lord was saying. The change was immediate and visible, as peace came into this frightened woman. It seemed as if she was embraced by the love of Jesus, and she went into the surgery with a deep peace. Indeed, to my own surprise (and the surprise of her doctors!) the lump turned out not to be cancer.

As I reflected on this experience, I understood more clearly about the fusion of the divine and human dimensions in ministry, and I started to learn more about the dynamic of cooperating with the Holy Spirit. Later I would learn that the Bible refers to this sense of guidance as a "word of knowledge" and that it is one of the manifestational gifts of the Holy Spirit. Welcoming the gifts and manifestations of the Spirit is one of the Seven Dynamics of cooperating with the Holy Spirit that we will explore in detail later, but I did not know any of this in 1991. All I knew was that the sovereign God, the Lord of the universe, had called me into a whole new dimension of working with him. I had read about it in the book of Acts but had never experienced it before in my own ministry. Frankly, this was a little overwhelming, but it was also immensely exciting!

Each of us three authors has traveled on a journey of learning and struggling to keep this fusion of the human and divine together. We each have fallen into most of these errors and misunderstandings at various times during our growing in leadership in the church. For each of us the real place where the breakdown began was in our own hearts, whether through sin and trying to be independent, through loving the institution more than Christ, or through ignorance and lack of experience. Similarly the restoration of the fusion of the divine and human also began within our own hearts. Indeed, regaining the dynamic of cooperation with the Holy Spirit begins not "out there" in the general context of the church, but within each of us. It is the inner dynamic of our own submission to Jesus Christ and the practical realization that the Holy Spirit is our helper who truly is present, ready to empower us, guide us, and transform us.

The Promise Is for You

When Peter concluded his Pentecost sermon, he made it clear that the Holy Spirit's dynamic work was not restricted to himself and his colleagues. The promise was good for his audience too. In the same way, we are convinced that the promise still holds for God's people today. Cindy discovered this on the shores of Lake George in New York and then in the wards of the hospital where she works. Brad discovered this in a prayer center in the remote mountains of South Korea and then in context of training retreats around the world. Paul discovered this through a vision on a bicycle ride and then in the daily work of pastoral ministry. The Spirit's power, authority, guidance, support, and compassion can be an experiential reality in our own lives. We believe this is a vital discovery for those who are entrusted with leadership, for they have a crucial role to play in the life of Jesus' church. So the first foundation that we will explore is leadership that embodies the reality of the kingdom of God.

Part 1

The Two Foundations

Chapter 3

Leaders Embodying the Kingdom of God

Leaders mold congregations. The leader's task is to so shape the culture and ethos of the church that it becomes a context in which the dynamic of cooperating with the Holy Spirit of God may take place. Leaders must therefore be living models of what it means to follow Jesus Christ, for only then can they shape the congregation into a dynamic expression of the kingdom of God.

When Jesus Christ set about growing his church, he started with a small core team of people whom he nurtured as leaders. This nucleus of 12 was later expanded to 72 and, at Pentecost, grew to a group of 120. He adopts the same approach today, nurturing people for leadership who then continue this work of growing his church in active partnership with him.

To understand why he does this, we need to appreciate how, from the very beginning, God chose to include us as his friends and coworkers. He created our first parents, Adam and Eve, in his own image, giving them all the gifts and endowments they needed to exercise dominion over the earth on his behalf. The privilege and responsibility of this dominion were ruined by their disobedience and resulted in the corruption of human nature. It also opened the door to demonic entities who capitalize on sinful human nature to thwart the Father's master vision of men and women sharing with him in friendship and partnership as coworkers in his kingdom. We truly are engaged in a struggle against the world, the flesh, and the devil as we labor and pray that his kingdom may be restored.

As a champion in the midst of this struggle, Jesus overcomes the corruption of sin and the schemes of Satan. He restores the original vision. When we are born again, we become a new creation and we enter the renewed reality of the kingdom of God. Here the privileges and responsibilities of dominion are restored, and we are called once again into dynamic cooperation with the Father, Son, and Holy Spirit. This happens initially with a cluster of leaders in whom Jesus has implanted the DNA of his kingdom, people whose own lives are being reshaped according to this spiritual blueprint, and who are called and equipped to shape reality, bringing it in line with the purposes of God as revealed to us in Scripture. Through the influence of their vision, example, and teaching, these leaders form a catalytic community. Around them gathers a growing number of people who are enabled to become active participants in this restored reign of God. The importance of leadership cannot be ignored. It is a critical factor.

Embodiment of Kingdom Reality as the Nature of Christian Leadership

The Holy Spirit will raise up many different forms and expressions of leadership to grow the church. All leaders, whether apostles, evangelists, teachers, prophets, or pastors—and indeed all the giftings of the Holy Spirit—have important parts to play in growing the church. However, common to all leaders who are called to work with Jesus Christ to build the kingdom is the foundational principle of *embodiment*. These are people in whom others can see the incarnate reality of what it means to live and work in friendship and partnership with the living God.

Jesus Christ himself is the best example of the principle of embodiment as the essence of spiritual leadership. The Bible describes him as a *pioneer*, a Greek word that refers to a "prince" or leader, the representative head of a family. The word also means a "trailblazer," one who breaks through to new ground for those who follow him. It is used some thirty-five times in the Greek Old Testament, and it is used four times in the New Testament, where it always refers to Jesus Christ (Acts 3:15; 5:31; Heb. 2:10; 12:2). He is our Pioneer who embodies the reality of the kingdom. He is the "Word [who] became flesh and made his dwelling among us" (John 1:14), and in him we see and know God the Father (14:9). Jesus exercised leadership for his disciples by bringing them into the new reality that was already being expressed in his own life. When Jesus asked the Twelve whether they intended to desert him like those who left because the cost of discipleship seemed too demanding, they chose to stay with him, saying, "To whom shall we go? You have the words of eternal life" (6:68). More than merely *speaking* words of life, Jesus declared, "I *am* the resurrection and the life" (11:25) and "I am the way and the truth and the life. No one comes to the Father except through me" (14:6). He embodies in himself the new reality of the kingdom of God, and as our Leader, he is able to lead others into this new reality.

Jesus compares the kingdom of God to yeast that leavens the whole lump of dough or to a small seed that grows to be a great tree. The kingdom is alive and growing, and this life and growth come first by becoming real in those whom he has called to be the seed for the new reality. Jesus himself, as the new Adam, is the first seed of the kingdom of God. Then, through the pioneering work of Jesus and the ongoing work of the Holy Spirit, the seed of the kingdom is planted in the leaders, who in turn become the seeds that grow the church. What is the nature of Christian leadership that grows the church? It is leadership that *embodies* this new reality.

The First Disciples Embodying in Themselves the Kingdom of God

Jesus' first disciples were able to lead others because the new reality of the kingdom of God was incarnate in their own lives. As they bore witness to Jesus among the nations, declaring and demonstrating his lordship, the practical reality of this kingdom was visible in them.

We see this, for instance, in Peter's leadership on the day of Pentecost. In the midst of an opportunity created by a questioning crowd, Peter seized the moment, stood before them, and explained about Jesus and his fulfillment of Scripture's ancient promises. His message cut through to people's hearts, leading some three thousand of them to repent and become followers of Jesus. The powerful impact of Peter's message was due not only to his faithfulness in proclaiming the Word of God, but also to the equipping from the Spirit that Jesus had promised: "You will receive power when the Holy Spirit comes on you; and you will be my witnesses" (Acts 1:8).

As this embryonic Christian community grew in faith and fellowship, "many wonders and miraculous signs were done by the apostles" (Acts 2:43). They embodied the new reality of the kingdom of God. The church was characterized not only by their devotion to apostolic teaching and by their authentic loving relationships, but also by the awesome deeds that served as signposts pointing to the presence, power, and reign of Jesus Christ in their midst. And so "the Lord added to their number daily those who were being saved" (v. 47).

We see the practical reality of God's kingdom visible in Paul's life too. In his role as a leader of Christ's church, he set himself forth as a living model of what it means to follow Jesus Christ. "Follow my example," he says to the Corinthians, "as I follow the example of Christ" (1 Cor. 11:1). Similarly, when challenged by King Agrippa, Paul's desire was simple: "I pray God that not only you but all who are listening to me today may become what I am, except for these chains" (Acts 26:29). This was not arrogant pride. It should be the invitation issued by every leader: "Look, learn, and live like this!" Paul understood well the nature of leadership in the kingdom of God. The way the Holy Spirit leads others into the new reality of Jesus Christ is by letting them see and experience this reality embodied in the leader who stands before them.

Throughout the church's history, we repeatedly find that those who have been instrumental in growing the church or in establishing new ministries have embodied in themselves that very aspect of the reality of God's reign that they were called to create on earth. The "Rules" of Saint Benedict were first seen in his own life before they brought a fresh, humble godliness into monastic living. Martin Luther championed the principle of justification by faith alone, because that reality had first led to his own salvation. The Reformation principle of *sola scriptura* was embodied in John Calvin as he sought to govern every facet of personal and social life by the Word of God. Hudson Taylor embodied Christ's great commission by going himself to China—the ends of the earth—with the gospel message. Martin Luther King Jr. embodied and campaigned for that kingdom vision in which there is "neither Jew nor Greek, slave nor free, male nor female" (Gal. 3:28). Mother Teresa, caring for the dying, embodied the love of Christ for the lost and suffering and inspired others to do the same.

We see this leadership principle at work in the way that we ourselves were born into the kingdom of God through faith in Jesus. Most of us are Christians today because a particular person embodied the reality of the Christian faith in his or her own life and was used by the Holy Spirit to lead us into the faith. Perhaps it was our childhood Sunday school teacher who not only taught us Bible stories but also embodied Jesus' love toward us. It may have been the youth pastor who gave us time and attention as we struggled through adolescence, and in whom we caught sight of life lived in hope and for a purpose. Maybe it was the friend who was alongside us during times of great need, embodying the love and presence of Jesus Christ and the reality of Christian faith, and speaking timely, God-given words. Or it could have been the pastor who preached on Sundays; not only did we hear the pastor's words and realize that God was speaking to us through his or her sermons, but we also saw in that pastor the transparent heart of a man or woman who loved Jesus and was willing to follow him anywhere.

This is a fundamental need. Those who are called to lead people into the new reality of God's reign need to embody that reign in their own lives. We simply cannot lead others into experiencing the fullness and reality of God's kingdom if we ourselves are not already part of it, experiencing that fullness in our own lives. We can only be ambassadors of that to which we already belong. From the outside, the best we could hope to do is point people toward it, but we would be unable to say with Paul, "Follow my example as I follow the example of Christ."

In our own leadership experience, we have seen that it is critically important that we embody the reign of Christ, because the role of leaders is to shape the culture and ethos of the church so that it becomes a context in which the dynamic of cooperating with the Holy Spirit of God may take place. Since leaders do inevitably shape the culture of the church, the vital question is whether we are shaping that culture into a living expression of the reign of God or an expression of a different agenda. Many will have experienced the pain of merely human priorities that were stamped onto a church by a few powerful personalities, or will have encountered situations in which the politics of denominational leadership drove the agenda of a church's life with little regard for Jesus' own priorities. How much better it is when such leadership power and influence are used to enable the church humbly to seek the Lord's agenda and to cooperate in the work of fulfilling it.

Nurturing a Leadership Team at Montreat Presbyterian Church

This principle of leaders embodying the new reality of God's kingdom and then shaping the culture of the church to do the same can be seen in Pastor Richard White's leadership at Montreat Presbyterian Church in Montreat, North Carolina.[1]

For thirty-three years this congregation was pastored by the Reverend Calvin Theilman, one of those remarkable, old-style pastors who did everything from pastoral care to administration, preaching, and teaching. When the Reverend Richard White succeeded him as pastor, people expected that he would simply follow in Calvin's footsteps of doing everything that Calvin did. But there was a problem: the church had grown! There were now about

---

1. This congregation is located in the unique environment of both Montreat College and the Mountain Retreat Association, a national conference center of the Presbyterian Church in the United States of America. This is the church in which I (Brad) was nurtured in faith. Since 1989 when I returned from the mission field, this has been my home congregation; and while I have not been on the pastoral staff, I have been friends and prayer partner with the pastor, Richard White. This congregation has been the living laboratory where many of the principles in this book have been practically tested.

three hundred active members in the congregation, and it was obvious that Richard could not fulfill all the needs. So the church hired a youth director, an administrator, and a worship pastor. But still Richard remained the pastor and the leader of everything. It was what the congregation expected, and the other leaders, elders, and staff all shared those expectations.

As the workload increased, this model of church leadership proved to be less and less effective, and it was Richard who was the target of the criticism. There was growing dissatisfaction among the leadership and the people. He was criticized for being a terrible administrator, and the elders began to clamor for a CEO pastor who would fix everything. What truly needed to be fixed, however, was not the pastor but the model of leadership that was used. The leaders needed to be formed into a team of which Jesus Christ was the head and in which the Holy Spirit had freedom to lead. In this model the reality of the kingdom of God would be embodied in a team of leaders, each with different gifting, working together in cooperation with the Holy Spirit. This was radically different from a CEO model of ministry, which, in truth, is little more than a modern expression of the pastor directing everything. Richard knew that he had to lead the church to adopt a dynamic new approach, but doing so was extremely difficult. He describes the situation:

> The first problem was in me! I was afraid that if I gave up my authority and made myself a part of the team, I would lose my position. So the first step was a breaking of my own pride, the idea that I could and should do everything. The second problem was that I needed to change not only my own concept of leadership, but also the concept of leadership that was in the minds of the other leaders and of the congregation. This was really hard, but what I did was to go back to the Bible and see the way that teams of leaders embodied the kingdom of God and therefore were able to shape the character of the early church. I pointed to Peter who was indeed the spokesman for the early church, but who was in a team with James and John and others, sharing in ministry together. I pointed to the way Paul spoke of a diversity of gifting all working together to build the body of Jesus Christ. Paul also was no loner in ministry, and while the letters were written by him alone, in actual ministry practice he is normally seen working in teams with others. We see him leading alongside Barnabas or Silas as coworkers [Acts 13:42; 15:40], or with some sort of a team on his travels and in his ministry [Acts 16:6]. And above all there is his emphatic teaching on the variety of gifts, all given by the Spirit, that all need to be working together in a corporate context

to build the church [Rom. 12:4–10; 1 Cor. 12:1–14:33; Eph. 4:11]. Probably this awareness grew out of Paul's very practical and sometimes difficult experience of working in team ministry alongside others.

All of this remained simply an abstract theory until we called an older, more experienced pastor, Bill Solomon, as an executive pastor to join me as an equal in ministry. Pastor Bill had this concept of team ministry not just in his head but also in his heart. First, we had to become a mutually submitted team in which the anointing of the Holy Spirit was shared. The place where we first embodied this team approach was in the Sunday worship. While I was often the preacher, Bill was the one there in coleadership with me, expressing his anointed gifting in prayer and making announcements that nurtured the life of the congregation. Often after I had preached, Bill would step forward to grasp a karios moment and lead the congregation into an appropriate response. Or in my preaching I would pick up on something that he had prayed about in the pastoral prayer. Essentially, in worship I was in up-front leadership, with Bill as a strong backup. These are small things, but in them is the embodiment of the kingdom reality of us sharing in anointed leadership together. It requires that Bill, an older and much more experienced pastor and a powerful preacher in his own right, shares in power and authority alongside me.

At staff meetings and elder meetings, our roles would be reversed. Bill was now the up-front leader, and I was his backup. This required that I give away power and authority—it sounds easy, but I had a real struggle giving these up. It went against all that I had been taught was the role of the "senior" pastor. It also brought to the surface a deep-seated insecurity, a fear that I would no longer have any place in the leadership of the church and indeed would be displaced. It was hard enough having Bill, who was much older and more experienced than me, leading worship. To step aside in the staff and session meetings felt like a major demotion and loss of position. But it was clear that Jesus was commanding me to let go and let him be the leader of this church.

This approach started to affect the rest of the staff. We began to function more and more as a team, and this change started to impact the rest of the congregation. As we embodied the vision of leadership as being a team of anointed leaders, there was a general revitalization of the whole church. Members started more and more to offer their gifting to the work of the church, and the result is a church in which the Reformed principle of the priesthood of all believers is not merely a cherished theological doctrine but is a living reality. A large number of people teach Sunday school; others form intercessory prayer teams; and when someone is sick, not only the elders, but also a number of church members, show up to anoint with oil, pray for healing, and offer comfort. By embodying a model of shared anointed leadership, the leaders have transformed the culture of the congregation and have facilitated a great release of spiritual gifting within the church. As we ourselves have become caught up in the dance of cooperation with the Holy Spirit, the rest of the congregation has also been set free and encouraged to join in the dance. The result is a shift in focus. No longer is it the case that we are working for God, but rather God is working more and more through and among us. We experience the felt presence of Jesus in our worship services, and we are seeing him move in the ministry of bringing people into salvation and into deeper, more faithful witness to him.

All my fears of losing position have not materialized! Instead of losing my place as a leader, I find that I am moving in even greater authority and leadership than before when I had tried to do everything myself. Yet still the leadership team and I face the constant temptation to rein in the anointed working of the Holy Spirit. We are tempted to try to control everything rather than nurturing others and then giving them the freedom and authority to minister in the anointing the Spirit gives them. The issue is one of trusting the people. It is also about trusting the Holy Spirit. As we learn to have that trust, we find that we can release people to work in cooperation with the Holy Spirit rather than grasping for control ourselves. It is by releasing power, and not grasping for it, that this model works. For that trust to be meaningful, the people also need to be filled with the Holy Spirit and to grow in the dance of cooperation.

One wonderful example of this is seen in the life of Diane, a lovely laywoman who has grown greatly in prayer ministry. Diane has been filled with the Holy Spirit and nurtured and equipped for this ministry through the training provided by PRMI. When a need arises, she will call me to say that a particular person needs prayer ministry and that she is forming a team to deal with it. My temptation is that I then want to be involved personally, yet by participating I would be trying to stay in control of the situation and be demonstrating my lack of trust in her! I have had to learn to let go and to trust her.

In these instances of Bill's pastoral ministry and Diane's prayer ministry, together with my own leadership role, we see the importance of anointing, trust, and accountability. We each have roles that are an expression of the Holy Spirit's anointing in our own lives—we are square pegs in square holes. We must trust one another enough to let one another exercise his or her particular gifting, and we must also remain accountable to one another and to the whole church for the manner in which our own ministries are expressed.

Least anyone be tempted to regard Montreat Presbyterian Church as the *perfect* example of a leadership team or to harbor the illusion that building such a team is a static achievement, we need to say that this dynamic team lasted for about a year, and then because of family reasons, Bill was called out of this role. Richard had the difficult job of finding another leader who could share the vision of team ministry and also had the gifts and experiences to complement the team. This is a reminder that putting in place the first and second Foundations as well as the Seven Dynamics is a constant process and an endless challenge for leadership. This will always be the case, because the church is a living system and not an inert mass that will keep its shape once given.

A Lack of Leaders Who Embody the Kingdom Hinders Church Growth

Leadership that embodies the reality of the kingdom of God will, in turn, shape the congregation into a dynamic expression of that kingdom. Such a congregation will be a fusion of the human and divine, because that fusion has been created first in the lives of the leaders. Together the people will be enabled to discern and cooperate with the intentions and activity of the Holy Spirit. Because of this the human aspect of the church's life—the programs, worship, committees, relationships, and everything that is needed to create a human social entity—will indeed work together well and be fruitful in fulfilling its purposes. The church's evangelism program will work, for people will come to Christ. The pastoral care program will work, for people will indeed experience the love and healing presence of Jesus Christ. The preaching and worship programs of the church will work, for the Word of God will be proclaimed with powerful, life-changing effect, and the worship will be "in spirit and in truth." The congregation will experience the work of Jesus as Prophet, Priest, and King in their midst, transforming their own lives and transforming the world.

The key truth is that for these things to happen, leadership is critical. When those entrusted with leading do not embody the kingdom of God in their own lives, cooperation with the Spirit cannot take place. The church ceases to grow, and the congregation becomes merely a well-oiled human organization instead of being the body of Jesus Christ, acting as the vanguard of the kingdom of God in the world. The human structures remain, but they are empty shells, no longer filled with the presence of Jesus Christ.

Let us not be mistaken. Numerical growth may take place that has nothing to do with the growth of Jesus' true church. We must avoid the simplistic conclusion that numerical increase is de facto proof that a congregation is functioning as the body of Christ, expressing the reality of the kingdom of God. Jesus warned that there is a well-populated, broad highway leading to a wide gate, a gate that gives access only to destruction (Matt. 7:13).

Our challenge is how to grow leaders who are able to embody the reality of the kingdom of God and thus grow the church. To this end we find that Jesus Christ has established some very clear guidelines about how such leaders are formed, guidelines that are essential to growing a church that is a true fusion of the human and divine. It is to these guidelines that we turn in the next chapter.

Chapter 4

Jesus' Four Requirements for Growing Leaders Who Will Grow the Church

Leaders have an influential, formative role within Jesus' church. Thus it is vital that they be developed for this work in the four essential areas that Jesus focused on with his first disciples. These four areas are *Incorporation* (being born again into the kingdom of God — John 3); *Information* (a knowledge of the Bible and doctrine — John 16; Luke 24); *Transformation* (the sanctified fruit of a Christlike character — John 15); and *Empowerment* (equipped with the spiritual "tools" for ministry — Acts 1–2). A full balance of all these areas is essential and, since different church traditions are prone to neglect one area or another, we need to acknowledge and redress these omissions in our own situation.

Churches are shaped by their leaders. As we saw in chapter 3, their personality, spirituality, and theology have a powerful influence, molding the character of the congregation and shaping the people's understanding and expectations.

Incorporation

By "incorporation" we refer to Jesus' teaching that people need to be brought into his kingdom, become children in his family. This is a fundamental requirement for any who would exercise leadership.

Conversion of the Clergy

William Haslam, a mid-nineteenth-century preacher in rural England, entered the kingdom of God during a Sunday sermon in 1851. As the preacher posed the Bible's question, "What think ye of Christ?" (Matt. 22:42 KJV), Haslam's eyes were opened to see himself as a Pharisee who had failed to recognize Jesus as the Christ, the Son of God; and the Holy Spirit seized that moment to bring about new birth. What is remarkable about this conversion is that it happened nine years after Haslam was ordained and that he himself was preaching the sermon! The effect of his conversion was so immediately noticeable that a man in the congregation stood and shouted, "The parson is converted!" and cries of "Hallelujah!" resounded through the church. Reverend Haslam was not the only person born again into the kingdom of God that day, and over the following three years, his church, nestled in the tranquil Cornish countryside not far from Truro in the West Country of England, witnessed a revival of Christian faith, weekly conversions, miracles of healing, and an attractive joy that drew others to Jesus.

Haslam's experience is not unique. Martin Luther had been a priest for twelve years before he declared, "Here I felt that I was altogether born again and had entered paradise itself through open gates."[1] Thirteen years after his ordination, John Wesley finally testified: "In the evening I went unwillingly to a society in Aldersgate Street, where one was reading Luther and preface to the Epistle to the Romans. About a quarter to nine, while he was describing the change which God works in the heart through faith in Christ, I felt my heart strangely warmed. I felt I did trust in Christ, Christ alone for salvation, and an assurance was given me that he had taken away my sins, even mine and saved me from the law of sin and death."[2]

Dramatic accounts stir our hearts. But let us not overlook the indispensable factor: to lead people into the kingdom of God, we ourselves need to be part of that kingdom. When Jesus said, "You must be born again" (John 3:7), he was speaking to a man who was already one of the nation's religious leaders.

I (Paul) received a telephone call one day from a local preacher who had a list of songs to give to my wife for her to prepare for the Sunday service. As we talked, she discovered that I was a minister and then asked plainly, "Yes, but are you a Christian? Have you been born again?" Indeed I had and could tell her so, but I am thankful for people like her who are prepared to ask church leaders this most basic question. It is too easy to assume, mistakenly, that everyone in a position of leadership has already been incorporated

---

1. *Luther's Works*, vol. 34, *Career of the Reformer IV* (St. Louis, MO: Concordia, 1960), 336–37. In these pages Luther dates his conversion as being "during that year," which, in the context of his comment, is the year in which the papal commissioner for indulgences, Johann Tetzel, died, namely, 1519.

2. *The Journal of John Wesley* (Kent, UK: STL Productions, Bromley), 64. The Methodist Church of Great Britain also includes the quotation on this page (displayed on October 15, 2008), http://www.methodist.org.uk/index.cfm?fuseaction=opentogod.content&cmid=1611.

into the kingdom of God. This was certainly not true of Haslam, Luther, or Wesley, and neither was it true of a Pharisee named Nicodemus.

Born Again into the Kingdom of God

Nicodemus's conversation with Jesus took place after sundown, initiated by this devout Jewish leader who was walking in darkness but seeking the light, curious to understand better. He had seen a dynamic difference in Jesus' life, teaching, and miracles, and he was convinced that somehow God was at work through the preacher from Nazareth. Nicodemus had caught sight of the kingdom of God and found it magnetic. As he listened to the Teacher, a searchlight illuminated the way ahead: "I tell you the truth," said Jesus, "no one can see the kingdom of God unless he is born again" (John 3:3). He spoke of a kingdom so radically different from the kingdoms of the world that the only way we can be incorporated into it is through the supernatural activity of the Holy Spirit. "Flesh gives birth to flesh, but the Spirit gives birth to spirit. You should not be surprised at my saying, 'You must be born again'" (vv. 6–7).

Unfortunately, the very phrase "born again" is heard by some people as being partisan and divisive, the jargon of a minority group rather than the terminology of the Son of God. Let us be clear that Jesus makes no statement about any particular type of religious experience. In the case of physical childbirth, the key issue is not whether the baby is born naturally or by cesarean section, nor whether the labor is brief or long. What matters is simply that the child is born. Similarly with spiritual birth, what matters is simply that the person has been born anew and is therefore incorporated into the household and kingdom of God.

Jesus emphasizes that this new birth into a living hope (1 Peter 1:3) is made possible only by the Holy Spirit and is centered exclusively in himself. He is the sole source of salvation, declaring unequivocally, "I am the way and the truth and the life. No one comes to the Father except through me" (John 14:6). The life of eternity begins with him, here and now, for "I am the resurrection and the life. He who believes in me will live" (11:25). The route to everlasting security runs uniquely through him, for "I am the gate; whoever enters through me will be saved. He will come in and go out, and find pasture" (10:9). All the signposts point us to Jesus, drawing us into the new reality that he embodies. It is a reality that we, like Nicodemus, may participate in through the agency of the Holy Spirit.

This is the absolute foundation for leadership in the kingdom of God, for unless we have been born again, we cannot embody this new reality of God's sovereign reign. The church is no mere human social organization.

Jesus intends the church to be a peculiar people, a unique fusion of the human and the divine, involving all the facets of a human organization fused with the spiritual reality that is brought about by the Holy Spirit. This dual, intermingled nature of the church is expressed by Paul's reminder that we human beings "have this treasure in jars of clay" (2 Cor. 4:7). If we are to participate in both of these realities and lead the church in doing the same, then we ourselves must be incorporated into them. The need for physical birth is self-evident. Spiritual birth is equally vital.

Clearly, for leaders just as for anyone else, being born again is necessary for their own eternal salvation. But we cannot stop at this point, for there are significant spiritual dangers inherent in appointing men and women to leadership roles who are themselves unconverted.

Dangers When Leaders Are Not Born Again

First, there is the spiritual leadership that such leaders *cannot* give. As Paul points out, "Those who are unspiritual do not receive the gifts of God's Spirit, for they are foolishness to them, and they are unable to understand them because they are spiritually discerned" (1 Cor. 2:14 NRSV). The Holy Spirit equips us with spiritual capabilities and insights that enable us to function as agents of the kingdom of God. But if our eyes are closed to the things of the Spirit, perhaps through ignorance or because we look down on them as something foolish, how can we fulfill this function?

During the Great Awakening that took place in the American colonies in the eighteenth century, Gilbert Tennent preached a sermon titled "The Danger of an Unconverted Ministry."[3] It was an audacious topic for a sermon, as he asked, "Isn't an unconverted minister like a man who would teach others to swim before he has learned it himself, and so is drowned in the act and dies like a fool?" Tennent's question provoked outrage, and he found himself attacked and rejected by an established church that was stung by his comments. In later years he is said to have regretted the tenor of this sermon, but its core challenge remains undeniably relevant. It is a simple, practical observation that those who have not been incorporated into the kingdom of God are not able to lead others to enter that kingdom; neither are they able to teach others how to live as citizens of that kingdom.

---

3. Gilbert Tennent, "The Danger of an Unconverted Ministry" (Soli Deo Gloria, Sermons of the Log College, out of print). The sermon with notes may be found at http://www.sounddoctrine.net/Classic_Sermons/Gilbert%20Tennent/danger_of_unconverted.htm. This site recommends for further reading on the setting for this sermon Archibald Alexander, *The Log College* (Carlisle, PA: Banner of Truth Trust, 1968), 35–37.

The second danger is the nature of leadership that is *actually* provided. Congregations are inevitably shaped to reflect these leaders' own "not-yet-born-again" reality, forming an alternative culture in which the dance of cooperation with the Holy Spirit is either greatly hindered or is stymied all together. Under the influence of such ministry, the things of the Holy Spirit, the supernatural expression of God's reign, and the spiritual nature of the kingdom of God itself, become marginalized and then lost behind the stage dressing of a performance based on an alternative script.

Tragically, the problem of such leadership has plagued the church from its beginnings. The apostle Paul had to deal with such a scenario, referring to these leaders in his letters as false apostles and teachers of false doctrines (2 Cor. 11:13–16; Gal. 2:4; 1 Tim. 1:3–7; 6:3–5). John Calvin believed that the problem of the corrupt Roman Catholic Church was due to having men in leadership who did not themselves belong to Jesus Christ.[4] This is no criticism of the sincerity of personality of the individuals. Such leaders may be well intended, compassionate, dedicated men and women but, not being born again, they have no clue of the spiritual realities woven in the human fabric of the church they serve. Like John Wesley they may be excellent at managing the organizational machinery of the church, have mastered the political or social process, and be able to direct programs. However, they are deaf to the guidance of the Holy Spirit and blind to the working of Jesus Christ in the world and in the hearts of people. To them the church becomes the buildings, the denominational or ecclesiastical structures, the liturgies, committees, and all the complex fabric of the earthen vessel; and by their leadership they cause the people of the church to adopt the same understanding.

Such leaders fundamentally alter the nature of the church so that over time it ceases to be the body of Christ and becomes merely a human organization, no longer consistent with the New Testament reality of the church. The fusion of the human and divine is lost, the congregation is no longer centered on the Word of God and the Son of God, and the dynamic of cooperation with the Holy Spirit is mislaid before it is even found.

Information

By "information" we refer to Jesus' desire that people should know truth, and that this involves both the intellectual knowledge of doctrine and practice

---

4. John Calvin, *Institutes of the Christian Religion*, ed. John T. McNeill (Philadelphia: Westminster, 1960), 2.15.1.

and also the personal knowledge of Jesus himself. This is a fundamental requirement for any who would exercise leadership.

Learning from the Teacher

Jesus strides onto the pages of Scripture proclaiming a message of good news with compelling words. From the uncomfortable challenges of the Sermon on the Mount via the vivid pictures painted in memorable parables, to the uncompromising correction of sin and merciful words of grace, Jesus spoke into people's lives. It is hardly surprising that John's poetical prologue describes Jesus as the *logos* — the Word that was made flesh (John 1:14).

Among all those who heard Jesus teach, a privileged few received private tutoring. For three years the small band of a dozen disciples had the benefit of personal attention as Jesus prepared them for the task of leading a new community of his followers. The faith that they would proclaim was to be built on a right understanding of his teaching and his ways. And so, after teaching the crowds, preaching with power, and ministering in signs and wonders, Jesus met with his little band of those who he had called into his inner circle, hosting a seminar with the Son of God, the greatest teacher in the world. The knowledge that Jesus imparted to his students was of two types: intellectual, academic knowledge and a personal, relational knowledge. Those who would lead his people need first to learn from him and of him.

Intellectual Knowledge — Using Our Heads

At the close of Matthew's gospel, Jesus indicates that the nurture of new Christians includes passing on his teaching so that it becomes the foundation for their living. Wise people hear and then act on his words (Matt. 7:24), not only reading Scripture but also doing what it says (James 1:25). The fledgling church "devoted themselves to the apostles' teaching" (Acts 2:42). It is therefore hardly surprising that those who were tasked with building Jesus' church were expected to know what they believed, as well as passing that knowledge on to others. To aid them in this role, the Holy Spirit would bring to mind the things they needed to know (John 16:13–15).[5]

Jesus himself was thoroughly acquainted with both the content and intent of Scripture, drawing on its teaching during his temptations and also during disputations with the Pharisees. Likewise, Paul exhorted Timothy,

---

5. We understand that the phrase "taking from what is mine and making it known to you" (v. 14) refers both to recollection of past teaching and to receiving further revelation as indicated by the immediate context of the quotation.

"Do your best to present yourself to God as one approved, a workman who does not need to be ashamed and who correctly handles the word of truth" (2 Tim. 2:15). Leaders in Jesus' church need to be informed about their faith. This is head knowledge, an intellectual grasp of truth that comes through time spent in study.

Doctrinal information alone is insufficient, but we should note that Jesus invested the three most important years of his life making sure that his appointed leaders understood the truth. One of the practical consequences is that we have our New Testament available to study, written by people who clearly applied their minds to understanding what Jesus had taught. Sadly it has become fashionable in some church cultures to belittle or dismiss the study of theology, adopting an anti-intellectual approach that boasts, "I haven't been to college, but I've been to Calvary." For the church in Asia and Africa who know well the difficulties of leadership without information and who are crying out for leaders who are well versed in Scripture and theology, this prideful approach is incomprehensible. Leaders do not have this "anti-intellectual luxury." It is not enough simply to stand at the foot of the cross and live, we must also sit at the feet of Christ and learn. Jesus' first disciples did both.

Personal Knowledge — Relating to Jesus

The invitation to discipleship is an invitation to walk through life in the company of Jesus. "Come, follow me," he says, "and I will make you fishers of men" (Mark 1:17). The context for learning is that of a daily, personal, experiential knowledge of Jesus. As they were educated for service, they ate with Jesus and walked, sailed, slept, and picnicked with him. They saw the passion in his heart as he drove corruption out of the temple. They saw the compassion and commitment as he sweat drops of blood in the garden of Gethsemane. They experienced his authority firsthand as, with their own eyes, they saw demons leaving, the lame walking, loaves multiplied, and waters stilled. They saw the empty tomb and watched the resurrected Jesus eat fish while enjoying a cookout on the lakeshore. When they proclaimed Jesus as the way of salvation, the Teacher of truth, the source of abundant life, and the only way to God the Father, these were testimonies born out of personal experience.

Peter and John were imprisoned and interrogated because of their part in healing the lame man at the Gate Beautiful. After Peter explained how this miracle had been wrought in the name of the very Jesus whom their interrogators had crucified, the court was dumbfounded. "When they saw the courage of Peter and John and realized that they were unschooled, ordinary men, they were astonished and they took note that *these men had been with Jesus*" (Acts 4:13, italics ours). Over the previous three years, these disciples had learned from Jesus, not only through the words that he spoke, but also through the priorities, passion, and purity of his living. They had come to know him personally and had learned to walk in his footsteps. This was doctrinal information coupled with a personal knowledge of the Master.

This heart knowledge comes not in the classroom, but in the laboratory of prayer and obedience. It is a knowledge that takes us beyond the mere accumulation of academic data and enriches it by opening our ears to hear God speaking. Through the ministry of the Holy Spirit, our study of Scripture moves into a dynamic encounter with God. He speaks to us in the words of Scripture, sinking them deep into our hearts and directing our lives. We become informed about the Living Word through the text of the written Word, quickened in the context of prayer, and find ourselves knowing the Author himself rather than knowing only his writing.

The Fusion of Head and Heart Knowledge

It is this fusion of head and heart knowledge — the conjunction of knowing facts and knowing a person — that the prophet Jeremiah glimpsed and wrote about:

> "This is the covenant I will make with the house of Israel after that time," declares the LORD. "I will put my law in their minds and write it on their hearts. I will be their God, and they will be my people. No longer will a man teach his neighbor, or a man his brother, saying, 'Know the LORD,' because they will all know me, from the least of them to the greatest," declares the LORD. "For I will forgive their wickedness and will remember their sins no more." (Jer. 31:33–34)

Here we see both a factual awareness of the teachings of God's law and also a personal knowledge of the Lord himself.

What was anticipated under the old covenant became reality under the new, as Jesus Christ poured out the Holy Spirit upon his disciples. Such knowledge is not only possible; it is an essential requirement for leadership. Those who lead the church must have a thorough knowledge of the Scriptures and of Christian doctrine. They must also have a good personal, relational knowledge of the triune God himself. As C. S. Lewis observed, our theology is "an experimental science" in which "Christian brotherhood is, so to speak, the technical equipment for this science — the laboratory outfit."[6] The Father discloses himself to us through the working of the Holy Spirit in the context of living Christian community consisting of born-again brothers and sisters growing together in Jesus Christ.

In practice these two forms of knowledge often become separated, even opposed to each other, and the result is that leaders become unbalanced. At one extreme we may find professors who excel in academic studies, mastering Scripture and doctrine, but with no direct experience of the living God. At best, the result is dead orthodoxy. At worst it may become prideful skepticism that dismisses faith with the familiar question: "Did God *really* say?" (Gen. 3:1, italics ours). At the other extreme, we may find those who have experiential knowledge but no grounding in the Word. The result is often a great enthusiasm marred by flimsy theology. If leaders are to embody the reality of the kingdom of God and shape the culture of the church as a place where cooperating with the Holy Spirit may take place, they need both forms of knowledge fused together in their own lives.

We see this fusion in the life of John Calvin. His *Institutes of the Christian Religion* and his various commentaries are a theological tour de force, displaying an overwhelming breadth and depth of knowledge, synthesized into a clear, systematic expression of Reformed faith. But when we read, for instance, his writings on prayer, we become aware of something richer and deeper lying behind the manuscript. This is Calvin's piety bubbling through, as he thinks and writes out of a firsthand experience and love for God. Beneath his academic writings lie an intimate acquaintance with the majestic power and love of almighty God, and this twofold knowledge—heart and mind—is the root of this Reformed theology.

A similar fusion of head and heart knowledge is characteristic of the teachings of St. Ignatius, founder of the Jesuit order. Alongside his profound erudition in areas of philosophy, Scripture, and the classics, there is also a passion and piety that is caught up in knowing the presence of the living God. Ignatius's spiritual exercises practiced in the context of faith in Jesus Christ and under the guidance of the Holy Spirit lead people into a deep personal encounter with the Lord. Head and heart knowledge merged together are the crux of the Jesuit order and made the order a remarkable movement for advancing the gospel around the world.

My (Brad's) studies at Union Theological Seminary, a well established academic community, introduced me only to intellectual knowledge. The balanced blend of personal and academic knowledge of God did not happen

---

6. C. S. Lewis, *Mere Christianity* (London: Fontana, 1972), 139–40.

until I visited Jesus Abbey and encountered a more complete environment for knowing God. There I found a living, loving, struggling Christian community in which the rigorous and systemic teaching of the Bible and theology took place alongside the ongoing work of faith-filled prayer, all interwoven with the daily tasks of cooking meals and working on various projects required to keep the community going. Above all, it was a fellowship in which the Holy Spirit was welcomed and free to work. Supernatural signs and wonders had a normative place in the daily life of the community in which Jesus healed people, cast out demons, and brought the gift of wisdom to solve life's problems. Here I saw Jesus at work, experienced his presence, learned practical theology about how God was speaking and working, and discovered what my role was in it all. This was like Bonhoeffer's underground seminary, which he wrote about in *Life Together*.[7] Leaders with this union of head and heart knowledge are so essential to the existence of the church that the Holy Spirit has consistently gone to great lengths to create such living laboratories.

Transformation

By "transformation" we refer to Jesus' teaching about the need for personal character and integrity that reflect our status as citizens of God's kingdom and are molded by the Holy Spirit. These are fundamental for any who would exercise leadership.

Carved into the wood of many pulpits are the words "Sir, we would see Jesus." These words are a permanent reminder of a vital truth: people need the chance to notice Christ. This is the case, not only in our words, but also in our living, and we are given a hint of this in Jesus' Sermon on the Mount. Repeatedly he raises the bar, setting standards for life in the kingdom of God that treat the pinnacle of Old Testament morality as a mere baseline from which to start. Lust is on a par with adultery; hatred is tantamount to murder. Materialism, reconciliation, and trustworthiness all receive provocative attention, and good deeds are to be visible to a watching world like beacons drawing others toward Jesus. Personal character and lifestyle are significant, because "by their fruit you will recognize them" (Matt. 7:20).

This emphasis is maintained in the New Testament letters. A Christlike character in which love, joy, peace, patience, and kindness blossom, good-

---

7. Dietrich Bonhoeffer, *Life Together* (New York: Harper & Row, 1954). During the Nazi era, Bonhoeffer and other evangelical pastors who refused to accommodate to the Nazi heresies and control of the church formed an underground seminary for the continued preparation of pastors faithful to Jesus Christ and to orthodox biblical faith.

ness is seen, and faithfulness, gentleness, and self-control are hallmarks is described as the fruit of the Holy Spirit's activity (Gal. 5:22–23). This fruit is the visible evidence that a person has come out of the domain of darkness and into the realm of God's glorious light (1 Peter 2:9). The transformation is wrought by the working of the Spirit, not by our human endeavors; and it is our responsibility to "keep in step with the Spirit" (Gal. 5:25). As Paul wrote about attitudes and practices within Christian worship, he embedded in the heart of that topic a reminder that love is to be paramount (1 Corinthians 13). And love is the theme of the symphony that John's letters play: "Since God so loved us, we also ought to love one another" (1 John 4:11).

When Paul counseled Timothy and Titus about appointing people to leadership roles within the churches, he gave, not a job description, but specifications for the kind of character required.[8] Such people are to be worthy of respect, self-controlled, gentle, able to resist the allure of drunkenness, money, and quarreling. The grace of God at work in our lives "teaches us to say 'No' to ungodliness and worldly passions, and to live self-controlled, upright and godly lives in this present age" (Titus 2:12). What a contrast this was for the Christians of Crete who knew well their population's reputation as "liars, evil brutes, lazy gluttons" (Titus 1:12). If anyone was to be entrusted with leadership responsibilities, their lives would need to be markedly different from the society that surrounded them.

Where does this difference come from? It would be easy to make the mistake of focusing on ethical behavior, as if diligent effort at keeping up outward appearances were what mattered. But faith needs to be more than skin deep. The Pharisees of Jesus' day created catalogs of permissible deeds, and they were reasonably successful at adhering to them. Evangelical Christians could easily follow in their footsteps. But Jesus pointed deeper within, knowing that it is out of the overflow of the heart that the mouth speaks (Luke 6:45), and that God's words and ways need to be embedded into the core of our very being (Jer. 31:33). We need to be a people of transformed character, not merely a people of conformed lifestyle. We need heart surgery.

This surgery takes place, and the character of Christ is created in us, as the Holy Spirit does his work within. God promised: "I will give you a new heart and put a new spirit in you; I will remove from you your heart of stone and give you a heart of flesh. And I will put my Spirit in you and move you to follow my decrees and be careful to keep my laws" (Ezek. 36:26–27). The Spirit's work in the human heart produces a renewed attitude and desire

---

8. The personal characteristics are listed in detail in 1 Timothy 3:1–13 and Titus 1:5–9.

to live the whole of our lives—thoughts, speech, choices, relationships, actions—in a manner that pleases our heavenly Father because it is part of our new spiritual DNA.

This is the process of sanctification in which we become holy just as he who called us is holy (1 Peter 1:15–16). In his passionate and poetic writing, John declares that "whoever lives in love lives in God, and God in him. In this way, love is made complete among us so that we will have confidence on the day of judgment, because *in this world we are like him*" (1 John 4:16–17, italics ours). Paul earnestly desired to see this kind of spiritual renovation in people's lives, writing to the Galatian Christians, "My dear children … I am … in the pains of childbirth until Christ is formed in you" (Gal. 4:19). As a leader of God's people, Paul could also encourage others to follow the example of his own transformed life, emphasizing that "I have been crucified with Christ and I no longer live, but Christ lives in me" (Gal. 2:20). These are words that should be on the lips of all who lead.

Sadly, this has not always been the case, and in recent years the church in the Western world has been rocked by the scandal of unsanctified leadership. But away from the banner headlines and the glare of cameras, the behavior of leaders in local churches remains crucially important. Sharp words, a critical spirit, moral inconsistency, and a general lack of grace all can undermine our credentials. For those outside the church, hypocrisy and lack of integrity on the part of church leaders may provide a good excuse for ignoring even Jesus himself. For those who are part of the church, such issues can destroy their confidence and trust in the leadership and erode relationships. When Paul wrote that a leader "must also have a good reputation with outsiders, so that he will not fall into disgrace and into the devil's trap" (1 Tim. 3:7), he was being spiritually pragmatic. Transformation of character is a fundamental requirement for leaders in Jesus' church.

Empowerment

By "empowerment" we refer to Jesus' intention that his followers should be receiving the power of the Holy Spirit to be his witnesses (Acts 1:1–8). This especially holds true for those who would exercise leadership.

The first leaders of the church were born again, had intellectual and personal knowledge of God, and were being transformed by the inward working of the Holy Spirit so that Jesus Christ could lead through them—incorporation, information, and transformation. Are these not enough? Indeed, many in the church have concluded that these three things are the only requirements for effective leadership. But in faithfulness to Scripture, we must recognize that Jesus adds a fourth aspect, even though it has proved controversial for many traditional and Reformed Christians.

Jesus' final commission to his church is to take the gospel to the ends of the earth; and knowing that this task is impossible in our own strength, Jesus adds the promise of the empowering work of the Holy Spirit. He told the believers at his ascension, "In a few days you will be baptized with the Holy Spirit. . . . You will receive power when the Holy Spirit comes on you; and you will be my witnesses in Jerusalem, and in all Judea and Samaria, and to the ends of the earth" (Acts 1:5, 8). This is a fourth, distinct aspect of the Spirit's work, and it begins with what Jesus refers to as being baptized with the Holy Spirit. The phrase has been the subject of much controversy, but as with "born again," it is one that Jesus himself uses, and therefore it is vital that we give it proper consideration so that we may be clear in our understanding of what he means.

Jesus and the Holy Spirit

Luke's account of Jesus' birth is replete with references to the Holy Spirit.[9] Zechariah, Elizabeth, John, and Simeon are all engaged by the Spirit as the Christmas story is told, but the most profound incident is Mary's pregnancy. Informed that she is to bear a child who will be the Son of the Most High and heir to the throne of King David, her response to the angel's message is bewilderment. "How can this be, since I do not know a man?" (Luke 1:34 NKJV) she asks, in words that echo the fact that Adam "knew" Eve and thus she became pregnant (Gen. 4:1 KJV). As the angel explained, Mary's pregnancy was due to the work of the Holy Spirit as the power of God came over her, and it is this absence of a biological father and the work of the Holy Spirit that leads to the conclusion: "*Therefore* the holy one to be born will be called the Son of God" (Luke 1:35, our italics).[10]

Jeremiah and Ezekiel had prophesied a new era in which the Spirit of God would dwell within, giving a new heart, a personal knowledge of God, and an innate knowledge of his Law (Jer. 31:31; Ezek. 36:25–27). Luke's brief account of Jesus' childhood reveals how these promises became reality in his life. While Mary and Joseph anxiously searched for the missing

---

9. Portions of this and the next section are adapted from the booklet by Paul Stokes, *Mission Enabled*, © 2005 GEAR Publications (Group for Evangelism and Renewal in the United Reformed Church in the United Kingdom) and are used by permission.

10. The NIV has "So . . . ," but we have used the word "therefore" (Gk., *dio*) to help clarify that this is the *reason* why Jesus is to be known as the Son of God.

Messiah, Jesus was at home in the temple, conscious that God was his Abba and revealing his knowledge of the Law as he amazed the teachers with his questions and answers (Luke 2:47). The writer of Hebrews tells how Jesus "learned obedience," was "made perfect," and was "holy, blameless, pure" (Heb. 5:8, 9; 7:26)—a process of maturation accomplished by the Spirit.

From the manner of Jesus' conception, the evidence of his childhood, and the unfolding of his life, it is clear that the Holy Spirit was active in Jesus. It is equally clear that, in becoming man, Jesus relinquished the privileges of divinity. Rather than clinging to them, he emptied himself, taking the nature, likeness, and appearance of a human (Phil. 2:6–11). This was no Clark Kent wearing a thin layer of human clothing, ready to burst forth in a blue spandex Superman outfit. Jesus' humanity was very real. Whatever wondrous works he performed, he did them as an authentic man. He was a human like us. There was no "cheating" involved! But the watershed came at Jesus' baptism. John the Baptist "saw the Spirit come down from heaven as a dove and remain on him" (John 1:32). The other writers provide us with more detail about the baptism, and all describe the fact that the Holy Spirit descended upon Jesus.

The crucially important fact is that only after the Spirit comes upon Jesus for power do we see the healings, deliverance, and empowered preaching. It is this coming upon—his empowerment by the Spirit—that makes the dynamic difference in his ministry.

Throughout the Old Testament era there was a consistent pattern to the Spirit's work. We repeatedly find that the Spirit came upon a person, who then engaged in some form of dynamic activity. Famously, the Spirit fell upon Samson, who then overcame the attacking lion. Later the Spirit fell upon Samson again, and he avenged himself on those who defrauded him (Judg. 14:5–8; 15:14–15). In a similar way, the Spirit fell upon such people as Othniel, Gideon, Saul, and Jehaziel (Judg. 3:10; 6:34; 1 Sam. 10:10–13; 2 Chron. 20:14–15). Looking at all the Old Testament prophets' writings, Peter affirms that their "prophecy never had its origin in the will of man, but men spoke from God as they were carried along by the Holy Spirit" (2 Peter 1:21).

We see the same pattern with Jesus. The Spirit came upon him, and only then was he empowered to act and speak. The notable difference with Jesus is that his empowering is permanent, for the Spirit came down and *remained* upon him (John 1:33). The wondrous works that he performed were possible precisely because the Holy Spirit was upon him, clothing him with power. He who was conceived by the power of the Holy Spirit and who emptied himself to be authentically human, was now clothed with power by the same Holy Spirit to do the works of the kingdom of God. Jesus himself well understood this, and so he pointed out: "If I drive out demons by the Spirit of God, then the kingdom of God has come upon you" (Matt. 12:28). Peter told "how God anointed Jesus of Nazareth with the Holy Spirit and power, and how he went around doing good and healing all who were under the power of the devil, because God was with him" (Acts 10:38).

It is hardly surprising, therefore, that Jesus' final recorded instruction before ascending to his Father's side was: "Do not leave Jerusalem, but wait for the gift my Father promised, which you have heard me speak about. For John baptized with water, but in a few days you will be baptized with the Holy Spirit" (Acts 1:4–5). Jesus knew this had been an essential requirement in fulfilling his own mission. It is equally essential for us in fulfilling the task that he has entrusted to us.

Baptized with the Holy Spirit

Tragically, the church has taken what Jesus said was essential and has made it controversial, a source of conflict, confusion, and hurt. Some have taught that the only evidence (indeed, the *required* evidence) of a person being baptized with the Spirit is for them to speak in tongues, and that such an experience comes only for those who have been fully sanctified.[11] It is an approach that emerged from within the Pentecostal Holiness movement after the great outpouring of 1906. Their doctrines required instantaneous, entire sanctification as a precondition for receiving this baptism. This precondition goes beyond the requirements of Scripture and turns baptism with the Holy Spirit into a reward for morally superior Christians. Sanctification is a lifelong process completed only at the resurrection; and in the meantime, confession of sin and walking in the light are certainly important preconditions for being clothed with power by the Holy Spirit. But "entire sanctification" is not a biblical prerequisite.

Another doctrine that complicates the issue further is the teaching that speaking in tongues is the definitive "initial evidence" of being baptized with the Holy Spirit. This is contrary to the biblical evidence, for while some did and do indeed manifest the gift of tongues when they first experience the Holy Spirit falling upon them, there are actually many diverse manifestations, ranging from no immediately visible sign to such things as speaking

---

11. David Petts, *The Holy Spirit: An Introduction* (Mattersey, UK: Mattersey Hall Bible College, 1998), 70–77. Dr. Petts was chairman of the board of directors of the Assemblies of God for more than twenty years.

prophecy, praising God, or engaging in evangelism.[12] The only universal biblical evidence that one has been filled with the Holy Spirit is that one becomes a more effective witness to Jesus Christ, the very purpose for which this promise is made: "You will receive power when the Holy Spirit comes on you; and you will be my witnesses" (Acts 1:8).

Pentecostal churches throughout the world have had a fresh vitality in worship and phenomenal fruitfulness in evangelism and extending the kingdom of God. We thank God for them and have no intention to denigrate part of the bride of Christ. But this specific aspect of their teaching about being baptized with the Holy Spirit has proved pastorally unhelpful for many Christians whose experience did not fit into the prescribed pattern, and we believe the teaching is biblically incomplete.

Shortly before the Pentecostal Holiness movement emerged, R. A. Torrey was called by the famous evangelist D. L. Moody to be superintendent of the Bible Institute of Chicago. A Congregational minister and excellent Bible teacher, Torrey was an effective evangelist in the United States and England, and each day he would read the New Testament in Greek and the Old Testament in Hebrew. Yet this intellectual giant and great man of God recognized his need for more than mere intellect.

> I had been a minister for some years before I came to the place where I saw that I had no right to preach until I was definitely baptized with the Holy Ghost. I went to a business friend of mine and said to him in private, "I am never going to enter my pulpit again until I have been baptized with the Holy Spirit and know it, or until God in some way tells me to go." Then just as far as I could, I shut myself up alone in my study and spent the time continually on my knees asking God to baptize me with the Holy Spirit.

Then later that week:

> It was a very quiet moment, one of the most quiet moments I ever knew; indeed, I think one reason I had to wait so long was because it took that long before my soul could get quiet before God. Then God simply said to me, not in any audible voice, but in my heart, "It's yours. Now go and preach." I went and preached, and I have been a new minister from that day to this.[13]

---

12. For examples, see Acts 2:1–4; 8:14–24; 9:10–22; 10:44–48; 19:6.
13. R. A. Torrey, *The Holy Spirit: Who He Is and What He Does* (Old Tappan, NJ: Revell, 1927), 198–99.

Torrey's experience helpfully illustrates that the baptism with the Holy Spirit is not about any particular emotional experience or any specific spiritual gift, but it did involve a genuine change in spiritual reality that began a new era in his ministry. Furthermore, he had to do the very thing that Jesus commanded his disciples: he had to wait, humbly acknowledging the fact that without the empowering of the Spirit he was simply not equipped to do the work to which God called him.

The heart of being baptized with the Holy Spirit is allowing ourselves to be immersed into the enabling, empowering activity of the Spirit. And this baptism is an integral aspect of life within the new spiritual reality that Jesus called the kingdom of God. Far from being a divisive doctrine, it is offered as the birthright of every Christian and is essential equipping for those who exercise leadership, for it is the only way that we can fulfill the mission that has been given to us. Spirit baptism is a shift away from our own efforts of leading or of working for God or for some other great cause and, instead, letting the Holy Spirit lead us as active partners in the dynamic dance of cooperation with three persons of the Trinity.

Baptized in the Holy Spirit

My (Paul's) initiation into the activity of the Holy Spirit came two years after I was converted. I was in my first year at university studying civil engineering, and I was living away from home for six months while I gained experience working on a construction site. I was a stranger in a strange town, and when my work was over for the day, I had time and space to pause, read, reflect, and pray. It was my own — slightly unusual — spiritual retreat. It took me the best part of those six months to read very slowly and thoughtfully through David Watson's book *Discipleship*, and as a fairly young Christian, I was being faced with the challenges of what it means to live as a wholehearted follower of Jesus Christ.

God met with me one evening while I was cycling back to my flat from the construction site. The Holy Spirit opened my spiritual eyes and over-whelmed me with a vision of the desperate state of those who are not yet Christians. I saw great crowds of people walking thoughtlessly past Jesus, across a hilltop and over the edge of a cliff, falling into the flaming chasm below. As I looked, the Spirit gave me a small taste of the Father's sorrow for those who ignore his Son. My heart was broken for those people, and I wept freely while trying to cycle safely.

Later that day I poured out my prayer in writing: "They don't know who they're rejecting.... I want to share you with them. Can't we stop them?

Can't we run a little faster, try a little harder to catch up with them before it's too late? I feel so futile, useless, unable to move before they fall. I want to help. I want to save them all. Do they have to die? Do they have to burn? Is there nothing I can do?" Toward the end of my writing, I had a sense that the Lord was also speaking to me, and I put those words on paper as well. One part reads, "Be brave, love truth, and I will help you win them."

Peter quoted Joel's prophecy: "God says, I will pour out my Spirit on all people. Your sons and daughters will prophesy, your young men will see visions, your old men will dream dreams" (Acts 2:17). This was my own experience as Jesus Christ baptized me with the Holy Spirit. The vision that I saw and the prophetic words God spoke into my life were an invitation to join in the dance of cooperation with the Spirit and play my part in the work that he purposed. Shortly afterward I began the interviewing process for training as a minister, taking practical steps of faith and obedience in response to the Lord's invitation. While the experience of being baptized in the Holy Spirit involved vision and prophecy, the key evidence of that baptism is that I am now playing my particular part in the church's mission of bearing witness to Christ in the world.

Please do not take my own vivid experience as normative. Each person's experience is different, as R. A. Torrey's example proves. Many simply ask for the baptism with the Spirit in the name of Jesus and quietly receive in faith. But they know that they have definitely been baptized, because as they obey the leading of the Holy Spirit, they can look back and see how God has been at work through them.

An Urgent Need

We have identified four key areas of Christian discipleship that are basic requirements for leaders who would join in the dance of cooperation with the Holy Spirit. All of us who lead in Jesus' church should profitably ask ourselves these questions about key requirements:

Have I been born again?
Am I growing in both intellectual and personal knowledge of God the Father, Son, and Holy Spirit?
Is Christ being formed in me?
Have I been baptized with the Holy Spirit?

If any of these cannot receive a clear "Yes" answer, we urgently need to take action, for they are fundamental factors in growing the church in the power of the Holy Spirit.

Chapter 5

Receiving the Empowerment
of the Holy Spirit

The leader's need for empowerment, in which we are equipped with the spiritual "tools" for ministry, is an oft-neglected area of preparation, leaving us ill-equipped for our task. Thus it is vital that we seek to be baptized with the Holy Spirit and continue to ask for and welcome his anointing throughout the course of our work.

In fact, the need to be baptized with the Holy Spirit is so vital that Jesus confined his disciples to Jerusalem until they had received this gift. Their mission field was the world, and they faced determined opposition from the same forces that had murdered Jesus. Taking the gospel to the world was a daunting, seemingly impossible task, and God's agenda for the believers was one of prayerful waiting rather than zealous working. The time for work would come, but first they needed to receive the spiritual equipping that would see them and future generations all doing the same things that Jesus himself had done — calling people into God's kingdom, driving out the forces of evil, bringing hope and healing, and witnessing the manifest presence of God in the midst of mundane life. Being equipped in this manner was a priority need. It is foolish and usually disastrous for untrained, unequipped solders to be sent into battle. It is equally foolish for the church to commission its missionaries or to ordain its pastors and elders without first ensuring that they receive the full equipping that Jesus Christ said they would need.

When my wife, Laura, and I (Brad) went to Korea as missionaries of the Presbyterian Church, we were expected to have all sorts of training. Alongside our seminary work, we also had studies in cross-cultural missions, a special eight-week "missionary orientation" program, and opportunity to learn the local language. But at no stage during our preparation was there any teaching, or even an expectation, that we should pray for and receive the empowering of the Holy Spirit. We were sent to Korea without having that essential equipping for missionary work.

The same is true for most people who serve as leaders in traditional churches, and the result is that many have failed in ministry. Leaders have been wounded or even destroyed in spiritual warfare because they faced it without proper spiritual equipping. Ineffectiveness and near fruitlessness are the consequences of a profound failure in theological education; this one basic aspect that has been provided for by Jesus Christ is inexcusably omitted. For this omission the church has paid a terrible cost. As a result of sending out leaders who are unable to take part in the dance of cooperation with the Spirit, we have a lack of growing congregations and a legion of burned out, wounded leaders.

The obvious solution to this problem is for leaders to avail themselves of Jesus' invitation and to claim his promise. As we learned from the examples in chapter 4, the baptism with the Holy Spirit is not to be approached in a programmatic manner. While R. A. Torrey was baptized with the Spirit after intentionally seeking the gift, Paul was simply caught up by God's unexpected, sovereign initiative. Moreover, their personal experiences were very different. By providing a series of practical steps for asking for—and receiving—the baptism with the Holy Spirit, we are not in any way suggesting that this is a mechanical process with a preprogrammed result. Nevertheless, we are persuaded that it is perfectly appropriate for Christians to come before the Lord and seek from him the fullness of what he has promised, patiently and persistently waiting upon him to grant our request. Unlike the first disciples, we do not need to wait until the day of Pentecost, but we certainly may join in their approach of prayerful waiting. The steps that follow—

1. Thirst for "more"
2. Expect God to give
3. Repent of sin
4. Ask the Father
5. Receive in faith
6. Obey the Holy Spirit

—are offered as a helpful guide for placing ourselves under a waterfall of God's grace as he baptizes us with his Holy Spirit.

1. Thirst for "More"

As the Jewish Feast of Tabernacles reached its climax with a dramatized focus on Ezekiel's vision of a river flowing out from the temple altar, Jesus commanded the crowd's attention and offered the living water of the Holy Spirit. He extended an invitation to all who were thirsting and promised that they would find refreshment. Thirst is what leads us to Jesus Christ so that we may receive the Holy Spirit. "'If anyone is thirsty, let him come to me and drink. Whoever believes in me, as the Scripture has said, streams of living water will flow from within him.' By this he meant the Spirit, whom those who believed in him were later to receive" (John 7:37–39).

This thirst is, first of all, for God himself. It is a deep yearning for him who satisfies our deepest need. David describes this in a psalm: "O God, you are my God, earnestly I seek you; my soul thirsts for you, my body longs for you, in a dry and weary land where there is no water" (Ps. 63:1). But it is also a thirst that arises out of a profound awareness of our own inadequacy, as we appreciate our utter inability to do the works of God in our own strength and realize that Jesus accurately describes our condition when he says, "Apart from me you can do nothing" (John 15:5). Being baptized with the Holy Spirit begins with recognizing our need and earnestly desiring whatever our heavenly Father is pleased to give.

My (Brad's) own experience of being baptized with the Holy Spirit began in a most unpromising manner. During my time at Davidson College and at Union Theological Seminary, I had a series of very bad experiences with people involved in the charismatic renewal, and these caused me to reject the whole movement. From seminary, Laura and I went to Korea in 1975 as missionaries of the Presbyterian Church (USA). For me this was a "homecoming," because I had spent my high school years there. We taught in the Presbyterian seminary in Seoul and saw the powerful prayer and dynamic moving of the gospel in the Korean church and in the lives of missionaries. But we ourselves were overwhelmed by our own inability to do this mission work to which we were called. Despite all our excellent theological education, we found ourselves embarrassingly powerless to witness to Jesus Christ.

We grew very hungry and thirsty for more power, more love, and more of Jesus. This thirst led us back to my roots at Jesus Abbey where I had often spent time with the Archer Torrey family starting in 1966. Finally, after a considerable period of extended study seeking answers to my theological questions, and with this hunger driving my prayers in preparation, I asked Archer and others at Jesus Abbey to lay hands on me. As they did, the Holy Spirit came upon me in a great torrent of love and power. I was caught up in ecstasy in the presence of Jesus Christ. With my spiritual eyes wide open, I saw him standing before me in resurrected glory calling me to follow him and to be his witness. As he called me, he then immersed me in the presence of the Holy Spirit. I was so caught up in worship and praise that I found myself speaking prophetically, speaking in tongues, and giving glory to God.

That encounter marked the beginning of my being able to be part of the dance of cooperation with Jesus. I started to experience the gifts of the Holy Spirit and found that the Holy Spirit would fall upon me again and again whenever I was seeking to follow Jesus Christ. Now, thirty-three years later, I look back and am astonished that through the power of the Holy Spirit, much of what Jesus called me into during that night in 1975 in Korea has become fulfilled reality.

2. Expect God to Give

Asian technology has become famous for miniaturization, fitting increasingly complex components into ever smaller packages. Today's laptop computers are massively more powerful than the roomful of machines that controlled the Apollo moon landing program. The adjectives *mini*, *micro*, and *nano* have been integrated into our vocabulary, and it seems that as our gadgets grow smaller, so too does our understanding of God. We have constrained him to fit within our own lack of knowledge and limited worldview, tamed him because of our fears, and conditioned ourselves to expect little.

But the God of the Bible is big. Job was invited to "stop and consider God's wonders," (Job 37:14) to recognize the awesome majesty of the Almighty who is "beyond our reach and exalted in power" (v. 23). His hand cast stars into space, and he calls the constellations by name (9:9: Amos 5:8), yet he is mindful of us mere mortals (Ps. 8:4) and numbers the hairs on our heads (Luke 12:7). He is an amazing God, joyfully celebrated in Dr. Shadrach Lockridge's glorious declaration, "My King is a sovereign King—no means of measure can define His limitless love. No farseeing telescope can bring into visibility the coastline of His shoreless supply. No barrier can hinder Him from pouring out His blessings."[1]

This is the God upon whom Paul invites us to focus our attention: "Now to *him who is able to do immeasurably more than all we ask or imagine*, accord-

---

1. Transcribed from an audio recording of "My King" by Dr. S. M. Lockridge, widely available for download from the Internet. See, for example, http://www.youtube.com/watch?v=yX_7j32zgNw.

ing to his power that is at work within us, to him be glory in the church and in Christ Jesus throughout all generations, for ever and ever! Amen" (Eph. 3:20, italics ours).

As we seek to be baptized with the Holy Spirit, we may come before the Lord with an expectant heart, assured that He is willing and capable, ready to "throw open the floodgates of heaven and pour out so much blessing that you will not have room enough for it" (Mal. 3:10).

3. Repent of Sin

Peter urged the Pentecost crowd, "Repent and be baptized, every one of you, in the name of Jesus Christ for the forgiveness of your sins. And you will receive the gift of the Holy Spirit" (Acts 2:38). This free gift of God's grace is promised for even the newest convert to Christ, so clearly we do not need to be "perfect" or to have reached a high level of sanctification before the Spirit will come upon us. There is no precondition of "entire sanctification" for which we are then rewarded. Rather, the promise is valid from the very outset of the Christian life.

But because sin blocks our relationship with God, repentance is therefore a basic criterion for spiritual growth, including the growth of being baptized with the Holy Spirit so that we may be empowered to do the same works that Jesus did. The Greek word for repentance — *metanoia* — speaks of an "inward change of mind, affections, convictions, and commitment [that is] rooted in the fear of God and sorrow for offenses committed against him."[2] This is the kind of repentance that took place in Peter after he denied Jesus. In the bitter tears that he shed immediately, and in the conversation after breakfast on a beach, we see him recognize his sin, affirm his love toward Jesus, and then receive a fresh commissioning from the Master (John 21:15–19).

Repentance opens the door to the Holy Spirit. He is, after all, a *holy* Spirit, and if we would enjoy his presence and power at work in our lives, sin has no place in us. R. A. Torrey helpfully counseled, "If anyone sincerely desires the baptism with the Holy Spirit, he should go alone with God and ask God to search him and bring to light anything in his heart or life that is displeasing to Him."[3] What is brought to the light may then be dealt with through confession and repentance, in the assurance that "if we claim to be

---

2. *Evangelical Dictionary of Theology*, ed. Walter A. Elwell (Basingstoke, UK: Marshall Pickering, 1985), 936.
3. R. A. Torrey, *Power-Filled Living* (New Kensington, PA: Whitaker House, 1998), 239.

without sin, we deceive ourselves and the truth is not in us. If we confess our sins, he is faithful and just and will forgive us our sins and purify us from all unrighteousness" (1 John 1:8–9).

However, we must diligently avoid spiritual complacency, for persistent disobedience indicates an unrepentant spirit. This is the attitude that cherishes sin and pursues its own pleasures whilst foolishly hoping to avoid the consequences. God is indeed mercifully patient, but we dare not be presumptuous about mercy and grace. The Bible does reminds us that "if I had cherished sin in my heart, the Lord would not have listened" (Ps. 66:18), and this is a warning not only for those who seek to be baptized in the Spirit, but also for those who have already known the Spirit's anointing. The testimony of Scripture reveals that God may, and in fact often does, withdraw his Spirit from those who cherish sin. This happened with Samson and King Saul who, as they chose to live in disobedience, lost the anointing of the Spirit and, ultimately, their lives. David faced the same consequences as his willful weakness with Bathsheba was compounded by deceit, manipulation, and murder, but Nathan's parable enabled the king to confess, "I have sinned against the LORD" (2 Sam. 12:13). In the psalm that flowed out of this episode, he acknowledged the reality of his own sin and earnestly prayed, "Do not cast me from your presence or take your Holy Spirit from me" (Ps. 51:11). Persistent sin and an unrepentant heart are like a sign that reads, "Keep Out!" telling the Spirit that he is unwelcome.

The way to growing in depth of relationship with Christ and the Holy Spirit's empowerment for the work of his kingdom is by "walking in the light" (1 John 1:5–10). This means not only a willingness to be vulnerable to the Holy Spirit, letting his searching light pierce to the secret places within us, but also having a readiness to confess and to repent of our sin and receive the forgiveness and cleansing of Jesus. I (Brad) have found that if I am to continue receiving the Holy Spirit's anointing for service, confession must be a regular spiritual discipline. This is sometimes done alone with God, before whom all our thoughts and desires are known. But I have also found that it is helpful—and keeps me honest—to follow the counsel given by James and confess my sins to a fellow Christian (James 5:16). I therefore regularly meet with a trusted friend who has permission to question and challenge me about any area of my life, who will hear my confession and repentance, and who will minister Jesus' mercy (and sometimes his discipline) into my life.

If we are serious in our desire to receive the promised baptism with the Holy Spirit, we will need to confront our faults and repent of sin that so easily entangles us.

4. Ask the Father

Young children tend to have a straightforward simplicity in asking for what they want. If we wish to receive this gift of being baptized in the Holy Spirit, we need to recover that childlike boldness of simply asking our Father, just as Jesus taught:

> "Ask and it will be given to you; seek and you will find; knock and the door will be opened to you. For everyone who asks receives; he who seeks finds; and to him who knocks, the door will be opened.
>
> Which of you fathers, if your son asks for a fish, will give him a snake instead? Or if he asks for an egg, will give him a scorpion? If you then, though you are evil, know how to give good gifts to your children, how much more will your Father in heaven give the Holy Spirit to those who ask him!" (Luke 11:9–13)

Every Christian already has the Spirit dwelling within, for conversion is itself a work of the Holy Spirit. But to have the Holy Spirit come upon us to clothe us with power, which is what it means to be baptized or filled with the Holy Spirit, is something that we must appropriate. We do this through asking in prayer, as John Calvin makes clear: "Nothing is promised to be expected from the Lord, which we are not also bidden to ask of him in prayers.... We dig up by prayer the treasures that were pointed out by the Lord's Gospel, and which our faith has gazed upon."[4] This prayer requires no special formula or words. What matters is simply that we ask because this is our heart's intent. Andy Buchanan had been a Presbyterian minister for many years before a sense of deep spiritual hunger led him to pray, "Fill me fuller Holy Spirit. I don't know what baptism with the Spirit is, but I am open to whatever you would do in my life."[5] While the words may not seem wonderfully eloquent, God's gracious response was to answer this prayer from the heart.

Andy's experience, like R. A. Torrey's, saw him baptized with the Holy Spirit without anyone else involved. When I (Paul) was baptized with the Spirit, it happened on God's initiative, just as when the Spirit fell upon Cornelius and his household (Acts 10:44–46). There was a general willingness to receive from God, but this had not even reached the stage of being

---

4. John Calvin, *Institutes of the Christian Religion*, ed. John T. McNeill (Philadelphia: Westminster, 1960), 3.20.2.

5. *Dunamis Project Manual: Gateways to Empowered Ministry* (Black Mountain, NC: Presbyterian Reformed Ministries International, 1997), 264.

articulated in prayer. In these situations it is very clear that Jesus is the one who baptizes us with the Holy Spirit, and he alone receives the glory for it.

Yet we also see that many find it helpful to have someone lay hands upon them and pray with them to receive the Spirit, and this practice is certainly well attested in Scripture in the examples of Paul (Acts 9:17–19) and of the converts in Samaria (8:14–17) and Ephesus (19:6). The person who prays with the laying on of hands may bring the gift of faith and expectation, born out of previous experience, and also a love of the person for whom they are praying. This was Cindy's experience when she attended a Dunamis equipping event, and it was also Brad's experience at Jesus Abbey. It is a biblical and helpful practice, and one that we have engaged in on many occasions, sharing the privilege and joy of seeing God fulfilling his promise in the lives of hungry individuals. We must be alert, however, to the danger that attention may become fixated on the person who prays rather than on Jesus who baptizes with the Spirit. So while we gladly lay hands on people and pray for them to receive the anointing of the Spirit, we are also very clear that this is not about any "special" individual doing the praying.

Jesus not only promises to baptize us with the Holy Spirit, but he also explicitly invites us to ask our heavenly Father for the gift of the Spirit. The praying may take any variety of forms, and we must not get hung up on some particular method or approach. The important thing is the intention of our heart and the sovereign grace of the Holy Spirit.

5. Receive in Faith

Our heavenly Father is faithful, trustworthy, and true. This is a fundamental affirmation throughout the Bible, which celebrates the truth that "the LORD is faithful to all his promises and loving toward all he has made" (Ps. 145:13). We have already noted Jesus' promise that "your Father in heaven [will] give the Holy Spirit to those who ask him!" (Luke 11:13), and the apostle Paul confidently declares that "no matter how many promises God has made, they are 'Yes' in Christ" (2 Cor. 1:20). We may take the Lord at his word, and that includes his promise about baptizing us with the Holy Spirit.

Receiving the baptism with the Spirit is not a matter of experiencing emotions or feelings or having some kind of "experience." Rather, it is the simple willingness to believe that God means what he says. It is simply an act of faith. Paul emphasized this point to the Galatian Christians, first asking, "Does God give you his Spirit and work miracles among you because you observe the law, or because you have faith in what you heard?" (Gal. 3:5, our translation)[6] and then declaring that "by faith we might receive the promise of the Spirit" (Gal. 3:14).

Jesus himself exhorts us to take this approach: "'Have faith in God,' Jesus answered. 'I tell you the truth, if anyone says to this mountain, "Go, throw yourself into the sea," and does not doubt in his heart but believes that what he says will happen, it will be done for him. *Therefore I tell you, whatever you ask for in prayer, believe that you have received it, and it will be yours*'" (Mark 11:22–24, italics ours). And years later John was able to affirm: "This is the *assurance* we have in approaching God: that if we ask anything according to his will, he hears us. And if we know that he hears us—whatever we ask—we know that we have what we asked of him" (1 John 5:14–15, our translation).[7]

These promises give us the confidence to ask for and in faith receive the baptism with the Holy Spirit. We know that it is God's will and intention that we are made useful in his kingdom and equipped to witness to Jesus Christ. Therefore, in faith we ask for it, and we trust and believe that we have indeed received. R. A. Torrey placed great emphasis on the importance of appropriating this promise by faith, knowing that it is a biblical emphasis that avoids the dangers of emotional manipulation and pressuring people and that recognizes the sovereignty of God. His comments are helpful, and so we quote them at length:

> Now apply this to the matter of the baptism with the Holy Spirit. You have taken all the other six steps,[8] and you have come to God and asked Him definitely to baptize you with the Holy Spirit (or, to fill you with the Holy Spirit, as the case may be). Then ask yourself, "Is this petition of mine according to His will?" You know that it is because Acts 2:39 and Luke 11:13 say so. Then read I John 5:14, *"this is the confidence that we have toward Him, that, if we ask anything according to His will, He heareth us."* Then say, "I asked for the baptism with the Holy Spirit, I know that is according to His will because God says so in Luke 11:13 and Acts 2:39; therefore, I know He has heard me." Then read the fifteenth verse, *"and if we know that He heareth us, whatsoever we ask, we know that we have the petitions which we have asked of Him."* The petition

---

6. NIV: "because you believe what you heard." The Greek *pistis* is translated as "believe" (verb) and "faith" (noun).

7. "Assurance" is translated "confidence" in the NIV.

8. R. A. Torrey lists seven steps. 1. Accept Jesus as Savior. 2. Renounce all sin. 3. Be baptized in the name of Jesus Christ unto the remission of your sins. 4. Obedience and unconditional full surrender of the will to God. 5. Thirst. 6. Just ask him. 7. Receive in faith.

I asked was the baptism with the Holy Spirit; I know He has heard me; I know I have what I asked; I know I have the baptism with the Holy Spirit. And what you thus take upon naked faith in the word of God, you shall afterwards have in actual experimental possession.[9]

For me (Cindy) these words are so helpful. Paul and Brad's experiences seem very dramatic, with prophetic visions, tongues, and encounters with Jesus Christ. My own experience was nothing like theirs. There were no emotions, no visions: it was a quiet, gentle occasion.

In chapter 2 I described how I came to realize my need for something "more" in my life. After years of trying to hold together being a hospital chaplain, a pastor's wife, and a new mother, I was emotionally, physically, and spiritually exhausted. I reached the end of my ability and was utterly discouraged about how I was to keep going in pastoral ministry when everything depended on me and my own strength and gifting.

In the midst of this exhaustion, I went to the very first Dunamis Project event at Lake George, New York. This was 1991, and Archer Torrey and Brad Long did the teaching. During that week I did experience Jesus' love and healing, which were wonderful, but when a few people laid hands on me and prayed for me to be baptized with the Holy Spirit, it seemed that nothing at all happened. I just asked and, in R. A. Torrey's "naked faith," I accepted the empowerment of the Holy Spirit that I needed. There were no emotions, no tongues, no fireworks at all—just a deep peace. It was only later when I got back to work in the hospital that I discovered that the Holy Spirit had given spiritual gifts to lead me in knowing how to pray for the patients. As I stepped out in obedience, I saw the power of God at work through me.

That took place seventeen years ago, and since then I have experienced some times of great struggle in my life, such as when my husband, Steve, was diagnosed with brain cancer. But as I have walked in obedience, God has filled me with the Holy Spirit again and again, empowering me for teaching and for the healing ministry, and also for growing the Dunamis Fellowship. It truly has been a wonderful journey that just keeps getting more and more exciting.

6. Obey the Holy Spirit

When the disciples saw Jesus walking across the lake toward their boat, Peter asked to join him in this miracle. "'Come,' he said. Then Peter got

---

9. R. A. Torrey, *The Holy Spirit: Who He Is and What He Does* (Old Tappan, NJ: Revell, 1977), 189.

down out of the boat, walked on the water and came toward Jesus" (Matt. 14:29). To be part of this supernatural activity Peter needed to take a step of obedience, and the same is true when we ask to be baptized with the Holy Spirit so that we may join in with the great dance of cooperation with the supernatural activity of the Spirit. Indeed, this is the essence of our whole relationship with Jesus Christ. We are called to obedience, for this is the practical expression of real faith. James makes this clear when he writes, "Faith by itself, if it is not accompanied by action, is dead. But someone will say, 'You have faith; I have deeds.' Show me your faith without deeds, and I will show you my faith by what I do" (James 2:17–18).

At the heart of obedience is the matter of surrendering our wills to Jesus Christ. Every year the members of many Methodist churches in Great Britain renew their covenant of Christian discipleship with words that vividly describe a heart surrendered unto radical obedience:

> I am no longer my own, but yours. Put me to what you will, rank me with whom you will; put me to doing, put me to suffering; let me be employed for you or laid aside for you, exalted for you or brought low for you; let me be full, let me be empty; let me have all things, let me have nothing; I freely and wholeheartedly yield all things to your pleasure and disposal. And now, glorious and blessed God, Father, Son, and Holy Spirit, you are mine and I am yours.[10]

We concur with R. A. Torrey's assertion that "this is one of the most fundamental things in receiving the baptism with the Holy Spirit, the unconditional surrender of the will to God. More people miss the baptism with the Holy Spirit at this point, and more people enter experimentally into the baptism with the Holy Spirit at this point than at almost any other."[11]

In our experience this is how the dance of cooperation begins. When we were baptized with the Spirit, we discovered opportunities to step out in faith-filled obedience, and then, as we acted, we experienced the power or saw evidences that we had indeed been empowered. For me (Paul) this meant approaching my church leaders and applying for training as a minister, a challenging step, because it would involve a large drop in my potential earnings! More recently there was a time when the Spirit made it clear that I should preach a few particular sermons without any notes prepared and, instead, rely on him to provide the words to speak. This was an anxious time, as I normally prefer to have a good sermon outline in my hands, but I

---

10. *The Methodist Service Book* (St. Albans, Hertfordshire: Campfield, 1975), 180.
11. Torrey, *The Holy Spirit*, 168.

took the risk of obedience and experienced the joy of watching God's Word draw people closer to him in worship and discipleship.

When the Holy Spirit first fell on me (Brad) at Jesus Abbey, I had an immediate opportunity for obedience. My tongue started to move, and though I could have stopped it or ignored it, I was aware that this was the invitation to yield my volition to the Holy Spirit by letting Him speak through my tongue. As I did, the gift of tongues as a prayer language flowed out of me. The inspiration for the words (which I did not understand) came from God, but the instrument of the speaking was my own tongue, offered in obedience to the prompting of the Spirit.

The call to active obedience can vary enormously, for not only is each person unique, but so too are the circumstances that we face and the work that the Lord wishes to accomplish through us. It may involve speaking particular words to someone or engaging in a sphere of ministry, such as healing, intercession, evangelism, or pastoral ministry. It may address the way we conduct business or how we handle relationships in the home or workplace, a matter of ethical conduct, or a call to financial generosity. It may tackle a small issue or reorient our whole life.

As we seek to be baptized with the Holy Spirit, welcoming his empowering work in our lives, we are called to "step out of the boat" in obedience. As we do so, we will see again and again the power of the Holy Spirit being expressed in and through us.

Receiving This Baptism with the Holy Spirit

In March 2008 I (Brad) was on a mission trip to Korea where we taught a group of 150 pastors and leaders about the person and work of the Holy Spirit. After five days of systematic teaching, we had set aside time to pray for people to be baptized with the Holy Spirit and for those who had already received this initiatory experience to receive a fresh infilling. The leadership team had received very specific guidance that we ourselves were emphatically not to lay hands on the people. I really struggled with this as I dearly wanted to lay hands on these servants of God and pray for every one of them! My struggle was compounded by the fact that I was present as Archer Torrey's spiritual son and anointed by the Holy Spirit for power ministry. I could feel the Koreans' attachment to me, looking to me to "impart" the Spirit to them. I was in grave danger of shifting their attention away from Jesus Christ and onto me. I appreciated the guidance but was struggling to yield to it.

After leaving the leadership team meeting, I went out to prepare myself for the evening session. John Chang, a ministry colleague, found me wandering around in the dark praying. We prayed in Chinese together, and with his help I was able to confess my struggle. We prayed together, but there was still the nagging struggle in my heart about letting go and trusting Jesus. As I started back to my room, I received a cell phone call from Cindy in the United States, saying that she and other intercessors had received clear guidance: "You must step aside! I [Jesus] will baptize these pastors with the Holy Spirit." I was amazed that she was getting such clear guidance from the other side of the world, but then the Holy Spirit is not bound by time and space. I returned to my room and took a shower. I found myself praying in tongues and asking the Holy Spirit to guide me. Right in the middle of the shower, naked and feeling rather weak and very human (which seems to be a way God likes us best), the awesome, wonderful presence of Jesus surrounded me like a waterfall. He spoke vividly to me, commanding, "Let it all go! And you will be amazed at what I am doing through you! I am going to baptize these Koreans who are seeking me so earnestly in the Holy Spirit and with fire in the same way I did with Cornelius. Your role is like Peter's; it is to preach! Mine will be to pour out my Holy Spirit upon them. Do not lay hands on them; I am going to do that myself." With this powerful encounter, I found that the struggle had ended and I had only a deep peace that Jesus was planning on working.

During the evening session, the jubilant and very Korean praise team had led the group into an emotional intensity of expectancy. I knew we had to come out of this state of high excitement, because asking for the Holy Spirit's empowerment is an act of the will and of receiving in faith, rather than through emotional excitement. So I called the whole group to be very quiet and to wait on the Lord. In the silence I prayed for faith and for us all to be thirsty for the Holy Spirit. The Lord led us into a long period of reaffirming the calling or vision that he had given each person, and we became very aware of how it is impossible to fulfill that calling in our strength. We then moved to an extended time of repentance and surrender to Jesus Christ, all very peaceful, with everyone on their knees waiting in a deep expectant silence.

In the midst of this, I suddenly saw a vision. The roof of the meeting room became transparent, an open window to heaven, and I saw Jesus with extraordinary love gazing down on these men and women whom he had called into his service. He then reached down his hand and said, "Now tell them just to stand when they are ready to receive from me the equipping of the Holy Spirit to do the work I have called them to." I spoke this word, and as one by one the people stood up to receive from Jesus, the Holy Spirit was poured out upon them.

Within myself I was aware of a great rushing of the Holy Spirit, like a river running through me and leading me in the dance. Jesus started giving guidance as to what to do in my part of the dance, saying, "Now I am calling out intercessors and empowering them." As I spoke the word, so it happened. "Now, I am empowering those whom I am calling as evangelists." Again, I spoke and it happened. Again and again he spoke, and wave after wave of the Holy Spirit's presence swept across the room. There was great joy, and the power of God kept overflowing. Then the Lord commanded me, "Now leave, lest they look at you instead of me." So I pushed the Korean-American leadership team up front and quietly slipped out the back, rejoicing in what Jesus was doing and well aware that this was his sovereign work of grace as he baptized these church leaders with his Holy Spirit.

Pray for the Empowering of the Holy Spirit

We have listed these six steps, not because they are theoretically interesting, but because they are theologically urgent. In Korea we saw them acted on in the course of an evening's meeting, producing men and women who are equipped to work with Jesus through the power of the Spirit. John the Baptist promised that Jesus would baptize us with the Holy Spirit. It is up to us to appropriate that promise, humbling ourselves before the Lord and welcoming all that he wishes to accomplish in our lives. Have you sought and received this baptism?

When empowerment is added to the other leadership requirements of incorporation, information, and transformation, the leader is fitted to the dance of cooperation, embodying the kingdom of God and serving in Jesus' work of growing the church in the power of the Holy Spirit.

Chapter 6

Growing Congregations That Embody the Kingdom of God

Jesus provides leaders for his church so that they can facilitate growth in discipleship, and this includes the whole body of Christ learning to cooperate with the Holy Spirit. Leaders must therefore nurture an overall context in which disciples may be prepared and equipped for active service, become Christ-centered and united in their work, and grow to mature wholeness in their faith. When this happens congregations truly embody the kingdom of God.

When Jesus entrusted his apostles with the global work of making disciples, he emphasized two specific issues that would need to be included. First was the task of "baptizing them in the name of the Father and of the Son and of the Holy Spirit" (Matt. 28:19), the symbolic act associated with a person's incorporation into the kingdom of God, a drama of the gospel that provides a threefold testimony about the individual, the Lord, and the church. For the individual, it spoke of personal repentance and dedication, of dying to sin and self, of turning toward God and submitting to his sovereign rule; it was a confession that Jesus is both Savior and Lord. For the Lord's part, it was a testimony of divine love, grace, and power, washing away sin and giving new birth into resurrection life. The church, by administering the sacrament, bore testimony that this believer belonged with them in the whole fellowship of the body of Christ. Water baptism gave a dramatized acknowledgment that a person was born again into a living hope.

New birth alone, however, merely fills a nursery with spiritual babies, whereas Jesus speaks of actively discipling people so that they grow from infancy to maturity. In order that spiritual growth may take place, the disciple-making process also involves "teaching them to obey everything I have commanded you" (Matt. 28:20). This is the second specific issue, and it is amazingly broad in its scope. The *entire* corpus of Jesus' teaching is to be transmitted to all future generations of Christians, not as a mere academic exercise, but as the model for a living faith that is put into action. It is a comprehensive commission from which nothing is to be omitted.

In the previous few chapters, we have highlighted key aspects of discipleship in connection with leaders, which we labeled *incorporation, information, transformation,* and *empowerment.* These are not exhaustive, but they certainly are essential, and they are an integral part of the "everything" that Jesus mentions. The need to be born again, the importance of growing in knowledge of Jesus and in Christlikeness, and the invitation to be baptized with the Holy Spirit—these apply to every individual and not only to leaders.

When Paul bade farewell to the elders of the Ephesian church, he could affirm, "I have not hesitated to preach anything that would be helpful to you.... I have not hesitated to proclaim to you the whole will of God" (Acts 20:20, 27). He knew that he had been faithful to Jesus' commission. In a similar way, Peter exhorted those who were young in the faith: "Like newborn babies, crave pure spiritual milk, so that by it you may grow up in your salvation" (1 Peter 2:2). And on the other hand, we can almost feel the author of Hebrews' frustration about the lack of growth among some Christians: "In fact, though by this time you ought to be teachers, you need someone to teach you the elementary truths of God's word all over again. You need milk, not solid food!" (Heb. 5:12). All of these leaders took Jesus' instruction to heart, knowing that new converts need to be nurtured into mature disciples, growing in understanding and learning to put faith into action. The responsibility of making that happen rests squarely on the shoulders of those who lead. Their task is to grow disciples.

The Nameless People of Pentecost

As we read Luke's account of life in the early church, we naturally find our attention drawn to key leaders. Philip's evangelism, Peter's cross-cultural outreach, James' leadership, Barnabas's encouragement, and Paul's missionary journeys all provide concrete expressions of how the Holy Spirit was at work. But we do not know the identities of the vast majority of disciples. On the day of Pentecost the Holy Spirit fell upon a host of nameless people—men, women, and children—who were all anointed and called to play their unique roles as members of the body of Christ. These anonymous saints of the Bible are an encouragement for the rest of us who will never be named in history books, but whose names are written in the Lamb's Book of Life and listed among those who labored in God's vineyard. These are the people who, having turned to Christ, then grew in discipleship as they "devoted themselves to the apostles' teaching and to the fellowship, to the breaking of bread and to prayer" (Acts 2:42).

I (Brad) have witnessed this kind of growth in discipleship in the life of Montreat Presbyterian Church as members of the congregation have been nurtured in their faith and have learned to obey everything that Jesus commanded his first disciples. After pastor Richard White was baptized with the Holy Spirit at a Dunamis Project event, he invested his energies in nurturing the leadership team, and they in turn helped the rest of the congregation to grow in knowing how to cooperate with the Holy Spirit. We began with teaching a few classes about the work of the Holy Spirit and then focused on Jesus' healing ministry. Out of this grew healing prayer ministry teams. As people continued to grow, we taught about intercessory prayer and nurtured a team of intercessors who provide prayer cover for the congregation. This combination has provided a wonderful dynamic of ministry at Montreat Church that has been expressed in many ways, including the situation with a member named Terry.

When Terry was diagnosed with prostate cancer, he and his wife, Caroline, came back from the doctor's appointment downcast and in despair. His checkup six months previously had shown nothing, but now the cancer was very aggressive and had apparently spread into his pelvic bone. The intercessory prayer team responded immediately to the call to pray for Terry and his family, and on the following Sunday, Richard informed the whole church about the seriousness of Terry's condition. He also said that the family had invited the elders — and anyone else from the congregation — to visit that afternoon to pray with the laying on of hands and anointing with oil, as described in the letter of James (5:14).

Richard called me (Brad) to ask if I could be there too. I arrived a little late for the gathering at the home. When I entered the house, it seemed that our whole congregation had gathered. The elders were all gathered round Terry and Caroline, and Richard was reading Scripture. There was a tremendous outpouring of love onto this family from the whole congregation, and I could also sense that this was a kairos moment. The Holy Spirit was already moving, using the reading of Scripture to build faith in Jesus, and then the command came to me, "Move in now and lay hands on him and anoint him with oil and watch me work."

I was reluctant to do anything, because I did not want to steal attention away from Jesus or to interfere with the role of the elders, but they were not moving, and it seemed that the moment was passing. Thankfully Richard was alert to the kairos moment, as also was Diane, the prayer coordinator, and he invited us to join in. I placed my hands on Terry to pray, and I felt a great surge of the Holy Spirit moving through me into him. At that same moment, Diane read Scripture about the Holy Spirit moving from Jesus in power to heal. I immediately started to feel heat in my hands, and Terry looked up in surprise and then was moved to tears as he stammered, "God, thank you! It is so hot inside my bones! I am burning up inside. I feel Jesus right here!" He broke down in praise and weeping.

The whole group began to worship, and I asked all the other elders to lay hands on Terry and Caroline and their children. There was a great outpouring of love upon them all, as many offered up prayers asking Jesus to heal Terry. Through all this I could feel the power of the Holy Spirit surging through me, and then suddenly I heard the Lord say, "Now stop. I am done. Bless them and leave." I asked Terry, "What are you feeling?" and he said, "Oh, the heat just stopped, but I feel a deep peace that Jesus is holding me in his love and that everything is going to be okay." Richard led us in a prayer of thanksgiving, and nudged by the Holy Spirit, I slipped out and headed home.

The next day Terry returned to the doctor for further tests, and they found that the cancer was no longer in the bones, only in the prostate. Now, after surgery and chemotherapy, he is fine, and the church has been full of rejoicing because of the grace God has shown. People are also excited about the way that they were able to participate in this ministry, joining in with this dance of cooperation with the Spirit. As a result, we have seen a deepening of faith within the congregation and also a growing participation in healing and prayer ministry, through which we continue to see Jesus at work.

Later I was invited by Richard to join with Diane and some of the elders to "debrief" the experience by analyzing and reflecting critically on what we were doing in response to the guidance of the Holy Spirit. We have found that time spent debriefing is extremely important for nurturing the congregation's spiritual awareness and their capacity to participate in this dynamic work. It is an integral part of the disciple-growing process as the leaders teach people the practicalities of obeying everything that Jesus has commanded.

Leaders Are Jesus' Gift to His Church

Scripture indicates a variety of ways in which the Holy Spirit equips people with spiritual gifts so that they can serve God's purposes. In Romans 12 the emphasis is on people actually using the gifts they have been given. In 1 Corinthians 12 the concern is for unity as the various giftings are recognized as integral parts of the whole body. But in Ephesians 4 the focus is a little different. Here Paul mentions that the ascending Christ gave gifts to people, but he focuses on the fact that Christ provided the church with certain anointed individuals to function as leaders. Walter Liefeld, in his commentary on Ephesians, notes: "The gifts named are not abilities given to people; they are people given to the church."[1]

> But to each one of us grace has been given as Christ apportioned it. This is why it says:
>
> > "When he ascended on high,
> > he led captives in his train
> > and gave gifts to men."
>
> ... It was he who gave some to be apostles, some to be prophets, some to be evangelists, and some to be pastors and teachers, to prepare God's people for works of service, so that the body of Christ may be built up until we all reach unity in the faith and in the knowledge of the Son of God and become mature, attaining to the whole measure of the fullness of Christ. (Eph. 4:7–8, 11–13)

Leaders are indeed Jesus' gift to his church, purposefully given to facilitate growth in all its forms. This is not merely institutional leadership, where authority is exercised by virtue of appointment to an office. Rather, this is charismatic[2] leadership, where authority is exercised by virtue of a person's spiritual equipping and calling. Ideally these would coincide and an individual would hold an office because her or his anointing was duly discerned and affirmed by the church. But this is not always the case, and it is easy, for instance, to find situations in which elders are appointed merely by a democratic voting process that has little to do with the Spirit's guidance or anointing.

The gift of spiritual leadership that Jesus provides for his church involves an interdependent mix of variously gifted people all working together toward a common goal of producing a community of Christians who are "mature in the Lord, measuring up to the full and complete standard of Christ"

---

1. Walter L. Liefeld, *Ephesians* (Leicester: Inter-Varsity Press, 1997), 103.
2. We use the word *charismatic* here to refer to ability that is given by the Spirit's gifting (Gk., *charism*) and not in the popular senses of either a dynamic, often forceful or persuasive personality, or of a particular style of worship.

(Eph. 4:13 NLT). Through spiritual equipping, unity, teaching, and cultivating character, leaders create the context of an active Trinitarian theology in which the Holy Spirit is truly welcomed as the new Immanuel (literally, "God with us") and is allowed to work among us "just as he determines" (1 Cor. 12:11). The Ephesians passage indicates some of the areas to which leaders should give attention.

Prepare God's People for Works of Service

When we start a new job or voluntary post, take up a sport, or begin driving an automobile, we normally receive some kind of preparation. Whether a task is simple or highly complex and requires casual assistance or formal training, we are unlikely to know what to do unless someone takes the time to coach us. On those rare times when we do have an idea of how to tackle the task, it is probably due to relevant past experience anyway!

It is no different when we begin a new life in the kingdom of God. Though we might wish it were so, spiritual infants are not automatically mature or ready to minister, and leaders have the responsibility of feeding and discipling them so that they do become ready to play their parts in the kingdom. Paul uses a word that speaks of being "properly equipped or fitted for the moment,"[3] and we saw this happening as people prayed for Terry. Richard, Brad, and Diane had all learned to discern God's kairos moments, and they were aware of the kinds of ministry that were appropriate (fitting Scriptures to read, proper focus for praying, experience in anointing with oil and laying on of hands). But they also knew how to draw others into the work that was taking place by building faith and giving directions. When we add in the debriefing that followed, people were clearly being prepared for the next opportunity when they would have a better awareness of how they, too, could be part of this ministry.

I (Paul) have seen this process of preparation taking place in the life of Lynne James, a wonderful servant of God who has worked alongside me on the leadership team for a Dunamis Project in the United Kingdom. Soon after she was ordained an elder, Lynne found that people from her church were approaching her and asking for prayer ministry; so she prayed for them "based on what I had picked up by being on the receiving end for several years!" She herself had received some measure of preparation simply through her own experiences, but the learning became more intentional as she began to attend the Dunamis events that I was leading. Through systematic teach-

---

3. Ephesians 4:12: *katartismos*—from *kata* ("according to") and *artios* ("fitted, capable").

ing and participating in praying for people and then debriefing afterwards, she found herself becoming better prepared for this work. Reflecting back on that period, she said, "Dunamis put my call into a context that I could answer it, and gave me the tools to enable me to answer it practically." Today Lynne not only provides prayer ministry herself, but she is also involved in teaching and mentoring others so that they, too, can be equipped for this sphere of service.

This is the leaders' task. By intentionally nurturing people in any and every aspect of Christian living, we prepare them for works of service. If we wish to see people involved in evangelism, small group leadership, healing and deliverance ministry, intercession, teaching, pastoral visiting, or any other area of Christian service, the leaders are responsible for preparing people to do these things. The preparation will obviously include opportunities for people to be baptized in the Spirit and to continue being filled with the Spirit so that we are equipped to work under his anointing and not in the limitations of our own strength and wisdom.

Foster Unity in the Faith

The leaders' task is also to foster and facilitate unity in *the* faith, which "refers to faith as a body of doctrine, not to faith as an act of trust."[4] It is the challenge of building a community of people who share a common conviction about the person and work of Jesus Christ. Earlier in this chapter Paul has already written about the need to "be patient, bearing with one another in love. Make every effort to keep the unity of the Spirit through the bond of peace" and reminds them that "there is one body and one Spirit" (Eph. 4:2–4). Producing unity within the church is, first of all, a fundamental function of the Holy Spirit. He is the one who initially creates that unity, who equips people for leadership with the responsibility to grow that unity, and who also brings glory to Jesus by guiding people into his truth (John 16:13–15) so that the one church truly shares one faith (Eph. 4:5).

But unity requires effort. Indeed, the very instruction to "make every effort" suggests that disunity would be an ongoing problem and therefore requires patience, forbearance, and a peaceable attitude among the people. Who would have expected communion to become a symbol of severe discord within a local church as it did in Corinth, prompting Paul to say that "your meetings do more harm than good" and that "when you come together, it is not the Lord's Supper you eat" (1 Cor. 11:17–22)? Whatever happened

---

4. Liefeld, *Ephesians*, 108.

to the idea of being "one body, for we all partake of the one loaf" (10:17)? Fallen human nature has a devious flair for taking even the gracious gifts of God and turning them into something divisive.

Perhaps this is why Jesus prayed in Gethsemane for the unity among those who would later believe in him:

> "My prayer is not for them alone. I pray also for those who will believe in me through their message, that all of them may be one, Father, just as you are in me and I am in you. May they also be in us so that the world may believe that you have sent me. I have given them the glory that you gave me, that they may be one as we are one: I in them and you in me. May they be brought to complete unity to let the world know that you sent me and have loved them even as you have loved me." (John 17:20–23)

Unity in Christian relationships is a powerful evangelistic witness. A world that is falling apart needs to see in Jesus' church a people who are coming together, reconciled not only with God but also with one another. Unity also has practical benefits for congregations themselves. It enables them to direct their attention and energies toward shared goals because, like oarsmen in a rowboat, the work is much easier and more effective when everyone pulls in the same direction! Unity also makes the church a "safe" context for learning about and encountering the person and work of the Holy Spirit.

It is therefore no surprise to find that Satan works to disrupt the church's unity. By doing so, he not only undermines the church's testimony and diminishes its effectiveness, but he also distracts people away from the Holy Spirit. One ironic but effective tactic is to pervert teaching about the Spirit so that the Spirit becomes a cause of division rather than a source of unity.

We have often encountered people who have been hurt by teaching or treatment in connection with the Holy Spirit. In many cases, the issue is the gift of tongues. Some believers have been regarded as deficient, "second-class" Christians simply because they do not have this one gift. Others have found themselves concerned by the manner in which some spiritual gifts have been exercised, or they have been troubled by rumors and reports that give a negative impression. Through ignorance, misinformation, and caricature, Satan fosters fear and cultivates resistance to the Holy Spirit. If this attitude infects the majority of a congregation, corporate resistance toward the Spirit blocks his freedom to grow the church. And where there are smaller clusters of people either zealously resisting the Spirit's work or passionately promoting it, Satan may easily use the situation to erode the unity of the body of Christ.

This is a spiritual battleground strewn with propaganda and land mines by the "father of lies" (John 8:44), and leaders must navigate through it with pastoral grace, gentle wisdom, and careful teaching of the truth. Most important, everything will need to be underpinned with prayer as they faithfully add their own voice to Jesus' petition "that all of them may be one" (John 17:21).

Grow Believers in the Knowledge of the Son of God

To unity in the faith Paul adds unity in the knowledge of the Son of God. Here is the reminder that the church is not merely *a* religious community, but a *Christ-centered* religious community, deriving its identity and raison d'être uniquely from him. Commenting on this verse, John Calvin emphasizes:

> It was the apostle's intention to explain what is the nature of true faith, and in what it consists; that is, when the Son of God is known. To the Son of God alone faith ought to look; on him it relies; in him it rests and terminates. If it proceeds farther, it will disappear, and will no longer be faith, but a delusion. Let us remember that true faith confines its view so entirely to Christ that it neither knows, nor desires to know, anything else.[5]

This knowledge, which leaders must establish clearly in people's minds, concerns first an appreciation that Jesus is none other than the second person of the Trinity. He is the Son of God and not merely some wonderful prophet or renowned religious teacher. Not only was Peter able to affirm, "You are the Christ, the Son of the living God" (Matt. 16:16), but a week later he heard a similar declaration from the Father himself: "This is my Son, whom I love; with him I am well pleased. Listen to him!" (Matt. 17:5). Knowing Jesus' identity should result in heeding his authority: since he truly is the Son of God, we are constrained to pay attention to his words.

As our focus here is on growing the church in the power of the Holy Spirit, leaders particularly need to ensure that the church heeds the words spoken by the Son of God about the Spirit of God. This is an integral part of the "whole will of God" (Acts 20:27) that Paul declared in Ephesus as he taught the believers there to obey everything Jesus had commanded (see Matt. 28:19–20). It includes Jesus' words about being baptized with the

---

5. John Calvin, "Commentary on Ephesians," *Books for the Ages.* USA Version 1.0 (Albany, OR: AGES Software 1998).

Spirit so that we may become worldwide witnesses to him, fulfilling the Great Commission.

Our knowledge of Jesus the Son of God also includes his self-description as the way, the truth, and the life, the only way to God the Father (John 14:6, 26). This is both a motivation for mission and the message the Spirit enables the church to proclaim. We call people into a living relationship with a heavenly Father whose love sent his only Son to bring the option of eternal life into a dying, alienated world (John 3:16). God, we are reminded, "wants all men to be saved and to come to a knowledge of the truth" (1 Tim. 2:4).

But growing in our knowledge of the Son of God means more than knowing him as Savior. The Spirit also enables us to know him as the Prophet, Priest, and King who brings healing, forgiveness, deliverance, grace, and wisdom, speaking into our circumstances and directing our living. We need to grow in discipleship. Asking WWJD (What Would Jesus Do?) is an easy, popular question, but in order to answer it, people first need to know WJDD (What Jesus Did Do). For those who came to faith following Peter's Pentecost sermon, it meant that they "devoted themselves to the apostles' teaching" (Acts 2:42) so that they grew in knowledge about the life and teaching of the Son of God. The apostles' teaching is preserved for us in Scripture. We too may know what Jesus did do, and thus the same growth is possible for us today.

Beyond the basic informational head knowledge about who Jesus is and what he did, the Spirit also enables us to *know him* through personal encounter. Saul fell to the ground blinded as he met with the glorified Jesus on the road to Damascus and received a vision from heaven that reoriented the course of his life (Acts 26:13–23). John similarly records his own awe-inspiring mystical encounter with Jesus in a vision mediated by the Spirit that provided pastoral purpose for his life in exile on Patmos (Rev. 1:9–18). In subsequent centuries, countless Christians have grown in their knowledge of the Son of God through similar supernatural encounters, occasionally recording their experiences for the benefit of others.[6] Through prophetic words, visions, dreams, and the whispered voice of holy stillness, the Spirit continues to provide people with firsthand encounters with the risen Christ.

So we see that the church, quickened by the Holy Spirit's ministry, becomes a community of faith that centers on the Son of God. Faith, assurance, and devotion are deepened as the Spirit directs attention to Jesus,

6. Witness, for instance, the testimonies of Julian of Norwich, Bonaventure, and Teresa of Avila.

mediates his grace, unites his people, and illuminates his words. Jesus said, "He will bring glory to me by taking from what is mine and making it known to you" (John 16:14). Apostles, prophets, evangelists, pastors, and teachers are fitted for their task by the Spirit and given by Jesus as a gift to his church to guide, teach, and nurture a fully informed and personal knowledge of himself.

Help Disciples Attain the Whole Measure of the Fullness of Christ

The combined outcome of all these growth factors is to see the church "become mature, attaining to the whole measure of the fullness of Christ" (Eph. 4:13). For leaders this can be a frustrating process, which Paul described as being "in the pains of childbirth until Christ is formed in you" (Gal. 4:19). But if we want the church to grow in the power of the Holy Spirit, then this crucial second foundation needs to be constructed.

People need to be incorporated into the kingdom of God by being born again. The fruit of the Spirit needs to be cultivated so that people are transformed into increasingly Christlike character. Unity in the faith and in the knowledge of the Son of God must be nurtured, growing people in their understanding and in their personal relationship with Jesus. And men, women, and children need to be baptized with the Holy Spirit so that they can be empowered to do everything that Christ commands, each playing their unique roles as members of the body of Christ. We are not called to partial growth, and while these are not the whole picture, nevertheless they are undeniably essential aspects of what it means to grow into full maturity. As they are nurtured in the life of a church, we discover that the whole congregation is enabled to become part of that great dance of cooperation with the Spirit, as St. Paul's Anglican Church discovered.

St. Paul's is a comfortable, upper-middle-class and mostly elderly congregation in Asheville, North Carolina, who found themselves called to minister among the homeless through the prompting of the Spirit, the support of the pastor, and the participation of the church. The Holy Spirit began stirring the heart of a recently retired businessman from the congregation, giving him a burden of compassion for the street people who lived under a highway bridge near the church building. Through this inspiration, coupled with his assessment of their practical needs in the wintertime, he started providing them with knapsacks of food and clothing. What began with just a few knapsacks has now grown to be a significant ministry to those in desperate need.

The pastor, John Green, made it clear:

Originally this was not my idea! It just looked like a real hassle to me to get involved with these people. But we have now called and commissioned a layman for this work, and we are taking part in the ministry as a whole congregation. Some of these street people, as they are experiencing Jesus' love in such a concrete way, are coming to our worship services. Some are getting saved, and some are receiving continued prayer ministry. We have given away several hundred knapsacks. But what is most important is the way that the whole congregation has caught the vision for this and is helping it happen through financial gifts, actually helping to buy the food and clothing, and helping to pack the knapsacks. A number have joined in the trips to the homeless people to deliver them. A project that started with one person is now pulling us out of ourselves into a ministry of compassion. As the whole church has shared in this mission, so their faith in Jesus Christ and their commitment to follow him in all areas of life has grown and deepened.

Here is a church in which the second foundation is being established. Through the guidance of the Spirit and the obedience of a man, we see evidence of Christlike compassion, prayer, generosity, conversion, unity, vision, and mission in the life of this congregation. The kingdom of God is being embodied, Jesus is glorified, and the church is learning that discipleship can be exciting and fulfilling when the Holy Spirit is at work.

In later chapters we will examine the Seven Dynamics of cooperating with the Holy Spirit and consider how we may incorporate these into the life of a congregation. But first we must look at the pressing question for leaders: How can we helpfully introduce people to the person and work of the Holy Spirit? Our next chapter therefore addresses the practicalities of providing gateway opportunities for people to learn about, encounter, and be equipped by the Spirit of God.

Chapter 7

Gateways for Congregations

Congregations need practical gateways through which people may enter into the dance of cooperation with the Spirit. Leaders create the context for this by doing the spiritual preparation of prayer and teaching. They also need to create gateway opportunities for people to enter the kingdom of God and to receive the empowering anointing of the Holy Spirit. Without these crucial steps, we will be seeking to lead people in a process that is fundamentally alien to their theological and experiential understanding of Christian life.

The crowd that gathered in Jerusalem on the day of Pentecost heard a twofold invitation from Peter. In response to the news that Jesus is the resurrected Lord and the Anointed One,[1] they were called first to repent and be baptized, and then they were promised the gift of the Holy Spirit. The same two facets of faith are highlighted in Philip's visit to a Samaritan town. First, Philip preached the message about Jesus and the kingdom of God and many responded by being baptized, and then Peter and John prayed for them and they received the Holy Spirit (Acts 8:5–17). In many congregations, especially those from within our own Presbyterian and Reformed tradition, these two areas—repentance followed by baptism and the receiving of the Holy Spirit—have become increasingly noticeable by their absence. The groundwork teaching about both of these aspects of discipleship, together with opportunities to respond, have been dropped off the agenda with devastating results.

In 1975 while at seminary, I (Brad) attended the prayer and praise services at the local Presbyterian congregation in our city where the Holy Spirit had fallen. This church was at the center of the charismatic renewal in the city, and I vividly remember hundreds of people gathered in worship, many people coming to Christ, exciting manifestations of the Holy Spirit, and

---

1. "Christ" (Gk.) and "Messiah" (Heb.) both refer to the Anointed One whom God had promised.

vital engagement in missions. The pastor was a brilliant Bible teacher, a man who was greatly anointed for ministry and who did everything.

Twenty-five years later I was invited to visit this church to provide teaching about healing ministry. I was able to attend the 8:00 a.m. traditional worship service, and I preached at the 11:00 a.m. contemporary worship service. The congregation for the traditional service involved mostly younger people (below the age of fifty) and was very sparsely attended. The ponderous liturgy, flavored by liberal teaching and saturated with inclusive language for a seemingly emasculated God, struck me as dull and lacking in vitality and Christ-centeredness.

It was a stark contrast with the contemporary service. This was the older congregation, full of people well past their fifties, with gray or white hair. Only a few younger people were present. The large sanctuary was filled with people caught up in worship, raising hearts, hands, and voices to the Lord in praise. Jesus was exalted and glorified, and wonderful manifestations of the Holy Spirit were taking place. I was amazed by the difference and pondered what had happened to cause it.

During the 1970s, this church had come alive through the work of the Holy Spirit, but then they had failed to build for the future. Over the years, there was a profound lack of teaching about the need for spiritual equipping and a failure to integrate future generations into the empowering work of the Holy Spirit. No "gateways" were built into the life of the congregation, no opportunities were made for ongoing conversions and for growing disciples, and no believers were being drawn into the empowering work of the Holy Spirit. They simply did not build into their common church life the components that enable growth to be sustained.

We believe this sorry neglect is a pervasive problem, a scenario that should prompt us to pose the Pentecost question, "Brothers, what shall we do?" (Acts 2:37). To avoid this neglect we need to address three areas.

1. *Create the spiritual context* through persistent, reality-shaping prayer, and by providing balanced biblical teaching about the person and work of the Holy Spirit.
2. *Open the gateway into the kingdom of God* by giving people opportunities for making a conscious decision to follow Jesus Christ and receive the new birth the Holy Spirit gives.
3. *Open the gateway for the Spirit's anointing* by giving people opportunities to pray for and to receive the baptism with the Holy Spirit as the initiatory experience into the empowering work of the Holy Spirit.

These are preliminaries. Together they enable people to learn about, encounter, and be anointed by the Spirit of God. They bring people into a place where they may then go on to grow in receiving the gifts of the Holy Spirit and learning the dance steps of cooperating with the Holy Spirit in practical ministry. These three areas need to be integral to the life of the congregation if it is to stay alive and keep growing in spiritual maturity and in reaching out with the gospel.

Create the Spiritual Context

Reality-Shaping Prayer

Jesus made it plain that the spiritual reality of the kingdom of God is not accomplished through mundane activities: "Flesh gives birth to flesh, but the Spirit gives birth to spirit" (John 3:6). As we look to see people born again into that kingdom, and to see congregations come alive in the power of the Holy Spirit, we must recognize that the only proper starting point is the place of prayer. It was clearly a priority for Jesus and a practice of the early church. For example, as Paul engaged in evangelism, he requested, "Pray for us that the message of the Lord may spread rapidly and be honored" (2 Thess. 3:1).

Another time, after emphasizing the importance of persistence in prayer, Jesus revealed that the Holy Spirit is given "to those who ask" (Luke 11:13). Indeed, here we have great grounds for confidence in our praying. Because we know that the Father "wants all men to be saved and to come to a knowledge of the truth" (1 Tim 2:4) and that he sent Jesus to be their Savior, we may pray plainly for their salvation. Likewise, because we know that Jesus baptizes with the Spirit, told his disciples to await that gift, and promised that the Spirit would be given in response to prayer, we may pray with the conviction that this, too, is in accordance with the Father's will.

Through personal petition and intercession for others, we play our part in preparing the way for God to act. Prayer is the spiritual groundwork that levels mountains, fills in valleys, and prepares in the desert places a highway for the Lord. It is a fundamental spiritual necessity, as even John Calvin acknowledged. Famous for his teachings about predestination and the sovereignty of God, Calvin placed an even greater emphasis on prayer, both as a man of piety and in his written works: "Words fail to express how necessary prayer is, and in how many ways the exercise of prayer is profitable. Surely, with good reason the Heavenly Father affirms that the only stronghold of safety is in calling on his name."[2] Reviving the life of the congregation begins with the work of prayer.

In their book *Prayer That Shapes the Future*, Brad Long and Doug McMurray explore the kind of dynamic prayer that proves to be a partnership with our heavenly Father, bringing forth his kingdom here on earth. Prayer changes hearts, softens stiff necks, opens closed eyes, and stirs a hunger in people's souls.[3] Before trying to change people's understanding and openness to the work of the Spirit through teaching and practice, we first need to prepare the way through prayer.

In 1998 I (Brad) visited City Temple, a United Reformed Church (URC) in London, to teach at an event on the subject of prayer. I discovered how the faithful prayers of a few had opened the doorway for transformation in this congregation. During the war years, this had been a vibrant, thriving congregation, sometimes packed with four thousand people in worship. But their famous pastor had drifted into unorthodox teaching and did not lay a sound biblical foundation on Jesus Christ. The drawing power was his gift of oratory, and when he retired the numbers dwindled until finally, like many congregations built on foundations other than Christ and the Word, a tiny congregation was struggling to exist in a massive building.

But a spiritual transformation had begun. The minister and elders had themselves come alive in the power of the Spirit and had started to embody in themselves as a leadership team the new vision of a congregation growing by cooperating with the Father, Son, and Holy Spirit. They were giving true spiritual leadership to this church, and the prayer event that I attended was part of the fruit of their leadership. It was exciting to see the Spirit moving powerfully among the people, and it was equally exciting to discover the hidden work of prayer that had prepared the way for the renewal of the leaders and of the church.

I was getting ready to walk out the door of the meeting room to catch the train to the airport when two very elderly ladies from Scotland came up to me. They were bubbly with excitement and radiant with joy as they enthused, "Reverend Long, we have been praying for years and years for a move of the Holy Spirit to take place in our Presbyterian congregations in Great Britain. Now after hearing your biblical teaching and seeing the Holy Spirit work tonight, we can die in peace because we know God is answering our prayers!" They both hugged me and left. I never saw them again and

---

2. John Calvin, *Institutes of the Christian Religion*, ed. John T. McNeill (Philadelphia: Westminster, 1960), 3.20.2.

3. Brad Long and Doug McMurry, *Prayer That Shapes the Future: How to Pray with Power and Authority* (Grand Rapids: Zondervan, 1999).

never learned what their connection was to the congregation. But I am convinced that it was their prayers and faith that had welcomed the Holy Spirit to do his igniting work in this congregation.

Balanced Biblical Teaching

Alongside the work of prayer, there is also the need to lay a broad, balanced foundation of biblical teaching as part of creating this spiritual context. This is true especially of the nature of the gospel and the role of the Holy Spirit.

Scripture describes the salvation that is accomplished by Jesus with remarkable breadth—not only as forgiveness for sin, but as reconciliation, new life, transfer of citizenship, hope, purpose, eternal destiny, adoption, healing, freedom from slavery, cleansing—the list goes on. Different personalities find themselves better able to relate to different aspects and descriptions of the gospel. For some it is the love of God that draws them to faith. Others are attracted by the power of God that is able to rescue and keep us secure. Yet others find themselves persuaded by truth and are glad to discover a purpose for living. That one small aspect of the gospel that helped us to be born again may not be the portion that others particularly need to hear; and any preacher, teacher, or evangelist is wise to take this variety into account. Balanced biblical teaching will weave all of these threads into the wonderful tapestry that portrays the salvation wrought by Jesus.

What if we believe the congregation is made up exclusively of those who have been born again? Is there any value in preaching to the converted? Certainly there is! Simply hearing the Good News that we already believe, not only prompts us to worship our Savior, but can also bring a fresh motivation for sharing it; and hearing the same message expressed in different words can better equip us for talking about the gospel with others.

Furthermore (and this is true for teaching about the Holy Spirit too), these topics do not necessarily need to be the main focus of the sermon or lesson. I (Paul) have found it possible to "drip-feed" congregations with a great deal of teaching about the Holy Spirit by simply including a relevant point when the Spirit is mentioned in a Bible passage. By including small portions of teaching and illustrations woven into the whole theme, people have begun to regard the Spirit as simply a "normal" and integral part of the whole understanding of Christian life and teaching. This is ordinary, everyday activity in the kingdom of God. On the occasions when preaching or teaching is focused explicitly on the Holy Spirit, people have then found that many of the key areas are already familiar, and the teaching is simply drawing these threads together into a coherent whole.

Alongside preaching and teaching, we have also capitalized on the value of testimonies for enabling people to learn more about how the Spirit is actively working in our midst today. When Miranda and Rita experienced miraculous healings, they each shared their testimony during the next worship service. When Dick was baptized with the Spirit, he spoke about it during a one-day retreat. When the Spirit gave guidance in the midst of a prayer meeting, that story was described in the church's next monthly magazine. Such stories have put flesh on the bare bones of my preaching and opened people's eyes to the ongoing activity of the Spirit.

As with presenting the gospel message, it is vitally important that teaching and testimony do not become "trapped" in giving a lopsided, partial impression. Both pastorally and for the sake of integrity, we must remain faithful to the whole breadth of biblical revelation about the Holy Spirit, and we need especially to avoid focusing on only one part of the work of one person of the Trinity. We have found it helpful to emphasize repeatedly that there are four basic areas in which the Spirit works in our lives today, and we have linked them mnemonically with the four points of the compass:

N: New life (or incorporation)—the Spirit enables us to be born again as a child of God, entering his kingdom and becoming part of the body of Christ.

S: Sanctification (or transformation)—the Spirit changes us from within, growing in us a Christlike character that is described as the fruit of the Spirit.

E: Empowerment—the Spirit clothes us with power, equipping us with a variety of spiritual gifts that express God's supernatural reign on earth.

W: We (or *koinonia*, fellowship)—the Spirit unites us, joining us together as a reconciled people, members of the one body and household of God.

Obviously this is not an exhaustive coverage of every aspect of the Spirit's work, but it certainly has helped provide a balanced framework that prevents a myopic view of the Holy Spirit.

Open the Gateway into the Kingdom of God

Jesus said that the road and the gate that lead into the kingdom of God are narrow, and only a few find the way in. He told of a master sending his servants far and wide to ensure that people attend the feast, and he commissioned his own disciples as worldwide witnesses with a commission to make new disciples. Their task, and our continuing task, is to help people find that gateway, enter the kingdom of God, and join in the feast.

We therefore need to present people with the challenge and opportunity to become Christians by accepting Jesus Christ as Savior and following him as Lord over their lives. Jesus himself extended such opportunities: "Come, follow me" (Mark 1:17), he said to Peter and Andrew, promising them new purpose in life. Peter exhorted the Pentecost audience, "Save yourselves from this corrupt generation" (Acts 2:40), and offered the chance to repent and be baptized. Whether such gateways are structured or spontaneous, built into the ebb and flow of church life or provided through special events and occasions, they need to be provided.

In many Baptist congregations, it became habitual to have an "altar call" during most worship services, but in many churches the call to conversion or recommitment to following Jesus is no longer given. This may be due to a variety of reasons, such as cultural inhibitions and awkwardness or the mistaken belief that everyone who attends a church service is de facto a Christian. Opening the gateway into the kingdom of God needs to be done intentionally and repeatedly, for people do not all rush through at the first opportunity!

I (Paul) was pleased to introduce the Alpha Course as a regular evangelistic ministry at Plymstock United Church in Plymouth, England. During the fifteen years of running Alpha, we have enjoyed repeated opportunities for people to take a step of commitment to Christ, for this is built into the program in the course of systematically presenting core teachings of the Christian faith. Christianity Explored, Emmaus, and other such courses can provide similar scheduled opportunities.[4] Alpha has been the single most fruitful means of evangelistic outreach in the church's life, but it has not been the only gateway that we have provided. During our children's holiday clubs (similar to vacation Bible school in the United States) we provide a chance for children to come to Christ, and we have seen not only children but also leaders convert during these times. At the end of a worship service in which several people shared their conversion testimonies, I gave only a brief challenge for people to consider their own response to Christ, yet it was the gateway that one woman needed, and a couple of people prayed with her during the final hymn as the Spirit birthed her into the kingdom of God.

In the course of a church's ongoing life, it is not difficult to find appropriate occasions for opening the gateway into God's kingdom. These include the

---

4. See www.christianityexplored.org and www.chpublishing.co.uk/category.asp?id=22601 for more information.

story of the Christ child born at Christmas, the accomplishments of the Easter cross and empty tomb, the fresh beginnings of a new year, the annual service of renewing membership promises, the regular reenactment of grace made tangible through communion, and the baptismal celebration of new life. All these, together with the Holy Spirit's prompting at the unexpected, opportune moment, provide a plethora of occasions for calling people to respond to Christ.

Whatever particular opportunities are provided, they need to include an acknowledged profession of commitment, or recommitment, to Christ as Lord. Jesus expected us to voice our faith to others. He said, "Whoever, then, acknowledges me before people, I will acknowledge before my Father in heaven. But whoever denies me before people, I will deny him also before my Father in heaven" (Matt. 10:32–33 NET). Paul affirmed the same truth: "If you confess with your mouth, 'Jesus is Lord,' and believe in your heart that God raised him from the dead, you will be saved. For it is with your heart that you believe and are justified, and it is with your mouth that you confess and are saved" (Rom. 10:9–10).

I (Brad) find it troubling to discover just how many people are faithful church members but have never committed their lives to Jesus simply because they have never been given an opportunity. An elderly Dutch woman in a traditional Canadian Christian Reformed congregation came up to me after a weekend Dunamis event in Ontario very excited. She said that she had been baptized as an infant, had been confirmed, and for years and years had been a faithful member of the congregation. When I had given people an invitation to recommit themselves to following Jesus as part of preparation for praying for the baptism with the Holy Spirit, she was shocked to realize that she had never really committed her life to Christ. As she had offered herself to Jesus and made this confession to the person sitting next to her, she was flooded with joy and found a new aliveness in herself. "It is like for the first time in my life, this faith in Christ is not just the tradition that I love and am so much a part of, or the doctrine that I grew up knowing, but is now my own and alive in me. I guess I have just been born again!" Many people never have this experience simply because they are never given the opportunity. For their sakes and the sake of the vitality of the congregation, these opportunities must be built into the life of the congregation.

Open the Gateway for the Spirit's Anointing

The church in Acts made sure that they gave people the chance to receive the promised baptism with the Holy Spirit. Peter did so on the day of Pentecost (Acts 2:38). Peter went with John to pray for the converts in Samaria to receive the Spirit (8:14–17). Peter saw God's sovereign grace in Cornelius's household as the Spirit fell midway through his evangelistic message (10:44–46). Ananias laid hands on Saul/Paul that he might see and be filled with the Spirit (9:17–18). And Peter himself had the Spirit come upon him in power on several recorded occasions (2:4, 14–40; 4:8). We, too, need to provide regular opportunities for church members and new believers to pray for and receive the Holy Spirit upon them for power.

We speak of the first occasion of a person's being filled with the Holy Spirit in terms of being baptized with the Holy Spirit, this being an initiation into the Spirit's empowering work. But we also need the experience of the Holy Spirit coming upon us again and again on subsequent occasions, empowering us for new forms of service or new phases of discipleship, as was the case with Peter. Leaders need to make intentional offers for both the initial baptism and for being filled again with the Spirit, usually with systematic and biblical teaching about the Spirit followed by opportunities for prayer and laying on of hands.[5]

I (Paul) helped the children's leaders prepare for such an occasion as part of the program at a weekend conference organized by GEAR (the Group for Evangelism And Renewal in the United Reformed Church). All the children, my own included, took turns laying hands on and praying for each other in groups of three, one asking the Spirit to grow a specific (requested) fruit in a friend's life, and the other asking for the empowerment of a (requested) spiritual gift. This was new territory for them, and children and leaders alike were intensely aware of the Spirit's almost tangible presence as they prayed. That took place six years ago, and all of those children are continuing to grow in faith, discipleship, and service.

But it is not only children who need to receive this baptism with the Spirit. Peter affirmed that "you will receive the gift of the Holy Spirit. The promise is for you and your children and for all who are far off—for all whom the Lord our God will call" (Acts 2:38–39). Every Christian needs

---

5. To understand this distinction between the baptism with the Holy Spirit and the infilling with the Holy Spirit we must go back to the Greek terms and the framework of meaning that is found in Luke and Acts related to the translation of "filled" with the Spirit. We find that there are two different meanings of "filled" that are consistent with the biblical motifs of the Holy Spirit upon or outside of people which is episodic and expressed in power and action, and the motif of the Spirit working inside of people which is "long term and constant" for salvation and transformation. For a complete study of "filled" and the biblical basis of our understanding, see the following: Zeb Bradford Long and Douglas McMurry, *Receiving the Power: Preparing the Way for the Holy Spirit* (Grand Rapids: Chosen Books/Baker, 1996), and PRMI's *Dunamis Project Manual: Gateways to Empowered Ministry.*

to be baptized with the Spirit, whether young or old, involved in leadership roles or serving on the front line of a school classroom or a grocery checkout. How do we make sure believers are not deprived of this promise?

Take People to Where the Fire Is Burning

It may be that the only way to get started is to identify events and opportunities that are available elsewhere and make the effort to travel. This was one of the ways that I (Paul) was able to bring people into a context where there was prayer for the infilling of the Holy Spirit and, indeed, was a valuable opportunity for myself too. I would take people along with me to events at other churches — some local and others a few hours' drive away — in order that they could learn about and encounter the work of the Spirit. This was especially helpful in the early years of ministry, but we still encourage people in the church to tap into whatever opportunities appear. Dunamis Project training events, weekend conferences organized by GEAR, and one-day events hosted by New Wine (a renewal network in the United Kingdom) have all provided occasions for people to catch the fire of the Spirit's flame.

When the Reverend David Hilborn became minister of City Temple United Reformed Church, he found himself serving a small congregation in the center of London, meeting in a building that used to host thousands of worshipers. An excellent evangelical scholar and teacher, David led Bible studies through the book of Acts and found himself faced with uncomfortable questions from the people in the group, such as, "Well, this is great, but why don't we see things happening like in the book of Acts? When are we going to start doing the stuff that we are reading about: people getting saved, the Holy Spirit filling people, demons being cast out, praying for the sick, signs and wonders?" The questioning persisted through the book of Acts until finally, toward the end of the series, David said, "I just don't know how! I have never read or studied anywhere any teaching on the Holy Spirit from our Reformed and biblical perspective. Please help me!"

The help came as James Gray, one of the elders, found and printed hundreds of pages of teaching about the Holy Spirit from the website of Presbyterian Reformed Ministries International (PRMI). He presented it to his minister, saying, "There is teaching on the Holy Spirit from the Reformed and Presbyterian perspective that will measure up to your excellent biblical scholarship." David read and digested all the teaching materials and came back to James, saying, "Okay! I get it now. I want to be filled with the Holy Spirit. What do I do next?"

"Next" involved James taking his minister and all the elders of City Temple to a conference about evangelism in the power of the Holy Spirit sponsored by PRMI and held in the mountains of North Carolina. On the very first evening, without any laying on of hands and praying, the Holy Spirit fell upon David and the elders, and they experienced the reality, presence, and power of Jesus Christ. Now they had, not just intellectual knowledge, but personal knowledge too. They returned to City Temple equipped by the Holy Spirit to embody the kingdom of God in their ministry and began leading that downtown congregation into active cooperation with the Holy Spirit.

Visiting a place where the fire was already burning was also the means by which God led me (Brad) to ignite renewal among churches in Taiwan. We arranged many trips for Taiwanese pastors to travel to Jesus Abbey in South Korea, giving them the chance to receive teaching and prayer and to be baptized with the Holy Spirit. When they returned to their homeland, they were equipped and able to spread the fire in the churches they served. If it is not yet the right time for events to be hosted in your own congregation, then taking people to where the fire of the Holy Spirit is already burning is a time-honored way of getting started. Indeed, it may be your only option for now.

Bring the Flame into the Local Church

I (Paul) have already mentioned how useful the Alpha Course has been for our church at Plymstock. One of the significant benefits has been the genuine Trinitarian emphasis throughout the whole of that course, together with a specific look at who the Holy Spirit is, what he does, and how we may be filled with the Spirit. For this we take the participants away for a day and provide time and space for praying for people to be baptized with the Spirit. In the early days of running this course, we simply used the video materials. Later we enlisted the help of a local minister who had experience providing this teaching and praying with people. In time I led these sessions myself, and now we have others who are also able to lead and pray for people to receive the Holy Spirit. This growth and development is wonderful, but bringing in people from outside the fellowship—first on video and then in the flesh—were valuable steps along the way. Furthermore, encouraging the whole church to participate in the course has proved a useful means of enabling everyone to be introduced to the Spirit personally and has thus helped to transform the outlook and understanding of the whole congregation.

However, it is not necessary to run a course like Alpha to provide opportunities for people to be baptized and refilled with the Spirit. In the United Kingdom the Lay Witness Movement has long experience running weekend programs for local churches. Through testimony, conversations, and prayer opportunities led by trained laypersons, it has provided a low-key environment in which ordinary Christians help others to grow in their spiritual lives and to receive the help and ministry of the Holy Spirit. In the United States the Spirit Alive program run by PRMI provided a similar means of congregational renewal for many years, bringing teachers and witnesses into a local setting with a specific focus on introducing people to the Holy Spirit. More recently this approach has morphed into the Ignite program in the United States, United Kingdom, and Canada.

Ignite was begun in the United Kingdom by the Reverends Andrew and Sally Willett in their role as Evangelism and Renewal Advocates for GEAR. The inspiration for the idea emerged out of a series of one-day events held at several local churches in central England in which Cindy Strickler taught about Jesus' healing ministry and the work of the Holy Spirit. Cindy had always endeavored to involve people in praying for one another, and this move from audience to participant seemed extremely valuable. Sally and Andrew describe their story:

> One of our first invitations in this role was to lead a day on the theme of renewal in a local church. As we prayed, we felt that their need was for us to lead a day of basic teaching about the Holy Spirit while offering an opportunity for worship and ministry, and this was the beginnings of Ignite. Since then Ignite days have spread, and on a number of occasions we have followed up with day events on other Dunamis Project topics, such as the gifts of the Spirit, prayer, healing, vision, and evangelism. In all cases, these involved a combination of teaching and personal testimonies, and then moving into some type of practical experience.
>
> A URC minister wrote to us after one Ignite to say that he had come to the day in a really disillusioned mood. He had been in a dry place spiritually, feeling battered by years of ministry during which he had been reliant on his own strength. He wrote to say that on that day God had met with him in a significant way and had re-enthused him for ministry. Another minister invited us to lead an Ignite day and followed this up with a series of services that he called "Ignition," focusing on Acts. The church has now been inspired to go out into the streets to share the gospel in an evangelistic campaign.

When there is an interest and openness, bringing in people from outside is a great way of providing gateway opportunities for being baptized with the Holy Spirit. It is, in effect, a case of temporarily importing the first foundation, and because of the greater local involvement, it has the advantage of creating a much broader impact on the life of the church.

Fan the Flame in Everyday Church Life

When a congregation is familiar with aspects of the kingdom of God, it nevertheless remains important to provide fresh opportunities for people to be filled with the Spirit as part of their equipping for serving, as well as recognizing that newcomers will still need to be baptized with the Spirit. For instance, as the founding pastor of Lakeside Community Church in Tampa Bay, Florida, the Reverend Peyton Johnson had the freedom from the very beginning to shape the life of the church. He has established a discipleship program that ensures that members receive a broad Reformed theological grounding for Christian living, and this includes systematic biblical teaching about the Holy Spirit and intentional opportunities to be baptized with the Spirit.

In Plymstock I (Paul) ensure that we regularly pray for people to be anointed and equipped by the Spirit. Sometimes this may happen as a specific focus within worship, following teaching about the Spirit's role. After preaching about evangelism, I simply invite those who have a burden for this work to stand and receive prayer from those around them. We invite the Holy Spirit to fall afresh on them and equip them for the task. Such opportunities can often be woven into the normal fabric of the congregation's life. When people become elders or a person is baptized or a leadership team is appointed for children's ministry, these are all opportunities to lay hands on them and pray for spiritual gifting and empowerment.

For churches that have already begun to grow in cooperating with the Holy Spirit's work, these are not significantly big steps to take. What is crucial, however, is that we do not forget to include these kinds of opportunities and lapse into taking the Spirit's work for granted. This is not about providing people with particular emotional experiences, or even about appearing to be spiritual. It is fundamentally a recognition that Jesus said "apart from me you can do nothing" (John 15:5), and therefore we need to enable people to remain "connected" with him and to be clothed with power by the Holy Spirit. This, he said, is the starting point for normal Christian life and witness. When God's people are growing into fullness in Christ, including being baptized with the Spirit, then the dance may begin.

Part 2

The Seven Dynamics

Chapter 8

Steps in the Dance of Divine-Human Cooperation

Like a woman in ballroom dancing, the bride of Christ must learn her own steps and also recognize and respond to the leading given by her partner. This is no rehearsed routine, but a living partnership requiring intimate contact and sensitivity. Leaders need to teach, cultivate, and intentionally put these "dance steps" in place within our human church structures. This is the dynamic of cooperation we see in the life of Jesus and his disciples. These are the disciplines through which the Holy Spirit will engage us and enable us to share with him in building the church.

From the beginning of this book, we have spoken of cooperating with the Holy Spirit as the key to growing the church. We have established the Two Foundations that make the dance of cooperation possible (see chart on next page). The first foundation (see chapter 3) is leaders who embody the reality of the kingdom of God, and the second foundation (see chapter 6) is congregations "attaining to the whole measure of the fullness of Christ" (Eph. 4:13).

Now we can introduce the nuances of the dance itself, the Seven Dynamics that must be built into the life of a congregation. These are the dynamic "dance steps" that enable the church to participate in advancing the kingdom of God through actively cooperating with the Holy Spirit. It is through this dance that the Holy Spirit grows the church as the body of Christ in depth of fellowship, in ministry, and in outreach.

As we grasp the dynamics of this cooperation, we see more clearly the nature of the church and how it is possible for us to do the same works that Jesus did (John 14:12). This fundamental biblical concept of cooperation opens up vistas as vast as the kingdom of God and changes us from passive bystanders into active participants with God in the great drama of redemption. Through his life, death, resurrection, and ascension, and by baptizing us with the Spirit, Jesus Christ restores the Father's original intention for all

The First Foundation:

Leaders Embodying the Kingdom of God

Jesus Christ provides the principle of embodiment as the essence of spiritual leadership. His criteria for leaders who will embody the reality of the kingdom of God are:

Incorporation

Information

Transformation

Empowerment

The Second Foundation:

Congregations "attaining to the whole measure of the fullness of Christ"

"It was he who gave some to be apostles, some to be prophets, some to be evangelists, and some to be pastors and teachers" (Eph. 4:11).

Prepare God's people for works of service

Unity in the faith

Knowledge of the Son of God

The whole measure of the fullness of Christ

humanity, including our active participation as his friends and coworkers in exercising his dominion over the earth.

In this chapter, we will consider the nature of the dance by examining the example of Jesus when he raised Lazarus from the grave. Here we see, in the life of the second Adam, a living example of this restored original intention. It is a case study of the dance of cooperation, and though raising the dead may not be our normal experience, we will see how the same principles or dance steps that were at work in Jesus' ministry can also be at work in ours. In subsequent chapters, we will then elaborate each of the various dance steps that are involved so that we can learn to cooperate with the Spirit as Jesus did.

Raising Lazarus — a Case Study

John describes the death and resurrection of Lazarus in chapter 11 of his gospel. It would be tempting to "hide" behind the truth of Jesus' divinity and persuade ourselves that the incident does not relate to our own lives, but we must take seriously the fact that Jesus "emptied himself" (Phil. 2:7 NRSV) and lived among us as authentically human, for only then can we see the parallels between his work and ours.

Like all of Jesus' miracles, this event takes place after his baptism, at which point the Holy Spirit descended upon him, clothing him with power. So although Jesus stands central in the story, we know that the Holy Spirit is also actively involved, leading, directing, and empowering him for this engagement. We know, too, that God the Father is present, because Jesus has already said, "The Son can do nothing by himself; he can do only what he sees his Father doing, because whatever the Father does the Son also does" (John 5:19). God the Father and God the Holy Spirit are Jesus' two invisible yet intimately present partners in the dance. Mary and Martha are drawn into the dance, along with the group of Jews who have gathered to grieve with the family, and also Lazarus who, being dead, has a rather less active role, at least until the end!

Love Provides the Context

This drama begins as an ordinary, human tragedy as two sisters, distressed by their brother's severe illness, send a message to Jesus, saying, "The one you love is sick" (John 11:3). It is clear that they themselves love their brother, and this message itself is an expression of love. With this plea for help, Jesus is brought into the tragedy of human life after the fall. While their request would have been sent via a human messenger, today it is through prayer that we invite Jesus to enter the tragedies of sickness and death among those whom we love and cherish.

We also catch a glimpse into the heart of Jesus, the reality of a deep love shared between them all, for Lazarus is "the one you love." Later Mary would show her own deep love and gratitude to Jesus by pouring expensive perfume on his feet and wiping them with her hair when he was guest of honor at a meal in Bethany (John 12:3). This love that Mary and Martha had for their brother and Jesus, and he for them, is the basis for God moving in supernatural power on earth. The love that Jesus has for all humanity is nevertheless personal and particular. He loves Mary, Martha, and Lazarus, and he weeps at their particular but universal human grief of the loss of one who is loved. It is love that draws Jesus into their agony over Lazarus's serious illness and death.

Recognizing God's Kairos Time

Considering the love between Jesus, Lazarus, and the sisters, his response to their message seems bewildering: he stays where he is for two more days. Our natural impulse is to hurry to the bedside when someone we love is unwell, but Jesus declares, "This sickness will not end in death. No, it is for God's glory so that God's Son may be glorified through it" (John 11:4). In doing so, he reveals that there is another agenda at work. He synchronizes himself with the activity of the Holy Spirit, stepping from *chronos* time into *kairos* time — from the relentless ticking of a clock to the "now" moment that is in the flow of what he sees the Father doing.

As Jesus delays, Lazarus dies, and when Jesus finally arrives in Bethany, apparently four days too late, he encounters a scene of grief, despair, and bewildered questions about why he hadn't come sooner. Martha is the first family member to meet Jesus, and she greets him with a reprimand born out of her grieving love: "Lord, if you had been here, my brother would not have died." We can almost hear the tone of her voice and see the tears in her eyes as her words reveal a broken heart. Yet in the midst of her sorrow she voices an extraordinary expression of faith: "And even now I know that whatever you ask from God, God will give you" (John 11:21 – 22 RSV). Even now, in this hopeless time, she may yet see the hand of God at work.

Faith Opening the Door to God's Activity

This mustard seed of faith in the heart of Martha is a gift from the Holy Spirit, and Jesus takes it as the first crack of the door opening for him to work. He then opens wider the door of faith by directly asking Martha to affirm the impossible. First, he states plainly his own identity, saying, "I am the resurrection and the life. He who believes in me will live, even though he dies; and whoever lives and believes in me will never die" (John 11:25 – 26). Then he takes this statement of universal truth and makes it directly personal for Martha. He requires her response as he asks, "Do you believe this?" On this pointed, terrible question hangs all the extraordinary possibilities of door-opening, mountain-moving faith or the blank, stone-cold walls of impossibility imposed by the power of death in the fallen human condition.

Notice that Jesus does not ask Martha to have faith for faith's sake, nor even to believe that her brother will be raised from the dead. Rather, the whole focus is on who Jesus is: "I am the resurrection and the life. He who believes in me will live, even though he dies; and whoever lives and believes in me will never die." The question, "Do you believe this?" is the invitation to trust that Jesus Christ truly is the "I am" in whom is life and impossible possibilities.

Martha responds with an affirmation of faith in who Jesus is: "Yes, Lord, ... I believe that you are the Christ, the Son of God, who was to come into the world" (John 11:27). This declaration by Martha is the open door of faith and is her second invitation to Jesus to enter into the situation. The first came from a heart of love for Jesus and his love for them; this second comes from Martha's faith in Jesus, that He is the "I am." Then, as Jesus heads into the village, he meets Mary and again receives that same reprimand of grieving love, "If you had been here, my brother would not have died" (v. 32). This time there is no talk of faith. But contained in Mary's lament about Jesus' absence during their time of need is an expression of faith; she knows that Jesus could have healed the sick man.

As the crowd of mourners arrives weeping, we gain another glimpse into the heart of God as John records, "Jesus wept" (John 11:35). In the tears running down his face, we see the Father's love for a world that is caught in the misery of sickness and death, held in bondage to the power of sin. This is the love that caused Jesus, the Son of God, to leave the eternal bliss of heaven and enter the tears and pain of a fallen world as love incarnate. We see in Jesus' tears the essence of the gospel of salvation, that "God so loved the world that he gave his only Son, that whoever believes in him should not perish but have eternal life" (3:16 RSV). While some in the crowd complain that if he could heal the sick, then he could have kept the man from dying, others recognize the tears and marvel, "See how he loved him!" (11:36). They, too, are becoming engaged in the unfolding drama that centers on him.

Jesus himself, deeply moved, goes to the tomb, and in that dusty place of death where all human hopes and dreams end abruptly, the dance of cooperation continues. He calls for a startling act of obedience, a corporate concrete expression of faith, commanding them, "Take away the stone" (John 11:39). Martha, having just affirmed her faith in Jesus, now voices the practical impossibilities of Jesus' request by protesting about the aroma that would accompany a four-day-old corpse. But he graciously encourages her to hold on to that statement of faith that he is the "I am" of resurrection life. As the stone is rolled away and people cover their faces against the stench of death, the drama pauses.

Time comes to a standstill as Jesus stands on the edge of an abyss praying to the Father. We do not know the contents of that prayer apart from the conclusion, as Jesus lifts up his eyes and says, "Father, I thank you that you have heard me. I knew that you always hear me, but I said this for the benefit of the people standing here, that they may believe that you sent me" (John 11:41).

By pausing to pray, Jesus demonstrates that God the Father and God the Holy Spirit are the invisible partners with him in this dance of cooperation. We may wonder what was happening in this prayer. Was Jesus beseeching the Father to raise Lazarus from the dead? Was he asking the Father, "Are You going to raise Lazarus from the dead?" Or were Jesus and the Father in such intimate communion that Jesus knew what he was going to do? It was not a matter of asking, nor telling, but of moving in unity of will and purpose.

Jesus Giving the Command and the Miracle

All of this time, from the moment Jesus received the sisters' message, is kairos time. This is the time of the moving of the Holy Spirit. The choice about timing, the words that spoke of love and of faith, and the faith expressed in obedience of moving the stone have all led to this culmination of the dance. Jesus stands before the tomb and speaks the word of God into the climax of this kairos moment. In a loud voice, he commands, "Lazarus, come out!" (John 11:43). And with this spoken word, all of these steps converge in the action of God the Father as the miracle occurs and "the dead man [comes] out" (v. 44). To the astonished crowd, Jesus gives another command, "Take off the grave clothes and let him go" (v. 44), and an extraordinary miracle bears witness to Jesus' identity and that in him death is not the end.

With this dramatic action of God, we return to the human participation as they obey and remove the grave cloths from Lazarus. John records that many saw and put their faith in Jesus, but others, witnesses of the same events, did not believe who Jesus was and instead went and reported him to the religious authorities (John 11:45–46).

Jesus—Fully God and Fully Human

Let us be clear about Jesus' role in this drama. In his writing, John repeatedly draws attention to Jesus' divinity: the Word was God; He came from the Father and became flesh (John 11:45–46). The whole of his gospel is "written that you may believe that Jesus is the Christ, the Son of God" (20:31). Yet it is equally true that Jesus is fully human. Having relinquished his equality with the Father, he shared our humanity and mortality (Phil. 2:5–11), and his ministry on earth was made possible as he was filled with the Holy Spirit, listened to the Father, received guidance, and then spoke the word of God into the situation. As a man, Jesus fits the role of a Holy Spirit empowered "prophet," one who speaks God's word into the human situation. He saw himself in this way (John 4:44), and so did the people around him (4:19; 6:14; 7:40–41; 9:17).

The dance of cooperation is an accessible reality for us because the Holy Spirit may come upon us just as he did with Jesus. The gift of prophetic insight and speech may operate through any Christian by the grace of the Spirit. We may do the same works that Jesus did (John 14:12) in the same way that he did them — as a human being filled with the Holy Spirit, listening to the Father and acting in obedience.

Identifying the Dance Steps

Contained in this extraordinary miracle are the dance steps of cooperation between Jesus, the Father, the Holy Spirit, and human beings. Yet the human and divine interactions are woven together as a whole in which the distinct steps may not be clear, just as in the dynamic movement of ballroom dancing the steps merge together in one fluid, graceful movement. When my wife, Cynthia, and I (Paul) began learning ballroom dancing, and still today when we learn new sequences, the instructor had to slow down the motion and teach us the steps one by one. We will do the same here, breaking down the drama to identify the discrete steps that take place.

These dance steps are what we have labeled the "Seven Dynamics" ("dynamics" because they are active movements rather than static building blocks). Below we give a brief overview of the steps, and in the chapters that follow, we will give extensive consideration to each, looking at how they may be nurtured and integrated into the life of a congregation so that we may participate in this dance of cooperation.

Dynamic 1: Divine Love Drawing Us into Participation

We place the dynamic of divine love drawing us into participation first in the list because it is the most fundamental. Jesus refused to "perform" miracles merely to satisfy curiosity, yet he gladly touched people's lives out of his deep compassion. Evidence of this love is clearly manifest in the account of Jesus' raising of Lazarus. Martha speaks of it, John notes it, Jesus' tears testify to it, and the crowd observes it. Love motivates Jesus' involvement and governs the actions that he takes and the words that he speaks.

Love is also the motivation behind the sisters' initial request. They involve Jesus because they, too, love their brother and want to see him healed of his sickness. They were not seeking a miracle to marvel at and talk about, nor hoping that it would persuade people to have faith in Jesus (though the miracle certainly did have that impact). Rather, it was love — both Jesus' and theirs — that formed the total context for this most extreme healing. The Holy Spirit works in the context of love relationships, and indeed, as 1 Corinthians 13 makes clear, he *requires* love to be the context.

Dynamic 2: Intercessory Prayer: Inviting God's Engagement

Within the mystery of God's sovereignty we find that he places a premium on prayer. He to whom all hearts are open and all desires are known nevertheless tends to wait for us to voice our requests. Certainly Jesus' involvement with Lazarus's sickness and death, his visit to the village, and the miracle that takes place at the tomb all occur precisely because the sisters invite him to engage with their situation.

Today the invitation is extended through intercessory prayer, as human beings ask for the activity of God and enter into dynamic engagement both with God and the situation. This is the beginning of an interactive partnership, and we discover that our own participation is truly an integral aspect of the dance.

Dynamic 3: Faith Clothed in Obedience: Opening the Door to God's Activity

Faith is the active conviction that he who invites us to participate in the dance is himself competent to lead us and able to act. Faith was already evident in both Martha's and Mary's statements that Jesus' presence would have prevented their brother's death. It is voiced again in Martha's affirmation, "I know that even now God will give you whatever you ask" (John 11:22), and Jesus draws from her an even bolder confession about his identity as the Son of God and source of life. This is not a "worked-up feeling," but a gift of faith that comes by the grace of God, sometimes out of previous experience of Jesus' miraculous intervention.

Faith is more than words alone, and as Mary takes Jesus to where her brother lies, and as bystanders obediently remove the stone from the tomb, we see that true faith is clothed in obedience. Even Lazarus's own exit from the tomb is an act of obedience in response to the command of Jesus. Here again we observe that human participation is a necessary part of the dance of cooperation, for faith opens the door for the activity of God.

Dynamic 4: Receiving Divine Guidance
for Cooperating with the Holy Spirit

Guidance enables us to work according to God's agenda rather than relying on our own partial wisdom and insights. As a man anointed with the Holy Spirit and perfectly obedient, Jesus stresses that he does "only what he sees his Father doing" and that "whatever the Father does the Son also does" (John 5:19). His initial delay before going to the grieving sisters and his prayer prior to raising Lazarus indicate this awareness of what his Father wished to accomplish.

Similarly, those who stood nearby were made aware of what action they needed to take because Jesus, the Son of God, gave them instructions. Today such guidance comes not only through the words of Scripture, but also with specific immediate revelation through gifts of the Holy Spirit, such as words of prophecy, knowledge, or wisdom, and makes it possible for us, like Jesus, to join in with what the Father is doing.

Dynamic 5: Spiritual Discernment:
Making Listening and Obedience Safe

Of the Seven Dynamics, spiritual discernment is not evident in the drama of Lazarus's resurrection. Yet it is crucial for us because, unlike Jesus, our "spiritual hearing" is imperfect, and without discernment we are prone to mistakes and open to abuses. This need for discernment is highlighted in Paul's instruction that "two or three prophets should speak, and the others should weigh carefully what is said" (1 Cor. 14:29), and John warns us to "test the spirits to see whether they are from God" (1 John 4:1).

By learning to discern what is and is not authentically from the Lord, we create an environment in which it is safe for people to listen for the Spirit's guidance and to take steps of obedient faith. Discernment is an oft-overlooked yet crucial discipline for the church as it considers an invitation into the dance.

Dynamic 6: Welcoming the Gifts
and Manifestations of the Holy Spirit

Spiritual gifts and manifestations of the Spirit's power enable us to act as agents of God's kingdom on earth. Revelatory gifts provide the necessary guidance, but other gifts are needed too. Jesus not only knew what to say, but also exercised miraculous powers, delivered people from evil spirits, and brought healing to people afflicted by a wide range of sickness and diseases (including a "mere" fever, blindness, leprosy, deafness, paralysis, and several other instances of death as well as Lazarus's).

He promised that we would do the same kind of works as he did. For this to happen, we need to welcome the full variety of the Holy Spirit's gifts and not place any constraints on his sovereign freedom. Gifts such as mercy, healing, evangelism, generosity, administration, prophecy, and hospitality continued to be seen in the life of the early church, and we need to welcome them equally in our own circumstances.

Dynamic 7: Seeing and Responding to Kairos Moments

Kairos moments are those spiritually significant occasions when the Holy Spirit is ready to act in a particular manner and place. They fall within the chronological passage of time yet stand out as notably different, being God's "now" moments of special activity. Jesus recognized the imminent kairos time as he delayed before journeying to Bethany. He knew the time was right when he told the bystanders to roll away the stone and when he called Lazarus forth from the tomb.

By learning to discern kairos moments, we discover and cooperate with God's timing, neither preempting his activity nor tarrying and missing the moment. We appreciate how to synchronize ourselves with the activity of the Holy Spirit, whether that concerns a particular season of a church's life or the right moment to speak out a word of correction or blessing. We learn not only to do what the Father is doing, but to do it *when* the Father is doing it.

Our human response to divine kairos moments may be seen this way.

Kairos Moments in *Chronos* Time

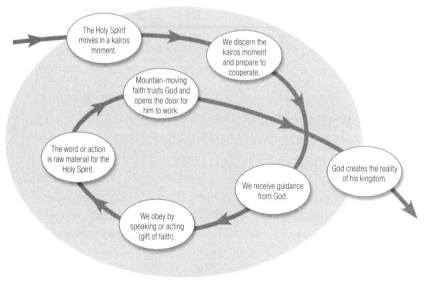

Dancing

Let us return to the image of a ballroom dance. At the beginning, the context is prepared as the room is made ready, musicians gather, dancers arrive with their partners, and the music begins. Throughout the event, there are a series of various dances, some slow and gentle, others fast and full of energy. Eventually it is time for the last waltz (why does the last dance always seem to be a waltz?), and afterward the dancers disperse. Within them linger the excitement, expectation, and necessary skill for dancing, all awaiting the invitation to return for the next dance.

So it is for us, too, as coworkers and friends of God in this dynamic dance of divine-human cooperation that grows the church and advances the kingdom of God on earth. While God is always the chief actor, our own actions play a vital part in expressing the kingdom of God; and as we learn to participate and put into practice what we learn, we find ourselves better equipped for future involvement. Let us therefore examine these Seven Dynamics and discover how each may be learned and integrated into the life of a congregation, bearing in mind that reality will always be a synergy of these steps flowing together in a complex whole.

Chapter 9

Dynamic 1: Divine Love Drawing Us into Participation

The only possible starting point, and therefore the first step in the dance of cooperation with the Holy Spirit, is love. Love draws us into the dance because love reflects the very nature of God. It was the starting point for Jesus' ministry and opens the door for us to engage in this work, too, for without it we are nothing. As leaders we need to cultivate love in our own lives and in our churches. When we do, the stage is set for the Holy Spirit to come and lead us into participation with him.

Love begins with God, and God begins with love. It cannot be otherwise, for that is his essence, his very nature. "God," declares John, "*is* love" (1 John 4:8, 16, italics ours). Within the intimacy of prayer, Jesus affirms that the Father "loved [him] before the creation of the world" (John 17:24), and Paul famously reminds us that the fruit of the Spirit is love (Gal. 5:22). The whole great drama of redemption and of our participation in the dance of cooperation with the Father, Son, and Holy Spirit begins with love. Jesus' advent and his self-sacrificial death demonstrate God's own love for us (John 3:16–17; Rom. 5:8). Indeed, "God has poured out his love into our hearts by the Holy Spirit, whom he has given us" (Rom. 5:5), and our own love is born as a response to this: "We love because he first loved us" (1 John 4:19).

This first dynamic, divine love drawing us into participation, is twofold. It speaks of the love that we know in our own relationship with God and of the love that we in turn express toward others. English Vicar David Watson highlighted the preeminence of love and how fundamentally necessary it is: "The world today is suffocated with words, but starved of love. A truly loving fellowship will therefore act like a magnet. Nothing can be a substitute for love; it is the greatest thing in the world, and it is the foremost concern of the Holy Spirit to pour God's love into the hearts of his people. Without that love we are nothing, and have nothing to offer to a hungry world."[1]

Knowing the Love of God in Experience

When our second child, Nicola, was just a year old, I (Paul) found myself late one night dealing with that typical parental task of a total cleanup after a baby has been sick. This was the second cleanup of the night (Ruth, our other daughter, had already begun the "fun"), and it came as the latest in a small catalog of setbacks and problems that had plagued the day. Probably the most frustrating was the unilateral action by my computer to decide to delete some crucial files and to keep turning itself off without warning! As I cuddled Nicola to sleep, I demanded a few answers from my own heavenly Father about why things like this should blight my nicely ordered life. Heaven was silent. I changed my line of questioning, asking if there was anything I could learn from these events, and immediately I had a profoundly clear sense that God was speaking right into my heart: "Look at the love you have shown your daughter. In the same way, I will never stop loving you or treating you in a loving way."

Now, I tend to be a very rational person, comfortable with lists and schedules and wanting things to be neatly organized. But I have found that the Father wants to deal with more than just my head and at times truly does choose to pour out his love into my heart through the working of his Holy Spirit. The day he gave me a vision of myself as a child held in his arms with him gazing down at me was a further reminder of the indescribable way in which I am loved.

Such encounters have a powerful impact, stirring our own hearts to respond. Since we are made in the image of God and are called to love him with the whole of our being (Luke 10:27), it is therefore right that our emotions should be part of that relationship. A personal awareness of the Father's love is not just the privilege of a few "elite" mystics, but of all of God's children through the ministry of the Holy Spirit. We may be caught up in worship and find our hearts are filled with praise as we are touched by the heart of Jesus. We may meditate on Scripture and find that the Holy Spirit stirs in us a deep response to the words and deeds of Jesus as we read of his life-changing compassion and mercy, his tenderness and his awful sacrifice. Or we may see him ministering to people in our midst and find ourselves overcome with feelings of love and joy for Jesus and for the person

---

1. David Watson, *I Believe in the Church* (London: Hodder & Stoughton, 1978), 175.

he is working in. Those who are touched by Jesus' forgiveness, healing, or salvation are often overwhelmed by feelings of love. The woman in Simon's house was overcome with love for Jesus because she had been forgiven so much. In response, she broke all social conventions and let down her abundant hair to dry his tear-drenched feet (Luke 7:44–50).

This experiential, "feelings," dimension of love means that when the Holy Spirit is welcomed to move in a congregation, believers will express joy and love. Some expressions may be emotional, with tears and other outward signs, but these should not be dismissed as emotionalism or a loss of control. Indeed, one of the first signs of the moving of the Holy Spirit in a congregation will be a greater freedom in expressing authentic feelings that accompany experiencing the love of Jesus.

Showing the Love of God in Action

Knowing and experiencing God's love for ourselves, however, is only part of the picture. John writes plainly, "If anyone says, 'I love God,' yet hates his brother, he is a liar. For anyone who does not love his brother, whom he has seen, cannot love God, whom he has not seen" (1 John 4:20). Authentic love shows itself in actions, and that is why Paul was pleased to point out, "My message and my preaching were not with wise and persuasive words, but with a demonstration of the Spirit's power" (1 Cor. 2:4). These were not gifts and manifestations for their own sake, but grace-filled expressions of God's love, signposts pointing people toward Jesus who is love incarnate. Without that love they would have been worse than useless (13:1–3, 13).

Love, like faith, is not primarily a feeling. It is an aspect of our relationship with God that is clothed with deeds. Jesus put it very bluntly: "If you love me, you will obey what I command" (John 14:15). Parables such as the parable of the good Samaritan show that love is not just a feeling or an abstract philosophical principle. Likewise, in the book of Acts, although the word *love* is never used, real-life stories reveal love in action as people sell possessions to share with the needy; bring healing to those who are lame, sick, or dead; and invite people everywhere to receive the salvation that came because of God's love for the world.

Paul uses the word *love* 120 times as he nurtures growing churches, and John uses it 50 times in his short letters. For both of these men, love *does* something because love is God's very nature. Love is the first step in our dance of cooperation with God in his work. It paves the way for all the other steps as Jesus Christ shares with us his own heart for those he loves.

Love in the Local Church

My (Brad) wife, Laura, is pastor of a small church in a North Carolina mill town. This town was once home to numerous textile and furniture factories, but in the last thirty years much has changed. In recent years, good jobs have been hard to find, and many people struggle financially.

Up the hillside from the church are houses built for mill workers of a previous generation. Now these small homes are occupied by a diverse population, including the elderly on fixed incomes, single mothers with children, people on disability, and immigrants from Latin America. On Sunday mornings the church bell would ring out clearly through the old mill community, but no one would come to church. The thirty or so people who were members drove from other parts of town. About the only way the neighbors used the church was to skateboard in the parking lot or smoke on the steps of the fellowship hall.

Nevertheless, this small congregation intended to live in love and service to the Lord Jesus Christ. But what did living in love and service mean? How could intentions become reality?

The pastor writes:

We tried to be optimistic through discouragement. Our outreach to the community over the years had been unsuccessful for various reasons. Should we just keep trying things that hadn't worked very well? We had already knocked on a lot of doors and offered invitations to come to different events. It would have been easy to give up, but we didn't. We continued to ask God, "What do you want us to be doing?"

We did know that we were successful in some things. We had done plays, programs, dinners, and fund raisers for ourselves and others. Through these things we were aware of one another's skills—like who could handle a computer spreadsheet and who enjoyed making phone calls, who had strong backs and who had free Saturday mornings.

At last God answered our prayer through Angel Food Ministries.[2] This is a Christian food cooperative that operates nondenominationally through most of the United States. Host sites distribute food that has been previously ordered and paid for.

Now things are different at the church. On the last Saturday of every month, the fellowship hall is alive with activity. Before dawn members are off to pick up the preordered food and bring it to the church. When the vans arrive, everyone pitches in to unload the boxes of frozen chicken, fresh eggs, milk, potatoes, and much more. Folks from other churches

---

2. For more information on this ministry, go to www.angelfoodministries.com.

help out; neighbors from up the street lend a hand. Soon we have the seventeen different food items neatly arranged on the tables along with the boxes of special orders and senior menus. By 9:00 a.m. people start coming through the door to pick up their food. Most of the food is ordered, but we do give food away to those who have special need.

Lots of good-natured teasing and hellos fill the room. A great-grandmother checks off the special orders and invites the guest to come to church. A church elder hands a package of frozen beef across the table and says, "Are you doing all right today? God bless you." A small woman with a big grin places a pumpkin pie and an evangelism magazine in the guest's food box. I chat with people as they load up their cars and sometimes have a prayer for them right there in the parking lot. One volunteer is playing the piano, another is serving coffee. Children are playing on the church lawn.

And so the morning goes. When we close up shop about two hours later, we have hugged, prayed with, blessed, and fed many families and individuals. We have had another great opportunity to share God's gifts of encouragement and love. And we know that Angel Food really is all about Jesus, and we are grateful to have this ministry by his grace.

Watching this small church overflowing with love and joy, turning into a place where heaven touches earth, is a deeply moving experience. God is using this Angel Food program to bless the community. But he is also using it to work in this little congregation as the love of Jesus is nurtured and given concrete, practical expression.

The Fruit of Growing in Love

For Laura's church this ministry began because a seed of love was planted in their hearts. God's love moved them to *feel* love toward others, stirred them to want to *show* Jesus' love, and moved them into *prayer* for the means of expressing that love. Divine love created the context within which the congregation could join the dance of cooperation with the Holy Spirit. And as they have participated in this ministry, the church has developed a new openness to Jesus Christ and the working of the Holy Spirit.

Several gifts of the Holy Spirit have become evident. Paul reminds the church in Rome: "If a man's gift is ... contributing to the needs of others, let him give generously; if it is leadership, let him govern diligently; if it is showing mercy, let him do it cheerfully" (Rom. 12:6–8). Laura clearly had an anointing for leadership, helping the church to seek and discern its proper sphere of ministry, uniting the congregation in its purpose, and giving direction to the work. The gift of generosity emerged as the congregation became aware of the needs in the community and began to buy extra boxes to give away to those who could not afford to pay for them. Mercy is shown joyfully to those who come seeking help.

Equipped by the Spirit, the church is acting as a witness to Jesus. A gifting for evangelism is evident as people speak about God's love and the hope that is found in Jesus Christ. Several families have now joined them for worship because they were drawn in by the food ministry. This has led to a changed atmosphere in the congregation, and hope has grown.

Laura herself has the encouragement of seeing that small church growing through the power of the Holy Spirit. Again, Laura describes the story:

> I am thankful to hear stories about how God is working in our church. I'd like to pass along some stories that members shared about why they joined our church.
>
> The first person to come our way was Amy. Her grandmother had been a long-time member of our church and was quite ill. I was at the grandmother's home for a pastoral visit, and Amy was there too. Amy joined in our prayer together. Later she started attending our church. She said that there had been "something about that prayer with Grandmother" that made her want to be part of our fellowship. She brought along her husband and two children.
>
> Amy's prayer ministry has continued to grow, and that is another story.
>
> Then there's Joe and Jenny. I was at the men's shelter one afternoon, and they were there waiting for a food delivery. I invited them to come to a dinner at the church the next Sunday. They came! And after our worship service, Joe asked one of our members, "Did you folks put on something special for us, or are you always like that?"
>
> "What do you mean?" the elder replied.
>
> "That passing of the peace — do you do that every Sunday?"
>
> "Yes, we sure do, every Sunday."
>
> And Joe and Jenny decided to stay and have become invaluable to us. They continue to give active testimony to God's faithfulness and provision, and that's another story.
>
> Andrew showed up early one Sunday to order some Angel Food and asked if he could stay for the service. We said, "Of course!" After church he told us he would be back again next Sunday. He's been back every Sunday since then. He had been hunting for a church for three years and decided to join us because, in his words, "The Holy Spirit is here. And, there aren't any 'big I's and little you's."

Andrew has a calling to healing ministry. Through his encouragement we have started a healing service. Now the session has asked for training in how to pray for healing for others, and the story is going on.

Sometimes God works in people, and then we don't see them again. One of the most memorable encounters was with Michelle. She came to us as an Internet friend of one of our members. Two Sundays she managed to come to church, but mostly she was too tired. Her doctor had said she had six months to live and only three months to be mobile. Soon her spinal cancer would keep her bedridden. The lesions in her lungs showed the cancer was spreading. Her husband had told her he didn't want to live with an invalid and had thrown her out. She was living alone in a small apartment. She avoided my visits.

A few months later, Michelle was hospitalized with pneumonia. When I stopped by to see her, she barely opened her eyes. I put my hands on her and prayed for the presence of Christ and her healing. I myself was aware of the sweetness of the presence of the Holy Spirit.

Two months later I got the word that Michelle was a new woman. She had gone back for another doctor's visit. The doctor was mystified; somehow her spinal tumor had shrunk and was no longer inside the spine itself. It was now operable. The lesions in her lungs had disappeared. He told Michelle she ought to be fine. She was ecstatic, and she told her friend that it all happened when "that lady came and prayed for me." She said she had felt heat going through her body and so much peace. We rejoice with her in God's good mercy. Michelle has now moved to another town, and we've lost touch with her, but her healing has blessed us all. Praise God!

This dynamic of love, poured into our hearts by the Holy Spirit and expressed in actions, is the first and most important dynamic needed within the church. It sets the context in which the dance of cooperation may take place. It is therefore crucial for leaders to nurture the love of Jesus Christ within the congregation.

Nurturing Divine Love in the Congregation

1. The Need to Embody Love

After washing his disciples' feet, Jesus explained, "I have set you an example that you should do as I have done for you" (John 13:15). In the same way, Paul tells the Corinthian church, "Follow my example, as I follow the example of Christ" (1 Cor. 11:1; cf. Phil. 3:17). The leaders of a congregation must embody Jesus' love for the people so that there is a working example for others to learn from and copy.

This comes automatically to some because it is part of their personality anyway. Among us three authors, Cindy is naturally a "heart" person, compassionate and caring. Paul is a "head" person who wants to see things organized and structured effectively. Brad is a "gut" person who focuses on purpose and action. These different centers of personality lead us to function with different emphases in ministry, so we simply recognize this fact and don't allow ourselves to feel guilty about it.[3] However, love truly is one of the fruits of the Holy Spirit and is of paramount importance. Paul and Brad, therefore, need to cooperate with the Spirit's work of nurturing love within our own lives, and sometimes that means deliberately choosing to engage in loving actions. If we don't do this, we will struggle to be a means of Jesus working in the church.

Leadership teams and churches need to seek out, encourage, and depend on those in our leadership team or in the congregation who do have the gift of mercy. Their hearts, which touch the heart of Jesus, may lead the church into tangible ways that Jesus wants us to express his love.

2. The Need to Pray for Love

As Jesus faced the cross, he prayed for all who would believe in him, saying to his Father, "I have made you known to them, and will continue to make you known in order that the love you have for me may be in them and that I myself may be in them" (John 17:26). He does not simply pray that they may be the recipients of God's love. Rather, he prays that the Father's love may also become their love. "The love with which they learn to love is nothing less than the love amongst the persons of the Godhead."[4] As this was Jesus' own prayer, we may echo it with absolute confidence, asking that God's love will increase within each of us and that love between us will also grow.

One Saturday evening I (Paul) was prompted by the Spirit to enter the church's sanctuary, place my hands on every chair in the room, and pray for

---

3. This reference to the "head," "heart," and "gut" centers of the personality is based on a Christian Jesuit (not New Age!) version of the Enneagram personality types that we have used in PRMI training. We have found this system and others such as Myers Briggs helpful as leaders are growing in self-awareness. However, these personality typologies are no substitute for the revelation of Scripture.

4. D. A. Carson, *The Gospel According to John* (Leicester: InterVarsity Press, 1991), 570.

each of the individuals who would sit there the next morning. As I did so, I found that love grew within me, and each person began to matter. The following day, as I led the service, there was a genuine desire in my own heart that each of these worshipers should connect with the living God.

Praying for love itself, and praying for people with the little love that we have, opens our hearts to allow the Holy Spirit to grow love in us. Leaders need to encourage people to pray for one another that they may experience the Father's love for themselves, that they may grow in love toward others, and that they may be a conduit of his love into a lost and hurting world.

3. The Need to Learn about Love

Jesus' message to the church in Ephesus was uncomfortable: "I hold this against you: You have forsaken your first love. Remember the height from which you have fallen!" (Rev. 2:4–5). The parable of the good Samaritan, probably Jesus' most famous parable, portrays the character of love. Paul wrote an entire chapter to the Corinthian church explaining the nature of love, and John's first letter returns repeatedly to the theme of love, like recurring phrases in a piece of music. The testimony of Scripture is that Christians need to be taught about love. We are a forgetful people.

One Sunday morning as I (Paul) was driving to church, I was venting my frustration to the Lord about people's offerings — it's the kind of thing ministers do when they are alone, and has a good precedent in the Psalms! As I prayed, the words "Teach them to love me" came to mind. It was hardly the most elaborate preaching plan ever devised, yet it goes right to the heart. As people learn about the diamond-faceted love of God, they move beyond a merely romanticized attitude on the one hand and escape from the dungeon of diligent duty on the other. The Bible's portrayal of love is at once tender and sacrificial, joyful and heartbroken, contemplative and practical. Let people learn about this love and it will pattern their living.

4. The Need to Remove Obstacles to Love

Near the climax of the Lord's Prayer lies a commitment to forgive those who sin against us, and Jesus warns of severe consequences "unless you forgive your brother from your heart" (Matt. 18:35). Unconfessed sin and unhealed hurts from the past can become blockages that prevent us from growing in love. These obstacles need to be removed. James encourages us: "Confess your sins to each other and pray for each other so that you may be healed" (James 5:16). Paul writes of the need to "bear with each other and forgive whatever grievances you may have against one another. Forgive as the Lord forgave you"

(Col. 3:13). The author of Hebrews warns us, "See to it that ... no bitter root grows up to cause trouble and defile many" (12:15). It is hard for the flower of love to grow among weeds or in stony ground. We need to clear away such hindrances to growth.

When a leadership colleague caused severe problems for me (Paul), I seriously struggled to work alongside her. Even being in the same room was emotionally painful as memories of the hurt surfaced yet again. It was hard to love the individual, and the ache in my heart could often be distracting. Over a year later, I was able to face and deal with the situation in prayer alongside two fellow Christians, though part of me would have found it easier to hold on to the hurt myself rather than place it in the Lord's hands. Yet removing that obstacle has freed me to love the person and no longer be distracted.

Obstacles may be individual or may affect a whole congregation. They may be current or be rooted in the past. The reality is that they need to be brought out into the light and dealt with so that love may be free to flourish.

5. Ask the Spirit to Guide into Love

Laura and her congregation asked, "Lord, how may we be a witness to the love of Jesus Christ in this neighborhood?" As they prayed, so the Spirit guided them to discover and become involved with Angel Food Ministries, and the surrounding community has seen clearly the truth that God is love. Each church's situation provides unique opportunities for demonstrating Christ's love. For some that is intensely local, while others may find their ministry touches lives overseas. What is crucial is that the church engages in the particular ministry of love that the Lord intends for them. Merely copying what happens elsewhere, without asking the Spirit to guide us, is little more than spiritual laziness.

Divine love drawing us into participation is the first of our Seven Dynamics. It creates the spiritual context in which congregations may join in the dance of cooperation with the Holy Spirit. It can be exciting to witness some of the more dramatic gifts of the Spirit, to recognize the arrival of a kairos moment, or to discover the power of reality-shaping prayer. But from beginning to end, love for God, for his church, and for his world has to be the context. Without it we are nothing.

Chapter 10

Dynamic 2: Intercessory Prayer: Inviting God's Engagement

During Peter's imprisonment and after his release, the early church was intentional about prayer. When battling the Amalekites, both Joshua's role of fighting and Moses' role of intercession were essential. Seeking vision in the context of prayer, and then the intercessory work of praying it into reality, are the key to engaging in the Lord's programs and initiatives. The leader's practical task is to cultivate this type of prayer in the local congregation, for prayer is the means that God has given us to invite his engagement in his own work.

When Lazarus lay sick, Martha and Mary "sent word to Jesus" (John 11:3). It seems a minor statement, but sending word to Jesus was a crucial part of the process, for without this message, Jesus would not have visited the village and healed their brother. We do not know how long it took for the news to reach Jesus—but his delay of two days, together with the traveling time, meant that Lazarus was four days in the tomb by the time Jesus and his disciples arrived. Today our communication with Jesus is more direct as, through prayer, we invite him to engage with our particular situations.

This capacity for prayer is made possible by the Holy Spirit who intercedes through us. The third person of the Trinity creates the medium through which prayer travels—that is, the relationship of love that exists not only between Father, Son, and Spirit, but that also involves us as God's children. This is the context in which prayer happens, and we see it in the case of Lazarus: the sisters' invitation captured Jesus' attention because of the love that already existed between him and this family. These two dynamics of love and prayer are inseparably interrelated. Love is the motivation, and prayer is the communication. Together they connect us to God and God to us.

The Sovereign God Awaits Our Invitation

Prayer is our human invitation for God to work. When Peter was next in line for the executioner's sword, the church engaged in earnest prayer. Peter was liberated even as they prayed, and having overcome their incredulity, the church was able to rejoice because of the miracle (Acts 12:1–17). But the communication is two-way, and within the context of prayer we also receive guidance through the Holy Spirit, inviting us to work with God. So, for instance, we find the Antioch believers were worshiping and fasting when the Holy Spirit said, "Set apart for me Barnabas and Saul for the work to which I have called them" (13:2). Intercessory prayer brings together the human and the divine, propelling us into the dance of working in a genuine partnership of cooperation with God.

Intercession is a heart cry born of helplessness, acknowledging our limitations and dependence on the Lord. It is also birthed and guided by the Spirit who intercedes through us with sighs too deep for words (Rom. 8:26–27), God himself evoking prayer, engaging us, and enabling the dance. Yet intercession also recognizes our responsibilities, realizing that God works where he is invited—an invitation that is given through prayer. How many situations are handled in our human strength alone because we abdicate this responsibility for intercession?

That the sovereign Lord of all creation should await our invitation seems strange, yet this is precisely how Jesus describes the situation. "The harvest is plentiful, but the workers are few. Ask the Lord of the harvest, therefore, to send out workers into his harvest field" (Luke 10:2). The implication is clear: No prayer results in no workers. God gives us the privilege of participation and waits to be asked. As John Calvin observed, "Nothing is promised to be expected from the Lord, which we are not also bidden to ask of him in prayers."[1] Here we see afresh the significance of our identity. We are created in the image of God and granted representative dominion over the earth. His original intentions for humankind included delegated responsibility, that we might accomplish his purposes as friends and coworkers. For us to be truly coworkers rather than slaves, we must have the freedom not to work with our Creator—a freedom exercised by Adam and Eve in their rebellion. A slave has no option. Friends and coworkers are involved by their own free choice.

---

1. John Calvin, *Institutes of the Christian Religion*, ed. John T. McNeill (Philadelphia: Westminster, 1960), 3.20.2.

A Parable of a House

A generous couple wishes to provide a house for their child. They purchase a plot of land and lovingly design the house and pay for the construction. As the work progresses, they take great pleasure in it, freely wandering through the unfurnished rooms to admire the development or to order changes. When the building is complete and the child is an adult, they hand over the deed and the keys, and the relationship changes. The house no longer belongs to the parents, for it has been gifted to their child. To enter they must first ask permission. The child has a choice, either to invite the parents in or to refuse permission and exclude them from the family activities that take place in the house. Of course the parents hope that the child will not exclude them, but nevertheless they take the risk of providing the house. Their love requires that they now honor the child as a free, responsible adult.

The parable is imperfect, but it illustrates truth. Our heavenly Father created a perfect world, made us in his own image, and gave us the faculties we need in order to exercise his dominion. Volition, reason, creative imagination, and faith are part of God's image in us. Finally, he granted us freedom to include him in our lives or to exclude him. We have a genuine option to live independently if we so wish, using the capabilities and resources that he has given to create a world that suits our desires. Alternatively, by prayer we can invite him to enter and engage with the world he has entrusted to our care, and resubmit ourselves to working under his authority and according to his will.

The life of prayer is the second essential dynamic that needs to be built into the congregation for the dance of cooperation to take place. Churches that do not cultivate this dynamic of prayer will be like children who have shut the door on their parents. They become a congregation in which there may be much human activity but little activity of the Father, Son, and Holy Spirit — a human institution or social entity but no longer the body of Jesus Christ. A church that prays is one that can grow in the power of the Holy Spirit because it is constantly engaging in this two-way dynamic of inviting God in and of God inviting them to cooperate with him.

Prayer and Provision

I (Paul) saw this dynamic interplay in a fairly simple manner when Plymstock United Church was in need of a new person to join the team of elders. For several years we had been operating with fewer elders than we needed, but rather than simply appoint someone to fill the vacancy, we called the church to pray for provision and waited until we had an unmistakable sense of God's guidance. At the monthly prayer meeting in October, Mary Ellis, Tracy Childs, and I were the only people present. When Tracy had left at the end of that meeting, Mary and I acknowledged to each other our inner sense that Tracy should be serving as an elder. We said nothing about this to anyone, including Tracy, but continued to pray.

During the church members' meeting in November, I drew attention to our need for an additional elder and urged people once again to pray about this. After the meeting, Tracy told Mary and me that she thought the Lord was calling her to serve as an elder and hoped this was not simply a response to my comments in the meeting. She said that this sense of calling had become strong after the prayer meeting in October. She and I then prayed together that the Lord would provide further confirmation.

The following Sunday evening, toward the end of the service, I gave an opportunity for people to receive prayer if they had sensed the Lord speaking to them about stepping into a new sphere of ministry. Tracy was one of just two people to respond, and in the context of that praying, someone said to her, "It's about being an elder, isn't it?" A few weeks later, on a Sunday morning in December, another person spoke to Tracy, saying that in the course of praying about eldership, he had sensed that the Lord was calling her to take on that responsibility.

It is easy for churches to appoint people to areas of ministry based on our own insights and then seek God's indulgent blessing on a decision we have made. But through patient, persistent prayer, we declared our dependence on him. In the midst of this prayer, the Spirit then invited us to recognize his specific provision, and by appointing Tracy to this role, the church took part in the dance of cooperation.

The Moses-Joshua Partnership

This second dynamic of intercessory prayer is broader than just the way that we invite God into situations and find ourselves in a two-way interactive process. It is also a crucial component in accomplishing our mission because there is very real partnership between the Joshua work and the Moses work—those through whom prayer is answered and those doing the work of prayer. Joshua himself was certainly a man of prayer, lingering in the Tent of Meeting after Moses returned to the camp (Ex. 33:7–11), but in the battle of Rephidim, Moses had a specific role of intercession, while Joshua's role was to lead the men in physical battle:

The Amalekites came and attacked the Israelites at Rephidim. Moses said to Joshua, "Choose some of our men and go out to fight the Amalekites. Tomorrow I will stand on top of the hill with the staff of God in my hands."

So Joshua fought the Amalekites as Moses had ordered, and Moses, Aaron and Hur went to the top of the hill. As long as Moses held up his hands, the Israelites were winning, but whenever he lowered his hands, the Amalekites were winning. When Moses' hands grew tired, they took a stone and put it under him and he sat on it. Aaron and Hur held his hands up — one on one side, one on the other — so that his hands remained steady till sunset. So Joshua overcame the Amalekite army with the sword.

Then the LORD said to Moses, "Write this on a scroll as something to be remembered and make sure that Joshua hears it, because I will completely blot out the memory of Amalek from under heaven."

Moses built an altar and called it The LORD is my Banner. He said, "For hands were lifted up to the throne of the LORD. The LORD will be at war against the Amalekites from generation to generation." (Ex. 17:8–16)

In this episode we glimpse the complex interrelationship between God working in the spiritual endeavors of the intercessor and God working in the physical endeavors of the warrior. Both men are working to accomplish God's purposes: Moses on the hill interceding, Joshua in the valley fighting. To a casual observer it would be hard to see any connection between the two men: one apparently watching the conflict from a safe vantage point while the other risked life and limb to overcome the enemy. But in the realm of the Spirit, there is a profoundly critical connection between Moses praying and Joshua fighting. God's presence and intentions are invisible and spiritual, but they are translated into physical reality by Joshua and the army defeating the Amalekites.

If either man abandoned his task, the battle would be lost and God's intentions of moving his people to the Promised Land would be thwarted. Both aspects are related in this second dynamic of intercessory prayer that invites God's engagement, and both are part of the dance of cooperation.

Moses and Joshua Teams

Neither Moses nor Joshua worked alone. Moses was supported, quite literally, by Aaron and Hur who held his arms high as he raised his staff before the Lord. Joshua was accompanied by an army of warriors who fought alongside him. This often is the means God chooses. In fact, from the beginning God noted that "it is not good for ... man to be alone" (Gen. 2:18) and promptly set about finding a suitable helper for his work.[2] Though there are inevitably times when a person must work alone, leadership is more commonly a corporate task, with teams of individuals each fulfilling the particular role for which he or she is called and anointed.

We see this Moses and Joshua partnership, for instance, when Paul is engaged in his mission trips. He and his team are the "Joshua" workers, but he is constantly asking for and acknowledging the prayer support of the "Moses" workers who are based in the established congregations of Rome, Corinth, Ephesus, Colossae, and Thessalonica. Paul himself is a man of prayer, but he knows that he also needs the intercessions of others so that his labors will be fruitful. In Paul's letters to the churches, he asks again and again, "Pray for us ..." (Rom. 15:30; 2 Cor. 1:11; Eph. 6:19–20; Col. 4:3–4; 2 Thess. 3:1–2).

We see this great interplay in church history, too. Charles Spurgeon was an anointed preacher of the Word, a "Joshua worker." He was supported in his labors by a host of intercessors who met, aptly enough, in the boiler room of the Metropolitan Tabernacle in London. Their prayers provided the powerful spiritual support that enabled his ministry to be effective. Charles Finney's name is remembered as the powerful revival preacher who brought many to Christ in the nineteenth century in America. Less well known is the man whose name history has forgotten but who contributed just as much to the revival as Finney did. "Father Nash" traveled with him, called to serve as Finney's intercessor, and as the preacher stood in the pulpit before the crowds, this man was alone on his knees before God doing the "Moses" work.

It is vitally important that both the Moses work and the Joshua work take place together within a congregation. Every church leader and missionary needs to be supported by the intercessory prayers of others, enabling him or her to labor according to God's agenda, with his resources and doing the work of his kingdom. Together they ensure that we operate in partnership with the Holy Spirit rather than depending on our own counsel and competence.

---

2. The Hebrew word for "helper" is normally used of God helping his people and should in no way be restricted to a husband and wife relationship.

Joshua and Moses at Montreat Presbyterian Church

These Moses and Joshua roles can be more fluid than fixed. Sometimes one is called up the mountain to pray, while at other times one is called into the valley to work. This tension is often felt most acutely by those in pastoral leadership. Part of their task is to intercede for the congregation, seeking provision and guidance for ministry. Yet they must often step aside from the Moses role to do the Joshua work of preaching, teaching, and pastoring.

Richard White and I (Brad) have shared this tension for many years in our roles at Montreat Presbyterian Church and in PRMI. Each Monday morning we meet and spend time in prayer for our families, the congregation, and the various works of PRMI. This is a wonderful time of Moses work, during which we serve as Aaron and Hur to each other. This is our time of engagement with God, inviting him to work and listening to his guidance of how he is calling us to work with him.

Once while we were praying for greater empowerment for the preaching of the gospel in the church, the Holy Spirit said clearly to Richard, "I am calling you to have a 'boiler room prayer group' to support you as you preach, just like the one I raised up for Charles Spurgeon." Immediately I knew this was from the Lord, and I heard the Holy Spirit saying to me, "And you are to be Richard's first intercessor. Your sole job at Montreat Church is to do the Moses work of prayer."

This guidance led to a prayer meeting that took place each week during the Sunday school hour. God immediately raised up other intercessors, beginning with Richard's wife, Portia. For a season Richard used to join us as we prayed for the preaching service, the Sunday school teachers, and the whole congregation to manifest his presence. This was our Moses work, while the Sunday school teachers and Richard, in his preaching and worship leading, were doing the Joshua work.

A profound change took place in the atmosphere of the worship service and in the Sunday school classrooms as a result of this work of prayer. We began to hear many stories of the work Jesus was doing in people's lives, and Richard's preaching took on fresh power and effectiveness. The other members of that "boiler room prayer group" have been called into other responsibilities, but the call upon me has not lifted. Each Sunday I sit in the back of the church or walk the halls, serving as a Moses worker, interceding for my brother Richard as he does the Joshua work of preaching. This work of prayer is contributing to the dance of cooperation taking place in the life of the congregation, with the result that the whole congregation is growing in numbers, in fellowship, and in works of service, advancing the kingdom of God.

Joshua and Moses in Korea

When I (Brad) returned to Korea in 2008, my role was that of a Joshua worker. I was joined in this work by Ben and Liz Torrey, John Chang, and Peyton Johnson, as together we shared in the upfront role of teaching 150 pastors and church leaders about the Holy Spirit. We did indeed take time to pray for each other and with each other during those days, but this was not the intensive intercessory prayer that was needed to cover the event. Like Joshua and his army, our main responsibility was to engage the crowd in front of us.

But supporting us in England, Canada, and America were a team of Moses workers. For the whole ten days of the trip, about twenty-five people were caught up in prayer for us, busy around the clock. Cindy was in North Carolina on "point," the one through whom the Holy Spirit was coordinating this divine-human effort. Dan in Oregon was mobilizing a network of intercessors over the Internet and was frequently on the phone with Cindy as they sought to discern insights that were offered through this group. Denny in Pennsylvania, a member of the PRMI board, seemed to be in a special position of spiritual authority to offer covering for me. Richard White also moved into the Moses role for me doing intercession, and he listened to my confessions when I called to make them. Lan in Alaska, Ruth in England, and Sandy in Canada were receiving visions, images, and words of knowledge that combined to reveal what was happening in the realm of the Spirit. All this information was "spiritual intelligence" that was analyzed, discerned, and then passed on to an extended network of intercessors. In addition, intercessors from John's congregation in New York City and Peyton's congregation in Florida were praying for this work.

As we taught, we witnessed a great outpouring of the Holy Spirit upon these leaders, and throughout this period we were intensely aware of the spiritual warfare raging around us. The intercessors were in touch by email, cell phone, and Skype, communicating their discernment, and we were able to give direct feedback on what was happening. Time and time again the guidance that they received connected perfectly with what we needed at that moment. For those intercessors in Canada and America, this was physically tiring, since most of our (daytime) activity was during their night time. The time zone difference meant that many could not sleep much during the whole ten days as most of their activity was during their night! Cindy reported, "I hardly slept this whole week and found the persistent call to engage in the battle of prayer really annoying. My son was home on spring break, and I was on call day and night, doing the Moses work for the team in Korea." Several other intercessors also reported being on high alert day and night as they engaged in intense spiritual warfare. Actually, I think the Moses workers were more exhausted than the Joshua workers; at least—thanks to the prayer covering—we could sleep at night.

Toward the end of the event, some major disagreements broke out within the Korean leadership team. Satan was stirring up conflict with a vengeance, working to undo all the blessing that we had just seen. Having taught for most of the week, I was so exhausted that, despite the conflict and warfare I knew were taking place, I felt a complete peace and knew that I was released to rest. I went to bed early and was soon in a deep sleep.

But on the other side of the world, the intercessors were wide awake and engaged in intensive spiritual warfare. My own "Joshua" role was clearly displeasing to the Enemy, who resented this major advancement of the king-dom of God. The intercessors were alerted to this through a shared sense of guidance. Realizing that I was about to come under major demonic attack that might be life threatening, they stepped up their praying.

They recorded that the prayer battle reached a decisive turning point at about 4:00 in the afternoon EST. At that very moment (4:00 a.m. in Korea), I myself was sleeping blissfully when my light was switched on and Liz Tor-rey came running into my room, knelt beside my bed, and laid hands on me, praying in tongues and in English for my protection. After a few minutes, she got up and left, and I went back to sleep as peacefully as before.

Later Liz told us that she had been awakened an hour earlier to go and lay hands on me and pray for my protection. The guidance became stronger and stronger, and she had awakened Ben and asked him to do it. But the guidance was that it needed to be her. The next morning we received news about what was going on with the intercessors. It became clear to us that the Holy Spirit had coordinated this prayer, calling Liz into the gap on site to provide prayers of protection for me locally, the same prayers that the intercessors were pray-ing at a vast distance. This is a strange and wonderful ministry in which, through prayer, we get to do the work of intercession that invites God into a situation, and then he tells us how to dance with him. The result is that the kingdom of God is advanced and Jesus gets the glory. The team and I made it safely out of Korea without any physical or spiritual attack, and the fruit of that teaching event continues to grow to the glory of God.

The Moses Role—Having Vision for God's People

In the life of Moses, we see several aspects of the work of the intercessor that relate directly to the local church. There is the area of spiritual warfare, in which the intercessor is engaged in a prayer battle with the forces of evil that seek to obstruct the church's mission. There is the work of "praying down" the necessary resources for God's work and his people. There is also the aspect of seeking wisdom, guidance, and direction for the tasks that we are called to do. Each of these is an invitation for God to work in the congregation, providing all that is needed to sustain his people in their witness in the world. But there is one particular aspect of intercession that will distinguish the Moses intercessor as a leader. Indeed, it is a primary means of spiritual leadership. This is the work of seeking God's vision of the reality that his people are called to create.

Let us be clear about what we do—and do not—mean here. The King James Version of the Bible translates Proverbs 29:18: "Where there is no vision, the people perish," and so leadership teams are urged to draw up the vision of the future they have planned for their congregation. It seems commonplace to talk about "visionary leadership" and the need for having a "vision statement." But this way of thinking is misleading. Vision is from God. It is *given*, not generated. The New International Version renders the proverb more literally: "Where there is no revelation, the people cast off restraint." Vision has to be *revealed* by God. Without this God-given awareness of the future into which he calls us, people are prone to adopt any and every course of action.

God's vision provides a congregation's particular role in making real the kingdom of God. Jesus' overarching vision for all churches is that they should take part in fulfilling the Great Commission and advancing the kingdom of God. But vision gives direction for a particular congregation in knowing how God is calling them to take part in this work in their specific time and place.

Receiving vision from God made Moses both an intercessor and a leader. When Moses went to see the burning bush, he was caught up in an extraordinary encounter with God. He was given a vision of liberating the people of Israel out of bondage in Egypt and taking them to the Promised Land where they would be made into God's own people, a kingdom of priests (Ex. 3:7–17; 19:3–6). This is actually a renewal of the vision God had already given to Abraham, of calling out from all the people of the world a chosen people through whom he would pour out his blessing on all the peoples of the earth (Gen. 12:1–3). This great compelling vision of a future reality sent Moses into the confrontation with the king of Egypt with the words, "Let my people go!" The same vision also led them during forty years of wandering in the wilderness through many perils and tests. After Moses died on the threshold of the Promised Land, the vision was caught by Joshua and a host of others. In the wilderness they had been formed into a community of God's people. Now Joshua led them into the Promised Land. This powerful vision has transformed lives and shaped history. The calling of God's people gave birth to the means of salvation for all humankind in Jesus Christ. It has persisted over the centuries, even calling the Jews scattered all over the world back to the land in the creation of the modern state of Israel. It remains alive, shaping the nature of the church as the people of God who await the return of Christ to create a new heaven and a new earth in which there will be a new Jerusalem (Rev. 21–22).

This vision came from an encounter with God in prayer, and over the centuries it has been sustained and renewed in prayer. It has resulted in obedience that has truly shaped history and continues to shape the future. This is the amazing power of vision that is given by God in the context of prayer. Through prayer we invite the Lord to engage with our lives, and he responds by giving us prophetic vision — his invitation for us to join him in creating his reality on earth.

God's Vision for Lakeside — "Build Disciples, Not Buildings"

Peyton Johnson is the leader of the growing Lakeside Community Church in Florida, and prayer is an integral part of his leadership. It is in the context of prayer that he receives vision and direction for the life of the church, and for years he has had the habit of regularly going "up the mountain" for extended times of prayer. Congregations have seen in his ministry a model of leadership that is rooted in the work of prayer.

In 1994 Peyton was called by the presbytery in Florida as a church planter. In contrast with the large Californian congregation where he had been the associate pastor, he was now faced with nine acres of land and zero people. It was a humanly impossible scenario, with nothing but the vision of founding a church, and he had little to do except walk on the public road beside the land, praying. As he did so, the Lord was birthing in him the vision of the type of congregation he was going to build — a church with the same dynamics of working with the Holy Spirit that he had seen in the book of Acts and had experienced firsthand at Jesus Abbey in Korea.

The first answer to these prayers came when "out of the blue" the rector of an Episcopal church called and offered a place where they could begin worshiping. So on Sunday afternoons at 12:30 a handful of people congregated and a new church was born. Under the Holy Spirit's anointing, Peyton's gifts of preaching and pastoring were used to establish the second foundation of a congregation growing in the fullness of Christ, and he also began nurturing the people in the Seven Dynamics of cooperating with the Holy Spirit.

Once again "out of the blue" Peyton received a call from a major developer and was offered a gift of twenty-seven acres adjacent to the original plot, including a wonderful nine-acre lake. A year after the church was planted, they put up their first modular office and classrooms, situated by the lake. The congregation kept increasing, outgrowing the Episcopal church's facilities, and they urgently needed a larger place for worship and classrooms. Peyton was often in prayer about the situation. He tells how the Holy Spirit conceived in him an unconventional vision that would profoundly affect the growth of the church.

> I was alone in our little modular office, looking out the window while praying and asking how we should take advantage of our thirty-six acres. "We can't afford to build anything, Lord. What do we do?" Then the thought came to mind: a tent, right over by the lake. That's the way Israel started. It's the way both my uncle and great-grandfather started in different venues![3] As I talked and prayed with other key leaders, we discerned this to be God's vision for the congregation. We had been so locked into the idea of constructing buildings that we couldn't see a simpler solution. We were also struggling with the desire to build a prestigious building like other prospering congregations in our area, but we sensed the Lord saying to us, "Build disciples, not buildings—buildings will come in my time."
>
> Two years later, as the congregation continued growing, we were back to the same concerns: "How do we get buildings up?" We received the same message—"build disciples, not buildings." So instead of bricks and mortar, we simply bought a larger tent—one that would seat more than four hundred people, and I concentrated on developing and running the "Acts 1:8 Course" as a means of nurturing discipleship.[4] We began to

---

3. Peyton's uncle is the Reverend Archer Torrey who started Jesus Abbey by pitching a tent in an isolated mountain valley on the east coast of South Korea. His great-grandfather is R. A. Torrey, the coworker of D. L. Moody who started his worldwide ministry and teaching on the Holy Spirit in revival tent meetings.

4. The Acts 1:8 Course developed by Peyton Johnston is a year-long course to be used in the local congregation that introduces basic Christian doctrine as well as biblical teaching on the person and work of the Holy Spirit as the key to the Christian life. These materials are very similar to the Dunamis Project that I (Brad) developed. They both come from the same root, the teaching of R. A. Torrey and Archer Torrey. The Acts 1:8 Course may be ordered through Lakeside Church at www.lakesidelife.com.

see the Spirit transforming lives and growing people as disciples of Jesus. The tent itself proved to be quite an attraction, drawing many previously unchurched people into our midst. For the eight years that we worshiped under canvas, more than half of the congregation was previously unchurched. Our slogan "Come as You Are" and the informal atmosphere of the tent were comfortable and nonintimidating. It's easy to escape—slip in and out—when there are no walls or barriers! We called ourselves the "Church of the Open Flap," a play on the Church of the Open Door my great-grandfather R. A. Torrey had founded in Los Angeles.

In a way that was not planned by us, our focus became transformation of people by the Spirit, not building church buildings and programs. With our focus on transforming discipleship in a "come as you are" environment, the Lord changed the spiritual DNA of Lakeside. The vision to "build disciples not buildings" has become part of who we are, even though we do now have wonderful premises. The buildings themselves have retained as much openness to the beautiful surroundings as possible, and while the "open flap" has now been replaced by an "open door," it remains open and inviting to the unchurched. The "tent vision" has shaped who we are and how we function.

Cultivating Intercessory Prayer in the Congregation

Cultivating this second dynamic depends heavily on the church's leadership. If the pastor and elders are people of prayer, their example and exhortation will encourage others to pray. If they are not, the whole congregation will be infected with an atmosphere of prayerlessness, and people's prayers will remain mostly personal and individual. I (Paul) find it helpful to have several people on the leadership team for whom prayer is a significant focus. They are certainly not the only ones who pray, but their passion and priority ensure that prayer remains woven into the church's life. I believe every leadership team benefits from having someone for whom prayer is a significant calling and anointing.

In our Reformed tradition, we hold dear the conviction that prayer is not confined to the priesthood. Yet it is easy for people to abdicate their privilege of access to the Father and to leave the practice of prayer in the hands of the leadership. So how can we avoid this and cultivate the practice of intercessory prayer in the life of the congregation?

Teach the People How to Pray

Both Jesus and Paul taught about prayer through modeling it and teaching it. The disciples witnessed Jesus rising early, staying up late, and going up the mountain to pray—a practice that prompted them to ask, "Lord, teach us to pray" (Luke 11:1). And so Jesus taught them, "This, then, is how you should pray: 'Our Father in heaven...'" (Matt. 6:9). As people saw the reality of prayer in his life, they themselves wanted to grow in it. Likewise, Paul modeled prayer, whether chained in prison, on a ship in a storm, or as a simple daily habit, and also gave specific instructions about prayer, such as praying on all occasions (Eph. 6:18) and praying in tongues and in one's own language (1 Cor. 14:15). This combination of both modeling and teaching is the best way for a leader to nurture the congregation in the work of prayer.

We have repeatedly found in all of the Seven Dynamics that learning takes place not just through teaching biblical principles, but through cooperating with the Holy Spirit in practice. One primarily learns to pray, not by hearing lectures on prayer or listening to inspiring stories of the prayer experiences of others, but by moving from teaching to actual praying.

Once I (Brad) was invited to teach a Sunday school class on prayer at Montreat Presbyterian Church. I told some of my own experiences of intercessory prayer and then looked at Jesus' teaching about asking in prayer. I could have just kept on teaching, but one of the men in the group looked very stressed and in need of prayer, so I asked, "Do you have something on your heart that needs to be prayed for by the whole group?" "Yes!" came the answer, "My wife has just been diagnosed with breast cancer. I am really struggling!" At that point, the whole class made the transition into practical application as we gathered around the brother and prayed for him; and afterward some from the class went and found his wife, and a group of women laid hands on her in prayer.

The next Sunday my class on prayer was packed out. I taught for only ten minutes; the rest of the class was spent praying for one another. On the third week, the pastor, Richard, talked about his own life of prayer, and we all ended up praying for him. The pastor's presence was important, for it reinforced what everyone already knew—that he is a man of prayer, and that this work of prayer in the congregation is led by the Holy Spirit and also comes under the authority of the pastor. Through this combination of teaching, testimony, and actively doing the work, the dynamic of intercessory prayer is being built into the general practice of the congregation.

Be Vulnerable Enough to Ask People to Pray for You and with You

Jesus wanted his disciples to keep watch with him as he struggled in Gethsemane. The apostle Paul cultivated prayer by asking others to pray for him and by giving them specific issues to focus on.[5] To the Christians in Rome, he wrote: "Now I urge you, brothers and sisters, through our Lord Jesus Christ and through the love of the Spirit, to join fervently with me in prayer to God on my behalf. Pray that I may be rescued from those who are disobedient in Judea and that my ministry in Jerusalem may be acceptable to the saints, so that by God's will I may come to you with joy and be refreshed in your company" (Rom. 15:30–32 NET).

Paul boldly and persistently asked for prayer, and so should we. It would be surprising to find people in our churches who opposed the idea of praying for their leaders! But while a few confident intercessors might simply get on with it, many more will appreciate having specific guidance and "permission." By having the humility to ask people to pray for us, as Paul did, leaders provide their people with motivation and direction for their prayers. These requests open the door for the Holy Spirit to involve and grow others in the work of prayer, drawing them into the dance of cooperation.

Leaders also must have the vulnerability to ask people not simply to pray for them, but to minister to their needs by praying *with* them. If leaders are the only ones who actually minister to people in this way, they reinforce the perception that prayer is only really for the "experts." So I (Paul) meet with others in prayer for a while before leading worship and preaching, and we pray for all who are taking an active role in the services that day, including myself. When I was about to take a sabbatical, I invited the congregation to gather and pray for me. At conferences I will normally call a few people to pray with me immediately before I do the teaching and will also have people interceding for me during the sessions. By providing opportunities such as these, we help people grow in the practice of cooperative prayer, joining in with the activity of the Holy Spirit.

Create Contexts and Opportunities for Prayer

If prayer is to take place in the congregation, it must be given time, place, and leadership. Different people will find different approaches helpful, and at Plymstock United Church, I (Paul) have sought to encourage prayer in a variety of ways. People gather for several prayer meetings each month, and

---

5. For examples of such prayer requests, see Eph. 6:19–20; Col. 4:3–4; 2 Thess. 3:1–2.

we encourage them to be alert to the focus of others' prayers and to join in along the same theme. Occasionally someone may find themselves unexpectedly burdened for an issue, or they may have a mental picture or a quiet conviction of what we should be praying about. We encourage them to share these things and then concentrate our praying on those topics. Sometimes I also tell the rest of the church what we focused on by sharing the story in the monthly church magazine.

Among the elders we have taken this process further, praying together at the start of our meetings and waiting to see if the Holy Spirit provides any specific guidance. On a few occasions, our agenda has been significantly changed because of the Lord's leading. These opportunities help the leaders themselves to grow in understanding and insight, better equipping them to give a similar lead to others in the church.

Through special events in the church's calendar, we draw people into prayer, often producing prayer bookmarks or a prayer guide with suggestions for focusing their prayers. We have also encouraged people to commit to pray for an activity and to regard this as their primary contribution for that event. By doing so we emphasize the significance of prayer, affirm those who may be called into this work, and provide them with practical ways of engaging in it. While some people deliver publicity leaflets door-to-door, others gather and pray at the same time. Each Sunday we invite people to gather beforehand to pray for the service and participants. A telephone prayer chain enables specific prayer requests to be communicated, and the monthly magazine includes topics for prayer in the church's life.

All these — together with teaching through sermons and special events — help saturate the life and ethos of the church with prayer. But while all Christians have the privilege of prayer, some are specifically called into the work of intercession.

Identify and Equip the Intercessors

Intercessors are a rich blessing. The leader who would nurture the dynamic of prayer should ask the Lord to raise up people for the work of intercession. These are Christians with a special gift and anointing for prayer, often painfully sensitive to the spiritual realm, with a deep personal relationship with Jesus and ready to stand in the gap as he calls them. Many are hidden away within the congregation, unrecognized and underused despite their anointing from the Spirit for this particular work. Often they are unwilling to step into the public view, conscious of Jesus' teaching that prayer is between them and God and is not for the applauding eyes of the public (Matt. 6:6). Some find that they have experiences with God and the demonic that are beyond the normal range of human experience, and so they simply keep quiet.

For others the call to intercessory prayer is embryonic, waiting for the opportunity and environment in which to grow. This is how Mary Ellen Conners, now serving as the prayer coordinator for PRMI, first became involved with intercessory prayer in her local church.

> I had long known the importance of prayer but never felt very effective at it. My first real steps forward came when I joined a group who met on a weekly basis to pray for the missionaries our church supported. In this group I met people who really believed their prayers made a difference. They talked to God, reminding him of his promises, praying in faith. As I listened to them pray, I was encouraged by their faith. I began to feebly add a few prayers and gradually gained confidence. About the same time, I joined a healing prayer team that was forming in our church. There, as we prayed face-to-face with people, we were able to see the immediate effects of our prayers. The principles of intercession that we learned praying for individuals we later applied to praying for Sunday morning services and other church meetings.

The invitation and opportunity to become involved with prayer must be accompanied by support, teaching, and encouragement, so that those who display a particular interest are equipped for it. This might involve offering useful reading materials, such as Brad's *Prayer That Shapes the Future*,[6] directing them toward conferences and teaching events that will nurture their prayer life, or linking them with someone with more experience in the sphere of intercession who can mentor and support them as they grow. Through the Dunamis Project, by giving people the chance to become involved in intercession, we have witnessed many people move from tentative participation to being wonderful prayer workers. The security provided by leadership and support from experienced intercessors, the difference made by their prayers, and thoughtful debriefing afterward have helped equip them for this ministry.

When people are learning to engage in a particular ministry, it is usually helpful for them to have a support framework and basic guidance about how to exercise that role. Similarly, within the local church, people need the invitation to become involved and then to have a context for meaningful participation. After all of this is in place, there then needs to be some way

---

6. Brad Long and Doug McMurry, *Prayer That Shapes the Future* (Grand Rapids: Zondervan, 1999).

that the intercessors can communicate with the leaders and also be balanced in what they are getting.

How can we get people involved in intercession in a way that is helpful to leaders and the rest of the congregation?

- Form prayer groups around something people have a passion about—for example, the church camp or the illness of a beloved church member. Have someone who is more experienced in prayer guide those who are less experienced.
- Help those who are less experienced by providing a starting framework, for instance, by focusing in turn on the four aspects of the ACTS acrostic: adoration, confession, thanksgiving, and supplication.
- Make time to debrief afterward, identifying how the Spirit was guiding and prompting the prayers.

One of the greatest challenges for church leaders is learning how to work with intercessors. When developing a "Moses-Joshua" relationship with one or more intercessors, it is helpful to negotiate expectations. For example, a pastor inviting a group to pray for Sunday service would do well to clarify:

- *How much will you interact with them?* Do you want to pray with them before the service, or do you need that time to mentally prepare to lead worship?
- *Provide a process for feedback.* If they receive discernment they think would be important for you to know, how would you like to receive it? A chat after the service? A note in your mailbox or email? A scheduled monthly meeting? It is often easier to funnel discernment through one person rather than trying to interact with the whole group.
- *Maintain the relationship.* Schedule a regular meeting (perhaps quarterly) to hear from the intercessors, to encourage them, and to agree on any changes that are needed.

In this chapter we have seen how the love that draws us into the dance of cooperation leads us into prayer. Through prayer God is invited into engagement with us, and we see him respond. His response also calls forth a response from us: faith and obedience, and it is to this third dynamic that we now turn.

Chapter 11

Dynamic 3: Faith Clothed in Obedience: Opening the Door to God's Activity

Faith is the conviction that God can and will act, and it is evidenced by actions based on that trust. Faith expressed in action saw Peter walk on water and saw him be an active participant in the healing of the beggar on the temple steps. Faith leads us to be willing to take risky steps of obedience, drawing us into the realm of depending on God where he may work supernaturally. We look now at how leaders can grow this mountain-moving faith and obedience in the congregation.

Hebrews 11:4–39 famously celebrates heroes of faith — men and women who lived with the conviction that God was to be trusted. This conviction is the spiritual gift of faith, "when you know, without a doubt, that you can give up control to God and be confident that he knows best and he will provide."[1] It is the soul-certainty that God can and will accomplish what he says, which then reveals itself in the actions that we take. Jesus describes it as faith that moves mountains (Matt. 21:21), a settled assurance that what is sought in prayer becomes reality in experience (Mark 11:24). This is our third dynamic — the combination of faith and obedience.

Faith and obedience flow naturally from the two dynamics of love and intercessory prayer. The love that calls us into involvement will take us not only up the mountain with Moses in prayer, but also onto the battlefield with Joshua. On the one hand, intercessory prayer invites God's engagement. On the other hand, it creates a context in which God gives vision, directs our participation, and calls us to take action. Obedient faith opens the door to God's activity in the world.

Abraham and Mary are two great paradigms of this type of faith in the Bible. Each stands at a hinge point of salvation history. Each had that gift of

---

1. This description of faith came from Charlotte Mackie, a teenager at Plymstock United Church, in a sermon she preached while this chapter was being drafted.

faith clothed with obedience, a faith that opened the door for God's crucial work of bringing blessing and salvation for all humanity.

Faith Opens the Door to God's Activity

Mary, the mother of Jesus, demonstrates this third dynamic of faith that leads to obedience in her response to the angel's message. As the prophecies of Scripture converge on the life of this betrothed maiden, Gabriel brings word of the role intended for her as mother of King David's heir, explaining, "The Holy Spirit will come upon you, and the power of the Most High will overshadow you" (Luke 1:35). The impact of these words has been blunted by familiarity, but for Mary the message must have been an outrageous absurdity. She was called into a physically impossible and socially embarrassing situation: to be pregnant before her marriage, with an unbelievable story about the child's father, risking rejection by her husband and condemnation by the community.

Mary's faith is extraordinary, displaying an untrammeled trust that God can and will do what the angel says. No wonder Elizabeth exclaims, "Blessed is she who has believed that what the Lord has said to her will be accomplished!" (Luke 1:45). Faith is an attitude of heart that trusts God and expects him to work. To this inner attitude we must also add faith's outward expression in the form of obedience. As James bluntly reminds us, "Faith without deeds is dead" (James 2:26). When stripped of active obedience, faith remains unclothed, mere intellectual assent that fails to connect with the Holy Spirit in the dance of cooperation. This is what James pinpoints in his reflections on Abraham. "You see that his faith and his actions were working together, and *his faith was made complete by what he did*" (v. 22, italics ours). Mary completes her inner attitude of trust with a most feminine yielding to God's plan. "Behold, I am the handmaid of the Lord; let it be to me according to your word" (Luke 1:38 RSV). Her faith expressed through obedience has changed human history. The Holy Spirit came upon her, and she conceived and carried and gave birth to the Savior of the world. Mary's faith opened the door to God's activity.

This dynamic of faith clothed in obedience is found again and again among those who work in partnership with God to shape history. For Abraham it meant uprooting his family to journey into an unknown future and becoming the founding father of God's people. For Moses it involved returning to Egypt for a power confrontation with Pharaoh. Ezekiel took the seemingly foolish step of proclaiming God's word to a valley full of dry bones.

The Moabite foreigner Ruth risked immigrating to Israel and became the great-grandmother of King David. Peter climbed out of the boat at Jesus' invitation and walked on waves. Martha and the crowd rolled away the stone from her dead brother's tomb and witnessed resurrection. Paul embarked on his life-threatening journey to Jerusalem, facing martyrdom for the Messiah.

This same phenomenon of faith clothed in obedience is integral to all great works of the kingdom of God, stretching from Pentecost to the present. John Calvin returned to Geneva, having just been driven out, so he could be used by God to grow the Reformation. Hudson Taylor, with no support, traveled as an evangelistic missionary to China. The Albanian Mother Teresa poured out her life caring for the dying poor on the streets of Calcutta. Jane and Archer Torrey pitched their tent in a Korean mountain valley and began a community of prayer. Peyton Johnson set up a lakeside tent in Florida and grew a congregation from among the unchurched. Myriad stories continue in the same vein, and behind these advancements of the kingdom of God, whether on a global scale, in the life of a congregation, or in the heart of an individual Christian, we always see the gift of faith clothed with obedience.

God's Astonishing Self-Limitation

In the miracle of Lazarus being raised from death, attention is focused on Jesus. Yet Martha also has a pivotal role, opening the door to the miraculous by her expression of faith. When Martha came out to meet Jesus as he approached her home in Bethany, he faced her with a choice: "I am the resurrection and the life. He who believes in me will live, even though he dies; and whoever lives and believes in me will never die. *Do you believe this?*" (John 11:25–26, italics ours).

With this question, history hung in suspense, its course dependent on her answer. Faith is the connector between the realm of the Spirit and this world. The all-powerful, sovereign Lord of all creation has chosen to work most of the time through human faith.[2] Without this open door of faith in the heart of Martha, Jesus would not have been able to move forward in the dance of cooperation with the Father and the Holy Spirit. Scripture records

---

2. We say "most of the time," because clearly God is sovereign and can work any way he chooses (as, for instance, with the creation of the world). But based on many examples of Scripture and church history, it seems that as a general rule God has chosen to work within the limitation of human faith and obedience. This fits with the larger biblical framework of God making covenants with human beings that include our participation in his plans.

that the absence of faith in Jesus' hometown was what robbed its citizens of miracles. The Father's grace, love, and power were the same in Nazareth as in Bethany, and Jesus had the same anointing with the Holy Spirit, but the door was closed. Jesus could do no great works there, and he marveled at their lack of faith (Mark 6:1–6).

Martha had genuine freedom to say, "No! I do not believe!" God, who knows all things and from whom no secret is hidden, already knew what her answer would be. But the choice was hers. Had she not found within herself the grace to say, "Yes, Jesus I believe," the power of God would have been blocked in Bethany just as it was in Nazareth. Lazarus would have remained in his tomb. Here we return to the first dynamic, for it was Martha's great love for Jesus, and his love for the sisters and their brother, which led to the possibility of great faith. And we see again, as with the dynamic of prayer, the Lord's astonishing self-limitation that incorporates *us* into his plans and purposes. Our choices have an integral role in determining what does — or does not — happen.

We still see this today in congregations that do not believe in Jesus Christ as the way, the truth, and the life, and the only way to the Father. Here, as in Nazareth, Jesus can do no great works, for faith is needed to open the door to the dynamic activity of the Holy Spirit.

Faith Clothed in Obedience

It is one thing to hear Jesus ask, "Do you believe this?" and give a verbal affirmation: "Yes, I do." It is a wholly different matter to clothe belief in obedience, yielding as Mary did in bearing the Messiah. This is the crunch moment when faith proves its authenticity. When Jesus told Martha and the weeping crowd to "take away the stone," the reality of their faith was made manifest in their deeds. Martha faltered for a moment, reminding Jesus that there would be a bad smell as Lazarus had been dead four days. But already her faith had opened the door to God's activity, and Jesus called her back to that place of trust, asking: " 'Did I not tell you that if you believed, you would see the glory of God?' So they took away the stone." Faith was clothed in action, welcoming God's powerful work into their midst, and Jesus spoke the command, "Lazarus, come out!" Death was superseded by life, and Lazarus emerged from the tomb (John 11:38–43).

We would be mistaken to regard the dance of cooperation as just one giant leap of faith. Sometimes this may be the case, but often it is one small step, followed by another and another, that enables us to walk by faith.

These incremental acts of obedience give expression to our belief, allowing God to work and faith to flourish one step at a time. So it is that Martha loved Jesus and could voice her trust in him yet struggled with the notion of rolling back the stone. She had not yet grasped the possibility that Jesus might actually raise her brother there and then. Yet removing the stone was the next small step of faith, the next step into the amazing reality of Jesus being the Resurrection and the Life. Jesus connected believing in him with active obedience to his commands. Once this step of faith was taken, Martha and the others saw the glory of God expressed in the miracle of resurrection, and the miracle in turn built up their faith.

It is the same in our own lives. As we step out in obedience to Jesus' commands, we place ourselves in the sphere of faith, opening the door for him to work in our midst. Then, as we witness his power at work among us, we grow in our capacity to trust him. We become more ready and willing to take steps of obedience; we see more of the Holy Spirit's activity—and so the dance goes on! The process of learning to cooperate with the Spirit may include many such incremental actions of obedience that both express our faith and enable us to walk by faith.

These actions of obedience may differ from one situation to another. But the one universal form of obedience, and sometimes the only means of clothing faith, is to offer praise and thanksgiving to the Lord as an expression of trust. Paul instructs, "Do not be anxious about anything. Instead, in every situation, through prayer and petition with thanksgiving, tell your requests to God" (Phil. 4:6 NET). The call to thanksgiving in every situation may sound utterly unrealistic until we remember the catalog of suffering in Paul's own life: being beaten, stoned, shipwrecked, left adrift on the open sea, endangered by bandits and false brothers, imprisoned, cold, naked, and without food (2 Cor. 11:23–28). It is amazing that he can have faith in God at all, much less retain an attitude of gratitude. How many times did Paul find that the only way faith could be expressed in obedience was by being thankful and giving praise?

Having journeyed to Philippi in obedience to the Spirit's guidance, Paul precipitated a riot by delivering a slave girl from the oppression of an evil spirit. Hauled before the authorities, he and Silas were stripped, beaten, thrown into prison, and locked in stocks. In these impossible circumstances, faith was expressed as they started "praying and singing hymns to God." This expression of faith later opened the door for God's direct and supernatural intervention of sending the earthquake. Ultimately it led to the conversion of the jailer and liberty for Paul and Silas (Acts 16:16–39).

When Paul insists that faith should be clothed in the obedience of grateful praise, he is speaking from personal experience of hardship. He chose to trust rather than be anxious, to offer prayer with thanksgiving. He had learned this third dynamic and applied it not only to his own life but also to the lives of the congregations he founded. Consequently, both Paul and the congregations were active participants in the dance of cooperation with the Holy Spirit. In this instance, the fruit of their obedience was to see the gospel of Jesus Christ spread into what is now the Western world, for Philippi was the first church planted on European soil.

A Pastor Learning the Lessons of Faith Clothed in Obedience

When John Chang founded the Grace Christian Congregation in Flushing, New York, he discovered the practical reality of faith clothed in obedience. After graduating from Princeton Theological Seminary, John was called to establish a Reformed Church of America congregation in Staten Island, New York. He himself comes from Taiwan, and this church grew into a flourishing congregation with services in Taiwanese, Mandarin, and English.

John was baptized with the Holy Spirit a few years after establishing this church and found himself gripped by a vision of reaching the Chinese world for Jesus Christ. On one occasion in prayer, he received a strong sense of leading from the Holy Spirit that he should start a new congregation among the vast ethnic Chinese population in Flushing, Queens, just an hour away. Some of the young professionals in the Staten Island congregation were driving from Flushing each week, and John saw how they could form the nucleus of a church, a mission base for reaching that area with the gospel. This would be a congregation that embodied the Seven Dynamics of the dance of cooperation with the Holy Spirit, although he did not use this language. All he knew was that he was called to build a congregation that functioned like the church he saw in the book of Acts and in Paul's first letter to the Corinthian church.[3]

John shared this vision with the group of commuting young professionals from Flushing, and they were immediately excited about the vision — mostly because it would save them the long drive on Sunday mornings! (Thankfully the Holy Spirit is able to work even when our motives start out wrong,

---

3. Specifically, 1 Cor. 12–14.

transforming our heart attitudes so that the right motives blossom within.) After sharing the vision and praying about it with this group, John took the proposal to the elders of the congregation and to his wife, Su. Their unanimous response was a resounding "No!" None of the leadership was in favor of adding to their pastor's workload, and none saw the potential for ministry in the Flushing area or shared the vision of founding a new congregation. Beneath the surface there was also the fear of splitting the congregation if some of the younger members were to start to worship elsewhere.

John was shattered by their response. With a heavy heart, he took this answer to the small, hopeful group of commuters, and they too were profoundly disappointed. His initial thought, born out of his pioneering personality, was to fight back and take on the whole session and his wife too! He was also tempted simply to resign and start this new congregation on his own. But after considerable personal struggle, John submitted to this guidance as coming from Jesus. Later he acknowledged: "For a while I was very angry at the leaders of the congregation and also angry at God! But during this time my own plans were put to death. I must confess that my ego was involved. I wanted to start a dynamic, Holy Spirit-empowered congregation that would make me famous in the R.C.A. I had to die to myself so that I could really have faith in Jesus rather than in my own abilities."

Having accepted the session's counsel, John returned to prayer with a submitted heart, asking, "Well, Lord, what do you want me to do now?" The guidance came clearly: "Start praying with this group. Start living with them the model of the church you see in Acts." John took this revelation to heart and started holding weekly prayer meetings with the group, as well as the church's traditional weekly prayer service. This was the first incremental clothing of faith with obedience, and it went on for about a year, during which many more young professionals became involved. Many of them were previously unchurched, and several came to faith in Christ through this prayer and fellowship group.

In the second year, Bible study and teaching were added to the practice of prayer and fellowship. John taught classes that started with basic Christian doctrine and then moved on to practical discipleship. He focused on biblical teaching about the gifts and power of the Holy Spirit, and by the end of this year most of the group had a deep grounding in Scripture and had been baptized with the Spirit. The empowering work of the Holy Spirit then led to growth in all sorts of areas, including healing prayer ministry and evangelism. They also began to see a lot of deliverance ministry (that is, casting out evil spirits), because as people from pagan backgrounds became

Christians and started growing in the work of the Holy Spirit, demonic manifestations would often occur. The healing and deliverance ministry was being modeled by Su and John who were themselves growing in the gifts and power of the Holy Spirit.

This activity was having a spillover effect on the whole Staten Island congregation. They were growing in depth of ministry, in fellowship, and in numbers, and now John was tempted to be content with this flourishing congregation. But the vision of starting a new congregation in Flushing persisted, and finally he took it back to the elders. This time the reaction was very different. The elders had learned better how to listen to the Holy Spirit, and the congregation had grown so much that they no longer felt threatened by the prospect of a few people leaving to form a new church. They gladly affirmed the vision, and a small team of fifteen from Staten Island left to form the core congregation in China Town in Flushing, Queens.

This new church had its origins in the vision given by the Holy Spirit to Pastor John as he prayed. It became reality as the Spirit drew first John and then the Staten Island elders and the small group of intercessors into the dance of cooperation. To John was given the gift of faith to believe that Jesus really wanted to form a new congregation that would be like the one modeled in Acts. This was not faith in his own vision, but faith in Jesus Christ who alone conceives and gives birth to all new works that are truly expressions of the kingdom of God.

Then came the successive steps of obedience that put faith into action, first submitting to the guidance of the church leadership by not leaving, then by continuing to pray, teaching the Bible, teaching on the work of the Holy Spirit, praying for people to be baptized with the Holy Spirit, and moving into ministry. What John had not realized at the time, but gladly acknowledges in retrospect, was that God was beginning this work within the safe place of the Staten Island congregation. Here he was able to grow and nurture the first and second foundations, which would later form the seeds of the new congregation, programming the DNA of a church in which the dance of cooperation with the Holy Spirit would readily take place. People's experiences of prayer, of growing in the gifts of the Holy Spirit, of seeing healing ministry take place, of people coming to faith in Christ and being set free from evil spirits—all these built up the foundational faith within the core group and in the whole Staten Island fellowship. God was now more welcomed to work than ever before.

After two years of preparation, growing a faith that was clothed in obedience, they reached the jumping-off place. On a particular Sunday, they had made the big leap and actually started. There was nobody in Flushing inviting them to come and start a congregation. They just had to clothe their faith with the very concrete action of starting the worship service. One of the commuters had given them use of a small room in the basement of an apartment building. The time was announced beforehand to the congregation, and posters in English and Chinese were put up around town. Everyone prayed that it would work. But when Sunday came, John had to act in faith, get in his car, drive to Flushing, and lead the service. A tiny, disappointing number of others had done the same, and at the appointed time, John stood before a small group of ten and led them in worship. The new church had begun.

Five years later this is a powerful congregation of about a hundred people. All seven Dynamics of cooperating with the Holy Spirit are integrated into the life of Grace Christian Congregation. When Cindy and I (Brad) came to the Wednesday night prayer group, it was packed with people, buzzing with electric faith and expectancy of what God was going to do, thrilled with what he was already doing. Today the church is alive with prayer ministry, healing, people coming to faith, and generosity in their giving to missions. They are a dynamic missionary sending base, empowered and directed by the Holy Spirit. They are reaching out with the gospel, not only to Flushing; but through their support of PRMI, they are enabling work to take place in mainland China and around the world. The church hosts a Chinese-speaking Dunamis Project track for their whole area. They are an amazing congregation, imperfect as any other church, but nevertheless reflecting the model that we see in the book of Acts of a church that is dancing in partnership with the Holy Spirit.

Nurturing Obedient Faith in the Congregation

If it is true that our faith and obedience do indeed matter, that God truly cannot work without the open door of our faith clothed in obedience, then we bear a terrible responsibility. Jesus intends his church to be more than mere puppets in the hands of an all-sovereign dictatorial deity, and the Father is willing to take terrible risks as he incorporates us into his work and limits himself to our faith and obedience. Our lack of faith and obedience truly can thwart his purposes. This third dynamic of faith clothed in obedience draws a congregation into the mystery and responsibility of truly being friends and coworkers with God the Father, Son, and Holy Spirit. To enable congregations to participate in the dance of cooperation, it is vital that we nurture obedient faith.

1. Begin in the Place of Prayer

Before choosing twelve disciples and designating them as "apostles," Jesus spent the night in prayer (Mark 3:13 – 14; Luke 6:12 – 13). John Chang's vision for establishing a church in Flushing was born in the context of prayer, and as he met with the small group of young professionals, they, too, were doing the work of praying. Through intentional and regular prayer, they were welcoming God to work in the congregation, seeking his guidance, and preparing themselves to act in faith. The Lord responded to this invitation by giving vision that provided direction for their work and by giving them the gift of mountain-moving faith.

Without this starting point of prayer, we face the danger of super-spiritual "believism," a Christianized "power of positive thinking" in which our own aspirations are clothed with enthusiastic pious-sounding declarations. But in the context of prayer, God brings us to the edge of what is humanly possible, inviting us into a future that is possible only because of his power at work, calling us to take the risky next step of obedience. This is no shallow spirituality. Instead, it is often profoundly challenging, sometimes frightening, and always for God's glory as he accomplishes what he wants to do through the congregation. If we would lead a church to clothe faith with obedience, we first must lead them into the place of prayer.

2. Tell the Stories of Obedient Faith

Scripture is saturated with testimony to living faith in a "can do" God who delivers people from the mouths of lions, the schemes of despots, and flaming furnaces. He is the one who provides food in the desert, by the brook, and on the hillside; the Lord who raises the dead, washes lepers clean, causes the lame to leap, and brings deliverance to the demon-oppressed. The Bible is replete with stories of obedient faith, "written to teach us, so that through endurance and the encouragement of the Scriptures we might have hope" (Rom. 15:4). Whether from the pulpit or in the context of small group Bible study, leaders need to retell these examples of lived-out trust and exhort people to follow in their footsteps. Teaching and preaching the Word of God in the power of the Holy Spirit will build faith and trust in Jesus Christ.

To compliment biblical teaching, there is the need for personal testimony. As John and Su Chang worked to build faith in God, there were many occasions when the people formally and informally shared their experiences of what God was doing in their lives. These were the stories of obedient living faith. They served as example and encouragement to others, and they increased people's expectations of what the Holy Spirit could and would do through them too.

Care is needed in telling these stories because it is dangerously easy for us to focus on what we are doing, how great our program is, or what we did to help in disaster relief. Sadly this merely builds pride in our own accomplishments. Instead, our aim must be to glorify the Father and nurture faith in him by describing the work he has done in our midst and how we needed to cooperate in it. This requires careful balance, being careful neither to focus on the sovereignty of God in such a way that we lose the human element and therefore end up with passivity, nor to focus on our own work in such a way that we lose the divine element and end up with faithless activism. When we tell stories of obedient faith, testifying to what God is doing and to the crucial role played by our love, prayer, faith, and obedience in this dance, the Holy Spirit builds people's confidence in what God can do and increases their readiness to trust him in practice.

3. Lead People Out of Their Depth

Jesus' disciples learned obedient faith by being pushed out of their depth — all Twelve sent out in pairs to heal the sick and drive out evil spirits (Mark 6:7–13; Luke 9:1–6). Seventy-two were urged to pray for workers in God's harvest field and then found themselves sent out with minimal resources to evangelize and bring healing (Luke 10:1–17). As John Ortberg writes, "If you want to walk on water, you have to get out of the boat."[4]

In November 2003 I (Paul) stood before a group of people at a Dunamis equipping event, reminded them of Jesus' promise about being baptized with the Holy Spirit, and then led them in prayer as we asked the Lord to pour out his Spirit upon us. It was one of the edgiest, most anxious moments of my life, standing on the borderline between faith and fear. I was out of my depth, with no control at all over whether the Lord would be true to his word. The future lay wholly in his hands. I had led people to the edge of a cliff and simply had to trust God to hold us safe and show his power as we cast ourselves upon his providence and promises. For me it was a moment of crisis, a step of raw obedient faith, as I exercised leadership among some of God's saints.

As John and Su Chang led people in prayer ministry, especially in healing and deliverance, there was a combination of receiving guidance, asking

---

4. John Ortberg, *If You Want to Walk on Water, You Have to Get Out of the Boat* (Grand Rapids: Zondervan, 2003).

for the gift of faith, and then clothing faith in obedient action. At first this was centered on them, as they were the only ones who had been baptized with the Holy Spirit. As others were filled with the Holy Spirit, they, too, were able to be incorporated into the dance. Faith grew amid the vivid, firsthand experiences of seeing the Holy Spirit healing people of emotional hurts and physical illness, demons being cast out, and people accepting Jesus Christ as Lord and Savior. We build faith within the congregation as we step out in obedience and help them to do the same.

As our faith is clothed with action, God moves in our midst. This gives us an experiential confirmation of God's existence and activity among us, which in turn grows our faith in God. The leadership needs to nurture this cycle of growing faith by sharing testimonies of what God is doing and inviting continued prayer and obedience.

Faith is the readiness to take God at his word and act upon it, which is why Jesus asks: "Why do you call me, 'Lord, Lord,' and do not *do what I say*?" (Luke 6:46, italics ours). Of course, this demands clarity about *what* it is that God is calling us to do. So this third dynamic leads inexorably into the fourth, namely, receiving divine guidance for cooperating with the Holy Spirit.

Chapter 12

Dynamic 4: Receiving Divine Guidance for Cooperating with the Holy Spirit

Receiving divine guidance ensures that we engage in Jesus' agenda and not merely our own good ideas. It is the key to our cooperating with the Father, Son, and Holy Spirit. Paul's visit to Philippi and Peter's visit to Cornelius were initiated by revelatory guidance from the Holy Spirit. Scripture is God's foundational, unchangeable revelation, but it also bears witness to the dynamic of his Spirit speaking into situations today, applying doctrine or leading into activities. Individuals and congregations need to become alert to and engage in the discipline of listening to the leading of the Holy Spirit of Jesus.

Every step of the dance of cooperation with the Father, Son, and Holy Spirit depends on us receiving guidance to which we can then respond in obedient faith. When my wife, Cynthia, and I (Paul) are ballroom dancing, she is constantly looking for guidance about what our next sequence of steps will be. This is a complex, multisensory interaction involving body language, balance, occasional eye contact, familiarity with each other, and whispered words of instruction. My human fallibility results in many occasions when she is left guessing or I tread on her toes, and I am grateful that love covers over a multitude of sins (1 Peter 4:8). But in our better moments, the guidance is abundantly clear, our interaction is effortless and intuitive, and the dancing is an overflow of spontaneity, freedom, and grace born out of love and familiarity with each other.

I have found that the situation is similar in the dance of cooperation with the Holy Spirit. Guidance comes in a variety of ways, a complex interaction of human reason, observed circumstances, commands of Scripture, and direct revelation from the Holy Spirit. Love for the Lord and his people motivates us to seek his guidance; often it is in the context of intercessory prayer that vision and specific guidance are given; and faith leads us to respond in obedience to the guidance that we receive. Already we can see that the Seven Dynamics belong together, blending in a vibrant synergy that displays the reality of God's reign in our midst. Divine guidance also plays a critical role in the remaining three dynamics: discernment, welcoming the Spirit's gifts, and responding to kairos moments. Without guidance we have no basis for cooperating with the Holy Spirit, no means of living according to God's will.

Guidance through Scripture and through the Spirit

The voice of creation declares the glory of God, a global testimony to the work of his hands (Ps. 19:1–4). As we look deep within our souls or explore the farthest reaches of space, we discover that our sovereign Creator has left his mark everywhere. Yet he is a personal God and not merely the cosmic "Force" of Star Wars fame, and so our observations of his handiwork give only a glimpse of his true nature. He is the God who speaks, and it is through his own word that we gain insight and understanding of his person and purpose. Creation provides testimony, but it is Scripture that provides instruction and a right understanding (Ps. 19:7–11). John Calvin highlights this distinction between the "mute teachers" of creation and God's self-revelation in the Bible:

> Just as old or bleary-eyed men and those with weak vision, if you thrust before them a most beautiful volume, even if they recognize it to be some sort of writing, yet can scarcely construe two words, but with the aid of spectacles will begin to read distinctly; so Scripture, gathering up the otherwise confused knowledge of God in our minds, having dispersed our dullness, clearly shows us the true God. This, therefore, is a special gift, where God, to instruct the church, not merely uses mute teachers but also opens his own most hallowed lips. Not only does he teach the elect to look upon a god, but also shows himself as the God upon whom they are to look.[1]

In the pages of Scripture, God has revealed his own nature and his purposes for the human race. It is his authoritative, once-and-for-all-time revelation of true, unchanging Christian doctrine and universal ethical

---

1. John Calvin, *Institutes of the Christian Religion*, ed. John. T. McNeill (Philadelphia: Westminster, 1960), 1.6.1.

imperatives. We affirm the orthodox, evangelical conviction that from cover to cover the Bible is God-breathed and fundamentally useful for molding our beliefs and our living (2 Tim. 3:16–17). It is God's written Word, his inscribed revelation.

The Scriptures, the Son, and the Spirit

The author of Hebrews directs our attention to Jesus, the living Word and incarnate revelation: "In the past God spoke to our forefathers through the prophets at many times and in various ways, but in these last days he has spoken to us by his Son, whom he appointed heir of all things, and through whom he made the universe" (Heb. 1:1–2). Therefore, through the life, teachings, works, and person of Jesus, we see God's complete self-disclosure, for "the Son is the radiance of God's glory and the exact representation of his being, sustaining all things by his powerful word" (v. 3). Paul affirms that "in Christ all the fullness of the Deity lives in bodily form" (Col. 2:9), and John refers to him as "the Word [who] became flesh and made his dwelling among us" (John 1:14).

The Father has spoken generally through creation, explicitly through Scripture, and ultimately through his Son. He also continues to speak through his Holy Spirit, a truth that is affirmed by both Jesus and by Scripture. The Holy Spirit not only directed the writing of the Scripture, but also provides direct guidance for God's people today. He speaks repeatedly into specific situations, teaching us how we may live in cooperation with him moment by moment as Jesus' friends and coworkers in the work of the kingdom of God. The disciples were assured that in moments of difficulty "the Holy Spirit will teach you at that time what you should say" (Luke 12:12) and promised that "the Spirit will take from what is mine and make it known to you" (John 16:15). Luke records how the Spirit spoke to people to give guidance (Acts 8:29; 11:12). Paul notes how the Spirit gave the ability to speak God's words into particular situations (1 Cor. 12:8). Throughout Scripture we find examples of the Father speaking through the Holy Spirit in ways that are not revealing true doctrine. He confirms doctrine that has already been revealed in Scripture, guides by the practical application of God's Word to contemporary situations, or guides in specific dance steps of cooperating with himself in building the church and fulfilling the Great Commission.

Here we need to make an affirmation as well as sound a caution. Some have taught that God speaks only through the Holy Bible and that the gifts of the Holy Spirit have ceased. This has discouraged many Christians from expecting and receiving what the Spirit has for them, including God's specific guidance. Yet we have to affirm the teaching of Jesus and of Scripture, together with the experience and witness of the church over the past two thousand years, that the Holy Spirit has not taken early retirement but continues to speak.

Alongside this we sound a cautionary note. Scripture, being God's written revelation, is the standard against which all other revelations must be measured. Thus, anything the Holy Spirit speaks to us today will be consistent with Scripture and consistent with the nature and work of the Jesus Christ revealed to us in the Bible. Again, Calvin's comments are helpful:

> Therefore the Spirit, promised to us, has not the task of inventing new and unheard-of revelations, or of forging a new kind of doctrine, to lead us away from the received doctrine of the gospel, but of sealing our minds with that very doctrine which is commended by the gospel....
>
> But lest under his sign the spirit of Satan should creep in, he would have us recognize him in his own image, which he has stamped upon the Scriptures. He is the Author of the Scriptures: he cannot vary and differ from himself.[2]

The vital practice of spiritual discernment is our fifth dynamic and will be considered in detail in the next chapter. But here our focus is on the dynamic of receiving guidance for cooperating with the Spirit as, for instance, when Philip's evangelistic work saw him leading an Ethiopian official to saving faith in Jesus Christ.

God's Immediate Revelation through the Activity of His Spirit

During the persecution that broke out after Stephen was stoned, Philip went to Samaria. There he exercised a fruitful evangelistic ministry as people were healed or set free from evil spirits, miraculous signs took place, and men and women were baptized as they put their faith in Jesus (Acts 8:4–25). In the midst of this effective work came a divine interruption as "an angel of the Lord said to Philip, 'Go south to the road—the desert road—that goes down from Jerusalem to Gaza'" (v. 26). Luke does not tell us whether this angelic visitation came as a dream, a vision, or a physical encounter,

---

2. Calvin, *Institutes*, 1.9.1–2.

and we may wonder about Philip's initial reaction: was he frustrated to be drawn away from a fruitful mission field? But he had learned to identify and respond to the guidance of the Holy Spirit, so he acted in obedient faith, leaving the town to remain part of the dance of cooperation with the next phase of work to which he was called.

This is the point at which traditional children's Bible pictures are unhelpful, usually portraying a solitary chariot making its lonely journey to a distant African nation. But this was the main route between two cities, an interstate highway carrying trade, pilgrims, and diplomatic traffic. Arriving at the roadside, Philip would have encountered a veritable selection of camel caravans, laden donkeys, and pedestrians like himself. What was he to do next, and how long was he to wait? Then "the Spirit told Philip, 'Go to that chariot and stay near it'" (Acts 8:29), but again Luke gives no indication of how the Spirit gave this guidance. It may have been an audible word or perhaps simply an inner "nudge"—a sense that this was what the Lord wanted him to do. Once again Philip responded with obedient faith.

As he came within earshot of the chariot, he heard the Ethiopian reading aloud from the scroll of Isaiah and discerned his opportunity. "'Do you understand what you are reading?' Philip asked. 'How can I,' he said, 'unless someone explains it to me?' So he invited Philip to come up and sit with him" (Acts 8:30–31). This final word may also have been guidance from the Spirit, spoken this time through the lips of a man.

In this example, as God spoke to Philip, it was not for the purpose of revealing doctrinal truth. Instead, the Holy Spirit was directing Philip, placing him in the context where he could cooperate with bringing a man to faith in Jesus Christ. In his conversation with the Ethiopian, Philip did indeed communicate true doctrine about Jesus, making it clear that he is the Son of God and the way of salvation. But through angelic encounter, direct words, and a human inquiry, the Holy Spirit spoke to Philip to provide divine guidance about his next steps in the dance of cooperation.

Philip was not alone in experiencing this kind of guidance. Ananias was instructed to visit the newly converted Saul, to lay hands on him for healing his blindness, and to speak God's word about his mission and calling (Acts 9:10–19). The Spirit instructed Cornelius to send for Peter and told Peter to journey with the envoys (10:1–23). Paul was led by the Spirit to visit Macedonia to proclaim the gospel there (16:9–10) and conversely was led to remain in Corinth despite the death threats against him (18:9–11).

In all these stories the Holy Spirit leads in a variety of ways, speaking directly, giving visions, sending angels, and working through other people who are listening and obeying, as well as through circumstances. A complete study of all these ways of speaking are beyond the scope of this book, but they do need to be included in any firm understanding and application of this fourth dynamic. The key point that we wish to make here is that the Holy Spirit does indeed continue to lead us in the dance of cooperation just as he led these people in the Bible. That guidance may be as far-reaching as proclaiming the gospel to a whole nation, or it may be to lead us to participate as God lovingly reaches out to touch someone in need of comfort with his grace.

The Reverend Laura Long found herself involved in one of these grace moments as the Spirit invited her to cooperate with his work in the life of a woman named Betty. Soon after Betty's husband died, Laura preached a sermon on how God speaks to us today. After the service Betty found that she had locked her car key in the car. In the past, her husband, Don, would have been there to help, but now he was gone, and she was overwhelmed by a wave of grief and loneliness. She told Laura, "If only Don were here, he would know what to do," and then she broke down crying. As the elders were trying unsuccessfully to open the car door, Laura received a "nudge" from the Spirit, a simple crazy thought: "Just try your own key in the car door; it will work."

She struggled with the question of whether this was actually from the Holy Spirit and surreptitiously tried the key in the trunk. It did not work. But the thought came again: "No, I did not say the trunk, but the door." Reluctantly she slipped to the other side of the car where no one could see her and tried the key. Effortlessly it worked and the door was opened. When she triumphantly handed Betty the key, Betty and the whole church were amazed.

Laura told how she had received the nudge to do this and said, "I think the Holy Spirit told me." Then Betty broke into tears again and said, "Well that just shows that God is real. He loves me, and that sermon about him speaking today is true."

Conditions for Receiving the Spirit's Guidance

Anybody with a cell phone knows what it is like to be in a "dead zone," when the only way to make or receive a call involves moving to a different location. Likewise, to receive guidance from the Holy Spirit, we need conditions that enable us to "pick up the signal." These conditions are not a checklist of spiritual achievements, but rather aspects of an active relationship with the living God.

These conditions are the foundations with which we began this book (incorporation, information, transformation, and empowerment) and are crucial for being able to hear from God in this dynamic way as his friends and coworkers. *Incorporation*—being born again into the kingdom of God—brings us into a relationship of communication with a heavenly Father. *Information* ensures that we are grounded in Scripture as the Word of God, the revelation of true doctrine concerning the nature of God and his ways of working with us. *Transformation* by the Spirit grows within us a heart that seeks to do the will of God and desires to conform our ways to God's ways. *Empowerment* comes as the Holy Spirit falls on us and through spiritual gifts such as wisdom, prophecy, and knowledge, speaks his guidance into the situations we face.

Let us be clear that these are not rigid rules. Rather, they are a description of our loving relationship with Father, Son, and Holy Spirit, which make genuine dialogue possible. They are the context for conversation, making possible the dance of cooperation.

In my own life, I (Brad) have discovered that the more I grow in loving and following Jesus, the more clearly I hear his voice directing me in the steps of the dance. This has required that I sustain my life of prayer, as well as regularly confessing my sin. It also requires that I submit myself to the discipline of radical obedience, doing what Jesus tells me to do when he wants me to do it. Even as I write this chapter, I find myself torn between several attractive options, only one of which is the Spirit's call on my life at the moment.

In June 2008 I struggled with whether to go to the Presbyterian Church (USA) general assembly in California. This year my wife, Laura, was a commissioner, so I had obvious reason to be there to support her. But beyond that, for the past eighteen years I have attended the assemblies to lead prayer and praise services, times of worship that exalt Jesus Christ and during which we have prayed for many to receive the empowering of the Holy Spirit so that they may be faithful witnesses amid the severe struggles within the denomination. The attraction was strong, but the guidance received by the PRMI board and the leadership team was that I was not called to that role this year and that Allen and Debbie Kemp were to go and lead the PRMI service. I passionately wanted to go, but Jesus was saying, "No! You are not called or anointed to do that—obey me. You are called to stay home and write this book." Had I gone, I would have contradicted the very truth I was writing about!

Yet it was harder still, for this guidance also collided with another strong desire to be in England to meet with the Dunamis Fellowship in Britain and Ireland. However, the Lord was speaking again, mostly by a strong unease in my own heart. "You are not called to do that. That is a work that has already been created, and others are anointed to lead that meeting. I am calling and anointing you to stay home and write this book, which will be the basis of future ministry in building congregations." This was a real conflict for me, as I love going to England and enjoy being with the fellowship.

On top of this there was also the guidance that I needed to be home for our son, Stephen, who had been at the Youth With A Mission base in Denver when a shooting occurred and was still experiencing post-traumatic stress.[3] I really needed to be home to be his father during this time of his need. As all these factors clamored for attention, I had a major crisis of obedience. I asked others to pray for guidance, and I tried to listen to what the Holy Spirit was telling me. I laid these options before the people to whom I am submitted for discernment. Laura, who was certainly called to be away from home that week to attend the general assembly, added to the mix by expressing her misgivings about both of us being gone from home for so long. I was torn between conflicting obligations and struggled to know what to do. But the guidance, confirmed by many others and in my own heart, was that I should not go to the general assembly or to England but should stay home, write, and provide emotional support for my son. As I acted in obedience, I found that my spiritual hearing began to improve. It became clearer that I was to write, and I also began to discern the next steps in various ministry directives. Our ability to hear the Holy Spirit is conditional upon our loving Jesus with all of our hearts and being willing to follow him.

Nurturing Congregations for Receiving Divine Guidance

The practice of receiving guidance is a learned art rather than a programmatic science, involving dynamic communication rather than formula and laws. Learning to hear God's voice accurately for oneself can be difficult, and to do so as a group can be harder still. It took young Samuel a while to learn to identify the sound of the Lord speaking to him, and he needed the help of someone else in the process (1 Sam. 3:1 – 18). Yet this is fundamentally a hope-filled process as we endeavor to hear and heed the Spirit who works to bring Jesus' guidance into his church, "taking from what is mine and making it known to you" (John 16:14).

---

3. In December 2007 a gunman entered the dorms and opened fire, killing two students and wounding two others. Stephen was in the hallway and witnessed the shootings. Miraculously, he was not hurt. In the summer of 2008 he had not fully recovered, and the question of his own well-being was weighing on me as I sought to hear from Jesus what he wanted me to do.

It is essential that churches develop this vital dynamic; otherwise congregations will not know their particular roles in God's work in the world. Mission groups that seek to be directed by the Holy Spirit in fulfilling the Great Commission especially need to develop their ability to receive divine guidance. As we have sought to integrate this fourth dynamic into the life of the Dunamis Fellowship, some key components have emerged.

1. The Need for Leaders Who Listen to the Spirit

Paul exhorted the Philippian church to learn from his own leadership: "Join with others in following my example, brothers, and take note of those who live according to the pattern we gave you" (Phil. 3:17). Those who accompanied Paul on the initial journey to Philippi had ample opportunity to witness him seeking the Spirit's guidance as he was directed away from Asia and Bithynia and then called specifically to Macedonia (Acts 16:6–7). We who are called to lead people into the new reality of God's reign need to embody that reign in our own lives, providing a working model that others may learn from and copy. If we are not doing this, our well-intended and sincere efforts to lead Jesus' church will be molded by an agenda different from the Lord's.

I (Brad) learned a great deal about receiving guidance from the Holy Spirit by watching and talking with my mentor Archer Torrey. As he bared his soul, sharing the thoughts and impressions that were part of the process of listening to the Spirit, he modeled guidance for me. Local congregations need to be able to learn these things from the pastor and elders who lead by seeking to listen to God and being open and vulnerable in the difficulties and complexities of the process. For instance, during a major controversy in the congregation about ordaining women, the Reverend Richard White took the risk of sharing from the pulpit his own efforts of listening to the Holy Spirit through carefully studying Scripture, seeking wisdom from other leaders, and spending time in prayer. He shared not only his conclusions, but also the *process* of listening to the Holy Spirit in reaching those conclusions. In doing so, he gave the congregation a living example of a leader genuinely seeking the Spirit's guidance and then acting in obedient faith.

2. Teach People How to Listen for the Spirit's Guidance

From the descriptions in the Bible, it is clear that the Holy Spirit uses a variety of means to speak to us. At times people "saw" an image or picture and, with it, an awareness of what God wanted them to say or do, as in the experiences of Jeremiah, Amos, and Zechariah (Jer. 1:11, almond tree; 1:13, boiling pot; 24:1–3, figs; Amos 7:7–8, plumb line; 8:1–2, fruit; Zech. 4:2, lampstand; 5:1–2, flying scroll), and perhaps also with Ezekiel's valley of bones (Ezek. 37:1–14). Most frequently we find that people simply "heard" God speaking. This may have been audible (as when the Father spoke to Jesus and was heard by the crowd; John 12:27–30) or an inner verbal communication as an awareness of the Lord's message was impressed upon the person's mind, but the Bible is replete with affirmations that "the word of the Lord" came to a catalog of individuals.[4] Occasionally God's message comes by means of an angelic visitation, either as a physical encounter[5] or in a vision or dream.[6]

Leaders need to provide both the teaching that clarifies people's understanding[7] and the contexts in which they may learn through experiential practice. One of the ways that I (Paul) have done this is through a model that I first encountered at a Dunamis equipping event that dealt with prayer. After giving some introductory teaching about some of the ways the Holy Spirit guides us, I ask participants to move into groups of three — preferably with people they do not know — and to choose someone in the group who has a genuine need the others could pray for. However, rather than telling the others about that need, we invite the Spirit to speak to us and spend five minutes in silence listening. Next we spend another five minutes sharing within the small group whatever we think the Lord may be saying. Then we take time to pray for the person according to the guidance given. At the end of this prayer experiment, I give the groups an opportunity to tell what happened — not the specifics of the prayer, which are often personal, but how God spoke and whether it connected with the person's needs.

I have repeatedly found that people are amazed, having received guidance for situations they knew nothing about, and in a variety of ways. In one group they received guidance in praying for a minister who had arrived with deep concerns about a colleague. In another group someone "saw" a single word that described the person's feelings about their church work.

---

4. With over two hundred instances, it is impractical to list them here, and the reader is encouraged to search the Scriptures with the help of a concordance. Jeremiah, Ezekiel, and Zechariah are replete with such comments.

5. Besides a host of Old Testament examples, the New Testament mentions Matt. 28:5 (women at the tomb); Luke 1:11 (Zechariah); 1:28 (Mary); Acts 10:3–4 (Cornelius); 12:7 (Peter).

6. For example, Matt. 1:20–21 (Joseph) and the book of Revelation (John).

7. Systematic teaching and practical experience of listening to the Holy Spirit's leading are an integral component in the Dunamis Project training events; see www.prmi.org for details. *Can You Hear God?* by Joyce Sibthorpe (Glendale, AZ: Exposure, 2006) provides practical individual help in learning to hear from God.

One person received guidance about an individual's health issues but was reluctant to share it because he knew the person and knew there was nothing wrong. God knew better, and thanks to the Holy Spirit's guidance, that individual received prayer for which he had not asked.

These revelations have come in a variety of ways. Sometimes people find that a few words of Scripture come to mind, or a Bible reference, which, when looked up, addresses the person's situation. Others have a visual or mental picture and possibly also an idea of what it means. For some there is an awareness of particular words that need to be spoken, words they heard or that came to mind and stayed there. Occasionally people receive a "spiritual sympathy pain"—a physical sensation that comes as they seek God's guidance for ministering and that relates to the person's need. At times it is simply a dawning, inner awareness or "nudge" about what needs to be said or done next. In many cases the complete guidance comes only when the various messages are pooled together, combining to give a clearer sense of direction and guidance. Time and again I have witnessed people discovering that they truly can hear from God. All they need is teaching, encouragement, and a safe context in which to learn and reflect on their experiences. What they learn in the laboratory, they are then able to practice in everyday situations as they pray for and minister to each other.

3. Provide Real-Life Opportunities to Practice

Some years ago I (Paul) had to chair a potentially divisive meeting of church members at Plymstock United Church. The discussion concerned financial support for development of one of our buildings, with an evenly balanced three-way split in opinions. Some, including myself, believed it was right to pursue the funding partnership. Others were convinced it was definitely the wrong thing to do. And a final third of the people were genuinely uncertain what course of action we should take. Simply to take a vote in that situation could have been disastrous, but as the discussion continued, one of the members suggested we stop, pray, and ask for God's guidance. She was absolutely right, although I felt disappointed that it wasn't me who had made the suggestion!

So I led the meeting in prayer, and we paused to listen, asking the Lord to make his will plain to us. After a suitable wait in silence, I invited people to share whatever sense of God's guidance they had received. A picture of a highway stop sign had come into my own mind, and all who spoke told how they had a sense of God saying no to the funding partnership. We were able to make a unanimous decision at that meeting, convinced that the Holy

Spirit had spoken in our midst and that God was setting our agenda. Having sought and received guidance, faith was then clothed in obedience; we stopped pursuing the development at that time.

It is vitally important that all Jesus' followers have freedom and opportunity to express the guidance that they may have received. Often that freedom is missing, and we assume that it is the role of the professional pastors or the up-front leaders to hear from God. Yet Scripture reminds us that the Spirit would be poured out on men and women alike, regardless of age or social standing, enabling them to see, know, and speak God's words (Acts 2:17–18). One of the responsibilities of leadership is to honor this work of the Spirit. As believers hear from God, they need opportunities to share what God is saying to them.

At Montreat Presbyterian Church the Reverend Richard White has been integrating this theology into the church's life over several years. He acknowledges:

> I realized that I wanted the people to share in this approach—at least in theory. But actually I was afraid that if they did then I would lose my particular place of authority as the "preacher of the Word of God." Brad and I prayed about this, struggling together for release from this fear, and then I started teaching Sunday school classes about receiving guidance in the local congregation. I found that I once again had to give up my need to control even the Holy Spirit.
>
> One Sunday I sensed the Holy Spirit say to me, "Now it is time to welcome others to receive guidance during worship." This was very frightening for me, but I felt that the right time to do this was during the pastoral prayer. So this Sunday, after offering a word of prayer, I invited the congregation to listen to the Holy Spirit and then to pray as he directed them. It sounds so simple, but it felt like a terrible risk, as I did not know what would happen. Not only did I have to give up control to the Holy Spirit, but what was harder still, I had to trust that the people would truly listen to the Holy Spirit and not abuse the privilege I had just given them.
>
> What happened was very instructive for me and liberating for the three hundred people gathered that Sunday in worship. People began to stand and pray, and we discovered ourselves having a truly Holy Spirit–directed prayer service. Prayers were being woven together into a wonderful whole, and we were led into interceding for some very special concerns for the congregation. We did have a few people who nearly derailed everything, using the opportunity to preach at everyone instead

of actually praying to God. This is part of the risk involved in giving people opportunity to learn and practice for real. But overall this time was led by the Holy Spirit.

Giving people permission to be led by the Holy Spirit and to receive guidance has been helpful for the whole congregation. Now, for instance, people sense a greater freedom to come to me and share guidance they have received, and the whole church is learning better how to listen and hear what the Spirit is saying to us.

Isn't This Dangerous?

The Holy Spirit speaks to guide us, not to entertain us. The greatest way to learn to receive God's word is to start doing what he says to us through Scripture and through the Spirit, for "everyone who hears these words of mine and puts them into practice is like a wise man who built his house on the rock" (Matt. 7:24). Acting on his guidance is like faith: the more we follow the more he speaks. If, on the other hand, we choose to ignore him, it will be no surprise to find that heaven seems to grow silent.

But this is also dangerous territory. If we are to seek the Spirit's guidance and faithfully obey him, we need to be sure that what we "hear" is truly from God and not from any other source. Because of our human imaginations, wishful thinking, cultural conditioning, and the deceitfulness of Satan, we need spiritual safeguards in place. Therefore we advance from this dynamic of receiving divine guidance for cooperating with the Holy Spirit to the fifth dynamic: exercising spiritual discernment.

Chapter 13

Dynamic 5: Spiritual Discernment: Making Listening and Obedience Safe

Discernment makes it safe for us to welcome the guidance and gifts of the Holy Spirit for the dance of cooperating with God. Discernment is the practical theological safety net that enables us to avoid the extremes of unthinking gullibility and obstructive skepticism and, instead, identify and affirm what is truly from God. Without it churches may be led astray or be afraid to welcome the supernatural activity of God. Later in the chapter we introduce four guidelines for discernment of the authentic working of the Holy Spirit and the practicality and value of debriefing for education as well as safety.

For some of us, hearing is a problem. In my early childhood, I (Paul) was diagnosed with hearing loss, and since my teenage years I have used a hearing aid in my left ear. The disability is sometimes frustrating, occasionally amusing, and mostly ignored. I don't always hear when others are speaking to me, especially when there is a lot of background noise, and so I have to ask them to repeat what they said. The amusing occasions are when I do hear them speaking but "hear" the wrong words, as happened while writing this paragraph. My wife's query, "Would you like to have some toffee?" was actually "Would you like a cup of coffee?" which, frankly, left me a little disappointed with the result. Worse still, it can be a bit embarrassing when I hear a noise and assume that I missed a person's comment but, when I ask them to repeat it, discover it was a door creaking or a car going past. Thankfully I do hear most of what is said, but over the years I have learned to be cautious about my hearing, checking that I got it right.

When we consider listening to the Holy Spirit we need that same sense of caution. It would be wrong to assume that everything we *think* is God speaking to us actually *is* what he is saying. At times we will hear clearly, occasionally we will simply miss his guidance, and sometimes we will mistakenly believe that the Spirit is speaking when in reality the source lies elsewhere.

On one occasion I was praying for a woman, accompanied by my friend Annie Lewis. As we listened for what God had to say, I had a sense that he wanted to speak his peace into her situation, assuring her that there was no need to be anxious. I shared this with the woman, asking if it resonated with her, but she shook her head, and so we continued praying, asking the Spirit to speak into her life. Then Annie spoke up and described a picture that had come to mind, of a father caring for and carrying his child. Immediately relief and joy showed on the woman's face, and she began thanking her heavenly Father for this revelation and affirming her trust in him. She phoned me a few days later to say that God had been true to his word and had carried her through the situation for which she had wanted prayer. In this instance, I was mistaken, but Annie had heard rightly what the Spirit was saying.

Twin Dangers We Must Avoid

We have presented many testimonies in this book and said that Jesus had spoken to us through his Spirit. Of every one of those stories, it is right to ask, "How can we be sure it was the Holy Spirit speaking?" We believe this is a crucially important question whenever we consider God's guidance, for there are two equal and opposite extremes into which the church may fall concerning this. One is unthinking gullibility that embraces everything; the other is obstructive skepticism that rejects everything. Both scenarios are dangerous, and both run counter to Scripture.

By "gullibility" we mean the attitude that simply assumes that everything that is *claimed* to be from God truly is from God. Certainly this is not always the case (as, for instance, in Paul and Annie's story above). So if we are diligently obedient to the so-called "guidance" we receive, then sometimes we will be acting on the basis of inauthentic guidance, pursuing wrong agendas and speaking inappropriate or even harmful words. Similarly, if we fail to be critically discerning, we place ourselves at the mercy of everyone who claims to have a word from the Lord, leaving the church vulnerable to the whims of manipulative individuals. This all-embracing attitude easily gives way to an emphasis on emotionalism (in contrast with the proper freedom to allow emotions as an authentic part of our whole-person worship).[1] And most damaging of all, this approach can bring discredit to Jesus when

---

1. In Luke 10:27 Jesus commands that we love God with 100 percent of our being, which includes emotions.

alleged "guidance" is gullibly embraced yet turns out to be fictitious. No wonder the Bible instructs us to "test everything" (1 Thess. 5:21) and to "test the spirits to see whether they are from God" (1 John 4:1).

By "skepticism" we mean the attitude that assumes either that God no longer speaks and that every purported word from the Lord is unreal, or that we cannot be certain and therefore are better off avoiding the issue. These approaches have sometimes emerged as a well-intentioned way of protecting the church from the dangers of deception and abuse, yet they themselves are dangerous because they place us in opposition to the Holy Spirit's ongoing activity of distributing spiritual gifts and making real the lordship and leadership of Jesus Christ. Skepticism can give way to a proud intellectualism that exalts human reason above divine sovereignty. It also frustrates the effectiveness of the body of Christ by depriving the church of the very resources Jesus intended us to have. Thus the Bible instructs us: "Do not put out the Spirit's fire; do not treat prophecies with contempt. Test everything. Hold on to the good" (1 Thess. 5:19–21). Likewise, we should, "be eager to prophesy, and do not forbid speaking in tongues" (1 Cor. 14:39).

Neither skepticism nor gullibility honors the third person of the Trinity. One welcomes more than God intended, while the other rejects what God intended. Thankfully there is a pathway that lies between these extremes, one that recognizes the truth of the Holy Spirit's ministry in the midst of not-yet-perfect human beings. But before we consider the practicalities of discernment, it is helpful to appreciate some of the roots of the spiritual problem.

Why Might "Guidance" Not Be from the Spirit?

When Jesus mapped out for the disciples his need to travel to Jerusalem, die, and rise from the dead, Peter took him aside to talk him out of the idea. Jesus' rebuke is pointed: "Get behind me, Satan! You are a stumbling block to me; you do not have in mind the things of God, but the things of men" (Matt. 16:23). He saw that the guidance offered by Peter actually had its origins in the work of Satan and the concerns of humans, and therefore he set it aside. In another conversation Jesus describes the devil as "the father of lies" (John 8:44), and Paul reminds us that "Satan himself masquerades as an angel of light" (2 Cor. 11:14) who leads people astray.

Alongside Satan's efforts to deceive us, we also face the pressures and priorities of ordinary human concerns, the "things of men" that affect our own attitudes and outlook. The assumptions of society can easily mold our thinking and color our perceptions, unconsciously causing us to conclude that what society welcomes is what God wants. This is why Paul exhorts, "Do not conform any longer to the pattern of this world" (Rom. 12:2). He is well aware of this danger and wants us to discern instead what God's will is.

Closest to home there is the unreliability within ourselves, leading Jeremiah to lament that "the heart is deceitful above all things, and desperately wicked: who can know it?" (Jer. 17:9 KJV). Our vivid imaginations or our own good-intentioned, caring attitudes may be mistakenly regarded as guidance from the Holy Spirit. Or, less innocently, we may be proud of our own spirituality or desire to appear spiritual in other people's eyes ("See! I am one who hears from God") and therefore fall into the trap of "inventing" guidance in our eagerness to look good.

Together these form an alternative trinity, described in some baptismal liturgies as "the world, the flesh, and the devil." When I (Brad) was filled with the Holy Spirit and growing in Jesus Christ, I just assumed that I would be immune from these dangers. I was unsettled by Jesus' strong warnings, "Watch out that no one deceives you. For many will come in my name, claiming, 'I am the Christ,' and will deceive many" (Matt. 24:4–5). I have often been guilty of thinking that Jesus was talking about someone else, but the more I have come to know myself, the more I have realized that the dangers of deception lie with me. Jesus' warnings are especially for people like me who are growing in spiritual leadership and growing in the dance of cooperation with the Holy Spirit in the work of advancing the kingdom of God.

These difficulties might cause us to despair. But the Bible's working assumption is that the Holy Spirit is alive and active, distributing his gifts among God's people and equipping us to bear witness to Jesus Christ. We have a well-grounded hope that our Lord is more than able to overcome these communication problems, and that the Spirit's guidance can be rightly discerned so that we may join in the dance of cooperation.

When we observe a particular behavior, such as shaking or falling on the floor, prophecy or words spoken in tongues, or teaching or guidance from a person or a church council, discernment helps us to identify whether it comes from the Holy Spirit or an evil spirit or the human mind. The teaching may have come from a respected individual or committee—perhaps the denomination's national assembly, or the pope, or a high-profile preacher—but it should not be received blindly just because those who say it have authority or are good, sincere people. Particular manifestations may be beyond our normal experience, or they may be very familiar to us, but neither case is therefore genuine or automatically suspect. We are called to practice discernment so that errors can be set aside and the authentic work of the Spirit can be embraced.

Four Vital Questions to Help with Discernment

Discernment is the act of testing or examining something to conclude whether it is genuine. As the church in Corinth faced the challenges of handling prophecy, tongues, and other manifestations of the Spirit's activity, Paul told them that "two or three prophets should speak, and the others should *weigh carefully* what is said" (1 Cor. 14:29, italics ours). John reminded his churches, "Do not believe every spirit, but *test the spirits* to see whether they are from God, because many false prophets have gone out into the world" (1 John 4:1, italics ours). Paul pointed out that "the things that come from the Spirit of God ... are *spiritually discerned*" (1 Cor. 2:14, italics ours) and urged the Thessalonians to "*test everything*. Hold on to the good" (1 Thess. 5:21, italics ours).

This can be a complex process, and we have found that four key questions are vital in practicing discernment. They come from Scripture and from the accumulated practical experience of seeking to discern what is truly from the Holy Spirit:

1. Does it give glory to Jesus Christ in the present and in the future?
2. Is it consistent with the intentions and character of God as revealed in Scripture?
3. Do other people who are born again and filled with the Holy Spirit have a confirming witness?
4. Is there confirmation in objectively verifiable events or facts?

1. Does It Give Glory to Jesus Christ in the Present and in the Future?

Jesus said, "When he, the Spirit of truth, comes, he will guide you into all truth. He will not speak on his own; he will speak only what he hears, and he will tell you what is yet to come. He will bring glory to me by taking from what is mine and making it known to you" (John 16:13–14). We place this question first because it gives priority to Jesus, ensuring that he is the one who is lifted up, honored, and acknowledged. John the Baptist humbly declared, "He must increase, but I must decrease" (John 3:30 KJV). Everything that truly comes from the Holy Spirit will give glory to Jesus Christ both in the present circumstances and in future consequences. He points us to Jesus alone and brings to us only the words of Jesus and not of anyone else. The Spirit turns the spotlight on Jesus.

The Holy Spirit has a single-minded focus on Jesus Christ as the truth who became incarnate. John teaches his readers: "This is how you can recognize the Spirit of God: Every spirit that acknowledges that Jesus Christ has come in the flesh is from God, but every spirit that does not acknowledge Jesus is not from God" (1 John 4:2–3). In the nebulous sea of "spirituality" that is the New Age movement, many speak of a Christ or a Christ Spirit. But this will-o'-the-wisp fantasy is detached from the biblical revelation that Jesus is a real person who died on the cross for our sins. The Jesus to whom the Spirit points us, and on whose behalf he speaks, is the historical, walking-on-the-earth carpenter of Nazareth who was crucified and who died and was raised as recorded in Scripture.

At one Dunamis event as I (Paul) was being prayed for, I found myself unable to stand and falling to the floor. As I rested there I saw myself as an infant resting in my heavenly Father's arms, gazing up at his face and aware of his tender love toward me. Others in the room saw only a church leader collapsing and then lying very still while one or two people knelt by me, praying. The physical events were largely meaningless and thankfully were not as undignified as King David's dance of worship (2 Sam. 6:1–22). But the encounter itself brought a fresh assurance into my relationship with the God whom Jesus taught us to call "Abba." Jesus said that one of the ways the Holy Spirit would bring glory to him was "by taking from what is mine and making it known to you" (John 16:14). On this occasion he took what Jesus had revealed about Abba and made it into experiential reality in my own life.

2. Is It Consistent with the Intentions and Character of God as Revealed in Scripture?

When Paul visited the Jewish community in Berea and explained the gospel message to them, they were simultaneously enthusiastic and cautious. "They received the message with great eagerness and examined the Scriptures every day to see if what Paul said was true" (Acts 17:11). The words of the evangelist were weighed against the words of Scripture, and he himself later emphasizes the fundamental value of Scripture as a means of preventing error and promoting truth: "All Scripture is God-breathed and is useful for teaching, rebuking, correcting and training in righteousness, so that the man of God may be thoroughly equipped for every good work" (2 Tim. 3:16–17).

In the pages of the Bible, as the Holy Spirit directed the understanding of its human authors (2 Peter 1:20–21), God spoke to reveal his character, his will, and his intentions. Because the Bible is God's self-revelation, its words are the bedrock, objective standard by which all other revelations are to be measured. It is why the Bereans checked to see whether Paul's message about Jesus was consistent with God's existing revelation, and it is why John Calvin said about the work of the Holy Spirit, "But lest under his sign the spirit of Satan should creep in, he would have us recognize him in his own image, which he has stamped upon the Scriptures. He is the Author of the Scriptures: he cannot vary and differ from himself."[2]

When the Spirit speaks directly and personally to his people today, this guidance may not be *verbatim* from Scripture, but it will always be *in accord with* the teachings of Scripture and consistent with the character of God as revealed in Scripture. For instance, there is no chapter and verse saying, "I am calling Cindy Strickler to become the director of the PRMI Dunamis Fellowship," or "Paul Stokes, you are to serve the URC congregation at Plymouth." No passage of the Bible says, "I am calling Brad and Laura Long as missionaries for Taiwan." But these are certainly *consistent with the character and intentions* of God that are revealed in Scripture as the Holy Spirit calls and equips people for apostolic, pastoral, and evangelistic roles (Eph. 4:11) and calls them to specific locations (Acts 16:10).

3. Do Other People Who Are Born Again and Filled with the Holy Spirit Have a Confirming Witness?

To ensure that the spiritual gift of prophecy was handled correctly in Corinth, Paul gave instructions that "two or three prophets should speak, and the others should weigh carefully what is said" (1 Cor. 14:29). The task of "weighing" is not the democratic process of taking a vote and letting the majority rule, and neither is it merely working toward a group consensus or opinion. Rather, an inner witness comes from the Holy Spirit, a divine "Amen," a sense of peace that the message may rightly be received as coming from God. Luke tells us that after Paul's night vision of a man from Macedonia, they corporately[3] concluded this was direction from God. If guidance, teaching, or a manifestation is from the Holy Spirit, the same Spirit will confirm it in the hearts of others. Quite simply, "the Spirit recognizes the Spirit."[4]

---

2. John Calvin, *Institutes of the Christian Religion*, ed. John. T. McNeill (Philadelphia: Westminster, 1960), 1.9.2.

3. In Acts 16:10 the Greek verb is in the plural, indicating that this was not just Paul's conclusion, but that of the group.

4. Arnold Bittlinger, *Gifts and Graces: A Commentary on 1 Corinthians 12–14* (Eng. trans., Grand Rapids: Eerdmans, 1967), 121.

Some people understand passages of Scripture more readily than others, perhaps because of a greater familiarity with the Bible. In a similar way, some will more readily discern whether it is the Holy Spirit at work. At the most basic level, "the man without the Spirit does not accept the things that come from the Spirit of God, for they are foolishness to him, and he cannot understand them, because they are spiritually discerned" (1 Cor. 2:14). Discernment of spiritual reality is exercised by those who are walking with Jesus, people who have been born again and are being filled with the Holy Spirit.

I (Paul) have already told the story of how Tracy was called into the role of eldership. Several people in the church all had the same sense of guidance and in a variety of settings, sometimes quite unexpectedly. As well as this common witness, there was a corporate "Amen" among the existing elders and also from the church's members. In a similar way, when we sought the Lord's guidance in the church meeting about funding support and people spoke of God saying no, there was a corporate sense of peace and "rightness" about this decision. On another occasion, I was leading a small group of people involved in deliverance ministry[5] and paused to ask the rest of the team whether they had any sense of God's guidance. One person said she believed we were dealing with "lots," and the other two confirmed this by saying, "Ten," simultaneously. This confirming witness helped us to know how we should proceed and what progress had been made.

4. Is There Confirmation in Objectively Verifiable Events or Facts?

When God said, "Let there be light," light appeared. His words had objective, verifiable results that could be observed and studied, for when God speaks, things happen. "My word that goes out from my mouth ... will not return to me empty, but will accomplish what I desire and achieve the purpose for which I sent it" (Isa. 55:11). So when we are presented with guidance that we believe may be a word from the Lord, we should look to see whether it produces verifiable results. Moses had to deal with this issue and taught: "You may say to yourselves, 'How can we know when a message has not been spoken by the LORD?' If what a prophet proclaims in the name of the LORD does not take place or come true, that is a message the LORD has not spoken. That prophet has spoken presumptuously. Do not be afraid of him" (Deut. 18:21–22).

---

5. That is, praying with others in order that they may be set free from the oppression of evil spirits.

This concept of objective verification is extremely important. There are times when the Spirit speaks of things that will not come to pass immediately. Some Bible prophecies took hundreds of years before they were fulfilled, and we too may experience a delay between first receiving prophetic visions or words and later seeing them become reality. On these occasions, we enter the suspenseful time of waiting until there is indeed a confirmation.

But many words from the Lord simply have an immediate objective verification. When praying for someone, a word of knowledge will connect with actual facts in the person's life. A prophetic word, delivered in the grace and love of Jesus Christ, may be distinguished from simple criticism or judgmentalism because it will actually build people in their discipleship, for "the one who prophesies speaks to people for their strengthening, encouragement and consolation" (1 Cor. 14:3 NET).

Sometimes when praying for healing there may be physical manifestations, but if there is genuine healing, it will be confirmed by a doctor and not merely by our emotional excitement. In being led by the Holy Spirit and discerning what he is doing and saying, one must have not only faith, but also an unwavering commitment to reality. We open the door to trouble when, in the name of faith, we try to falsify reality to suit our aims or preconceptions.

When Cindy's husband, Steve, was diagnosed with a brain tumor at the start of 2004, the doctor described it as a nonmalignant tumor the size of a golf ball, self-contained and operable. A few days before surgery, several of us met with Steve and prayed for him. I (Brad) was feeling heat and power surging through my hands into Steve's head. Suddenly there popped into my head a picture: it was of the tumor being, not a nice little ball that could be easily removed, but an evil-looking mass of tendrils reaching out into Steve's brain. In the picture I saw light moving through his head, and with it the guidance, "Command the tendrils to withdraw from my servant's brain and come back upon themselves." As I prayed this, I was aware of power and authority and light moving through me into Steve, and in a crazy way I felt that Jesus was actually reaching into his brain, pulling the tumor back. This was all coming to me in a series of vivid, spontaneous mental images. After a while, the Holy Spirit lifted from me. The stream of images stopped abruptly, and so did the sensation of heat and power in my hands. I knew that I could stop praying.

The surgeon's report, and the pathology report a few days later, indicated that the tumor was not benign but was in fact a malignant stage-three *anaplastic astrocytoma*. "Astro" means "star," and the cancer has tendrils that grow into other parts of the brain. The doctor said that it was contained, and that he thought he had gotten it all. Obviously this was great news! It was also objective confirmation that the guidance I received in the form of a picture had truly been on track with reality. Steve's cancer has not returned, and with each passing year, recurrence is increasingly unlikely.

Applying the Four Questions— a Prophecy for Plymstock

During my first year as a minister, I (Paul) was handed a note by a well-loved member who believed this was God's prophetic message for us. It read:

> You people of Plymstock love your warm comfortable houses. But you have neglected your central place of worship, my temple. It is cold and uninviting. Can't you see what is happening? You hope for a large harvest but have received a small one. And what you have gathered, I have blown away with the wind. Make provision to restore the warmth in my temple, and I, the Lord, will be with you.
>
> For confirmation please read the short book of Haggai (only a page and a half).

This was the first time I ever had to work out what to do with a prophetic word! I brought the note before the elders and asked whether there was a shared sense of the message being authentic, and almost immediately there was a corporate "yes." It seemed too quick to me, as if the mention of a Bible reference had automatically made it "right," and I felt uneasy. So later that night I walked around the local streets, initially praying about the prophetic word but then dealing with other aspects of the church's life as well. I had almost arrived home and was no longer considering the prophetic word when I heard God say, "It's me." I don't think it was an audible voice, but the words were clear as well as unexpected. At that moment, I had peace in my own spirit, a confirming witness alongside that of the other elders.

The wording and thrust of the message itself was clearly an echo of God's word through Haggai. The Spirit sometimes takes portions of historically rooted Scripture and declares that they are his *current* message for our particular situation. This happened when Peter quoted from the prophet Joel in Acts 2 and when the church considered the question of Gentiles becoming Christians in Acts 15. Thus I could see that this particular message was consistent with the character and intentions of God as revealed in Scripture.

Did the prophetic word bring glory to Jesus? The answer is surely yes. Like the letters to local churches in Revelation, this word called us to be transformed, to seek first the kingdom of God, to make it our priority to honor him through practical action.

And what about confirmation in objectively verifiable events or facts? For the next few years, we welcomed many new people into membership and saw even more people leave us. The numbers fell by about 25 percent as the Lord "blew away" what we gathered. During that period, faith was clothed in obedience as the small church began to make changes to the premises with new heating, new well-insulated windows, comfortable chairs, new audio-visual equipment, and the refurbishing of one of the main meeting rooms and the kitchen facilities. Other changes took place, too, in areas of prayer, fellowship, evangelism, and growing in the Holy Spirit. Over the past five years, we have been increasingly aware of the Lord's presence and have seen the church grow in numbers by more than 60 percent.

All four discernment questions received a positive response, affirming that a cautiously presented message truly was a prophetic word given under the guidance of the Holy Spirit. So how can we integrate this practice of discernment into the life of a local church?

Cultivating Spiritual Discernment in the Congregation

1. The Need for Teaching about Discernment

People need to know that it is not only permissible, but actually proper to practice discernment. On occasion I (Paul) have chosen to teach through these four tests, and we have also provided people with Bible bookmarks that have the tests and texts printed on them for easy reference. But as well as this systematic teaching, discernment can also be highlighted when appropriate in the course of preaching, Sunday school teaching, or Bible study group discussions. These are the "incidental" occasions that "drip feed" the concept into people's awareness. Scripture passages that involve guidance or some manifestation of the Holy Spirit's work, for instance, provide valuable opportunities for highlighting the need for and practice of discernment.

Shortly after I was ordained to ministry, the Christian and secular media began carrying news stories about the phenomenon they labeled the "Toronto blessing." More recently the stories have focused on Lakeland, Florida. These provoke inevitable conversations, with a mix of fear and fascination, curiosity and criticism, and they provide informal opportunities to help people learn to discern rather than merely reacting at an emotional level. It doesn't take a lot of effort to pose the question: "So how should we work out whether this is genuinely the Holy Spirit at work?"

2. Learning through Practicing Discernment

When it comes to discernment, the laboratory is a better learning environment than the lecture theater. Occasions when the Holy Spirit appears to have been at work are great opportunities for learning to exercise discernment. I (Paul) had spent a day teaching a small group of people about the person and work of the Holy Spirit, and in the afternoon we set aside time to worship, to be still in God's presence, and to pray for one another. As usual, people responded in a variety of ways, and I had the privilege of praying for several of them. At the end of the day, as we sat drinking coffee and eating biscuits, I gave them the opportunity to talk about their experiences and to ask questions. As we talked I made sure that we mentioned these discernment tests. This was not a "checklist" approach, but a low-key conversation in which I was able to say things such as, "I know that experience was not 'normal' for you, but it's the kind of thing that happened in the Bible when Paul encountered Jesus. It fits in with what God has revealed about himself in the Bible."

On another occasion, a small group of people had been praying for me in the church. We laughed when, having finished praying, I then began asking about how they had received guidance from the Spirit, forcing them to reflect critically on what had happened. I was also able to talk about what the Lord had been doing in my own heart and how their prayers had been on track (or not, as the case may be). By debriefing together, we were all able to learn more about the practice of discernment.

Whether the group is large or small, leaders can help others learn to discern by making sure that reflective debriefing actually happens. I have found these kinds of questions helpful in the process:

- How was the Spirit guiding people?
- What persuaded us that it was the Holy Spirit and not some other influence?
- Did anyone think the Lord was guiding but stay quiet? What were you getting?
- Did we drift or go off track anywhere?
- Is anyone willing to talk about what the Spirit was doing in your life?
- How does this bring glory to Jesus?
- How is it consistent with the character and intentions of God as revealed in Scripture?

- Is there a sense of confirming witness among other people? What prompts that response?
- What "fruit" can we identify? Are there any objective facts that confirm this as being authentically the Holy Spirit's work?

3. Submitting Ourselves to the Discernment Process

Those of us who are leaders are not exempt from the need for discernment. By making sure that we ourselves are placed under the microscope, we help others to feel comfortable when it is their own contribution that is the subject of discernment. During one evening service, I (Paul) had led people from the sermon into a period of reflective prayer. I was aware that the Holy Spirit was stirring people but was unsure whether now was the time to move deeper and offer the opportunity for prayer to receive the baptism with the Spirit. Eventually I chose not to pursue that route but was not certain I had made the right choice. Immediately after the service, I called together a couple of the elders and a visitor who I knew had previous experience in practicing discernment and asked whether I had missed following the Spirit's lead. Besides holding me accountable, this debriefing also gave the elders an opportunity to learn more about exercising discernment.

When we are training others, it can be difficult for them to be genuinely discerning in the early stages, for they may be tempted to assume that their beloved leader "must" have been right. There is also the opposite danger, that people with a grudge may abuse the opportunity in order to be critical. So whenever possible—and in truth it is not always possible—we must make sure that we do submit ourselves to other leaders who have the spiritual maturity to hold us accountable. We do this in order that Jesus may be glorified in our leadership and the church be protected from our human imperfection.

Opening the Door to the Spirit

By learning the art of exercising spiritual discernment, congregations will be better able to open the door to the Holy Spirit, identifying and acting on his guidance. Yet the picture is broader than this, and we have given examples in this chapter that were not specifically about guidance. The practice of discernment helps create a pastorally "safe" context for our sixth dynamic, in which a church welcomes the full variety of manifestations and gifts of the Holy Spirit and does so in a manner that honors Jesus Christ.

Chapter 14

Dynamic 6: Welcoming the Gifts and Manifestations of the Holy Spirit

The gifts and manifestations of the Holy Spirit are normal and essential expressions of the Holy Spirit's power and presence given to help us in the practice of cooperating with the Spirit. In the congregational worship in Corinth, the Christian faith manifestly involved a supernatural component, and Paul provided guidance about how this should be understood and handled. Leaders and congregations need to develop an understanding of spiritual gifts and how to express them in the church's worship and witness.

Builders need tools. I (Brad) recently watched a team constructing a wooden deck at PRMI's Community of the Cross in North Carolina. Collectively this team of white-haired senior carpenters had more than two centuries of building experience. They had tools on their belts, tools in their kits, and power tools plugged in and ready to go. They did not move very fast, but they moved deliberately, reaching for the tool perfectly suited for each task. At just the right moment—as if in some kind of dance—they were reaching for different expressions of power and authority for shaping wood, stone, and steel into a new reality. To my unskilled hands, these were merely hammers for pounding nails and saws for cutting wood. But for these craftsmen the tools were their means of expressing dominion over the created world, shaping reality according to a vision that was clear in their minds.

Jesus shaped reality—he was the master craftsman with a vision of the kingdom of God and with tools provided by the Holy Spirit. Spiritual gifts expressed the power and authority of the Spirit at the right time and in exactly the right way. With a conversation in full flow by a Samaritan well, he received the gift of knowledge about a woman's previous five husbands and her current live-in lover (John 4:4–42). The conversation moved to a new depth, and she returned to her village, saying, "Come, see a man who told me everything I ever did. Could this be the Christ?" (v. 29). Many of the residents put their faith in Jesus all because Jesus was receiving the tools he needed for this expression of God's kingdom.

When an adulterous woman was hauled before him for judgment, Jesus received the words of wisdom for handling the situation (John 8:1–11). He was able to drive out unclean spirits because the Holy Spirit gave him the ability (Matt. 12:28). He received knowledge of what lay in Simon's critical heart and in the sinful woman's penitent heart (Luke 7:36–50). On each occasion, as he saw what the Father was doing, Jesus played his part in the dance of cooperation under the Spirit's anointing. He spoke prophetic words into people's lives, proclaimed the good news, and called people into the kingdom. He healed those who were sick and raised the dead. He gave leadership to his followers, served their needs, and taught them the ways and the truth of God. All these are portrayed in Scripture as gifts and manifestations of the Holy Spirit, made available to express and build the kingdom of God.

Imagine if the team of carpenters building the decking had simply sat around arguing about tools in their kit: Which ones were most useful? Should some no longer be used? Whose tools were more impressive? While they were disputing the contents of the toolbox, they would be making no progress in building the deck. It is a ludicrous scenario, yet this is how the church often behaves concerning the Spirit's gifts. We argue about whether they are in use any longer or whether prophecy is more important than tongues. Some people are fascinated while others are frightened, some rejoice while others resist, and in the meantime they make very little progress in the building work.

Yet Jesus has called us to work with him in building the kingdom of God on earth, a global commission to bring people from every nation into his realm. This is where the dance of cooperation finds its purpose — we keep in step with the Spirit as he builds the Father's kingdom. Our focus is not on the gifts and manifestations themselves, but on the great task to which we are called and the Lord who chose to involve us in it. The Holy Spirit distributes a variety of gifts among us in order that we may engage productively in this building project. Fundamentally these gifts are simply "tools." We bring to the task the natural capabilities that we have as people created in the image of God — our capacity to imagine, organize, and manage. We also require the supernatural capabilities that come as gifts from the Holy Spirit. Human and spiritual tools belong together, an intermingling of the mundane and the transcendent in order to create the new reality that is God's kingdom.

The Dangers of Quenching the Spirit

What happens when the spiritual aspect of this work is constrained? Once I (Brad) was invited to a large conservative Canadian congregation to preach an evangelistic sermon and invite people to accept Jesus Christ as Lord of their lives. When I met with the leaders beforehand, I shared with them my experience from around the world—including Canada—of what happens when people come to faith in Christ. Often there are emotional responses as the Holy Spirit begins to heal deep hurts, and sometimes evil spirits manifest themselves as Jesus asserts his holy authority and presence. So I asked whether prayer teams were available to minister to people after they had come to Christ. Immediately the pastor jumped up and said that any such emotional expressions were absolutely forbidden in his church and that I was not to mention healing or evil spirits or anything about the Holy Spirit. I submitted to him and said, "Yes, sir. You are the pastor and I am under your authority as long as I am in your congregation as your guest." He obviously was fearful of any manifestations of the Holy Spirit and had no idea what to do with them. I later realized that the leadership had been influenced by the dispensationalist teaching that the gifts of the Holy Spirit had ceased with the close of the biblical canon.

That evening the sanctuary was filled with the presence of God, and the Holy Spirit fell upon me in great power and authority. I preached an evangelistic sermon and then invited people to come forward to make a commitment or recommitment to Jesus Christ. About three hundred people—half of the congregation—came forward to kneel and pray, quietly making confessions of faith. Among them was an elderly, very distinguished woman whose face began to contort with what looked like a demonic manifestation. I went over to pray for her and silence the demon that was manifesting, but before I could get there, she suddenly convulsed and shrieked, writhing on the floor in the grip of a very powerful evil spirit.

The pastor rushed over immediately, demanding to know what I had done, and I told him, "I did nothing, sir, but I think Jesus is setting this lady free from evil spirits, as she has just committed her life to following him." The pastor frantically ordered the elders to get the woman out, and five men hurried forward to carry the struggling woman out of the sanctuary into a back room. A wave of fear and confusion swept over many in the congregation, while others were full of joy and wonder at the mighty working of God. I offered to explain to the church what was happening but was rebuffed. I pleaded with the pastor to let me go and cast out the demons, but he forbade me. So I merely stood off to the side as the pastor instructed people to be calm but gave no explanation of what was happening.

The impact of these decisions was painful. For the next hour the woman's screams and the yelling of the men trying to subdue her were clearly audible, disrupting the whole service. She herself was not ministered to and left deeply hurt. The congregation received no explanation and was left in confusion and fear. I was told that I was not welcome ever again to step foot in that church. The episode caused great scandal in the church and resulted in a major split. The deep tragedy is that these manifestations of an evil spirit happened because of a gracious move of God. Jesus was actively working in the congregation; his kingdom was advancing and the domain of Satan was being pushed back. This was an open door, a wonderful kairos moment of opportunity as God began to draw the church into this dance of cooperating with him. The profound hurt and missed opportunity happened because the pastor and leaders were not willing to welcome the gifts and manifestations of the Spirit.

This is a scenario that has been played out in many congregations when leaders who do not know how to respond to the Holy Spirit's activity quench his work and sow seeds of conflict among their people. We are convinced that it is vital for leaders to develop a practical understanding of the various ways in which the Holy Spirit's presence is made manifest, including the full variety of spiritual gifts mentioned in Scripture. It is not our intention in this brief chapter to provide a comprehensive consideration of all the Spirit's gifts. Our concern is more straightforward: for a congregation to participate in the dance of cooperation with the Holy Spirit, they must have an attitude, understanding, and practice that welcome the gifts and manifestations of the Holy Spirit. This is our sixth dynamic.

Having a Biblical Attitude: Four Keys to Using the Gifts

In four key passages, the New Testament describes a catalog of various expressions of the Spirit's power, and in every context, the need for *love* is mentioned. The reality is that if love is left out of the equation, people not only allow spiritual gifts to cause division and hurt, but also dishonor the Lord who gives them. So we find in Romans that "love must be sincere," together with the instruction to "live in harmony with one another" and the admonition "Do not be proud.... Do not be conceited" (12:9, 16). The Corinthians are reminded that no matter what spiritual gifts they may exercise, they are empty and meaningless without love. Paul describes love as being patient, kind, and hopeful; not envious, egocentric, boastful, or proud; concerned for truth and ready to protect (1 Cor. 13:1–7). And in Ephesians we find the instruction to be "gentle; be patient, bearing with one another in love. Make every effort to keep the unity of the Spirit." We need to be "speaking the truth in love" so the church "grows and builds itself up in love" (4:2, 15, 16).

An attitude of love and harmony sets the context in which spiritual gifts are used. People need the freedom to learn how to use their gifts in a loving manner and also need the freedom to make mistakes and learn from them without fear of being condemned by fellow Christians.

Three other attitudes are key.

First is *an informed attitude*, the willingness to grow in one's understanding of spiritual things. When Paul says, "With regard to spiritual gifts, brothers and sisters, I do not want you to be uninformed" (1 Cor. 12:1 NET), he is calling us to a deeper and fuller awareness of their place and function within the Christian life.

Next is the need for *an inclusive attitude* that is willing to welcome whatever gifts the Holy Spirit chooses to distribute, without attempting to censor his sovereignty (1 Cor. 12:11). Therefore we are specifically instructed: "Do not put out the Spirit's fire; do not treat prophecies with contempt" (1 Thess. 5:19–20); and "do not forbid speaking in tongues" (1 Cor. 14:39). Instead, we are meant to welcome the Spirit's gift-giving activity, gladly embracing the wonderful variety of ways in which he equips us to carry out the work that Jesus has entrusted to his church.

Finally, we need to have *a hungry attitude* toward spiritual gifts, a yearning personally to receive whatever spiritual tools the Holy Spirit chooses to give and to see others equipped too. We are told to "follow the way of love and eagerly desire spiritual gifts, especially the gift of prophecy" (1 Cor. 14:1). We must "be eager to prophesy" (v. 39) and should "eagerly desire the greater gifts" (12:31).

What Gifts Does the Holy Spirit Provide?

It would be good to explore each gift of the Spirit in depth, and we encourage the reader to do so. But for our purposes in this book, the following "thumbnail sketches" will have to suffice.

Functional Gifts — Romans 12:6 – 8

The gifts Paul covers in Romans 12:6 – 8 describe the different roles, or ways we function, within the body of Christ.[1] They are concrete expressions of God's grace at work in the life of believers for the sake of others.

Through *prophesying* God's message enters the heart and brings comfort, direction, and conviction. *Serving* shows love by meeting the practical needs of others. Those with the gift of *teaching* are able to clarify truth and enable others to understand it. Through the gift of *encouragement*, people are motivated and exhorted to grow in their faith in the ups and downs of life. *Giving* is the ability to contribute generously using material resources to advance God's kingdom. *Leadership* is the function of coordinating people, resources, and activities to achieve a goal. The spiritual gift of showing *mercy* is the ability to identify with, and comfort, people who are hurting or needy.

Leadership Gifts — Ephesians 4:11 – 13

The five gifts Paul lists in Ephesians 4:11 – 13 give us insight into the leadership that Jesus gives to his church. The gifts are persons rather than activities, made available to equip the body of believers to do the work of ministry. Their combined purpose is to create mature, effective Christians in a mature, effective church.

The work of an *apostle* (literally, "one sent") is that of laying foundations, establishing new leaders, ministries, and congregations.[2] A *prophet* is someone who communicates the "now" message of God for people. *Evangelists* act as spiritual midwives, helping people be born again into the Father's family. *Pastors* care for and feed Jesus' flock, providing protection and guidance. *Teachers* ensure that faith is rooted in biblical truth.

Manifestational Gifts — 1 Corinthians 12:7 – 10

The gifts listed in 1 Corinthians 12:7 – 10 are more noticeably supernatural and are the various ways that the Holy Spirit has chosen to express, "manifest," or "show forth" his power through human beings.

The gift of *wisdom* shows us how to handle particular spiritual situations. A *word of knowledge* often proves the key for unlocking issues. *Faith*, in this context, is not saving faith in Christ, but rather an extraordinary confidence

---

1. Romans 12:4 notes that the various members of the body "do not all have the same function," thus placing emphasis on what each part *does* or what its *function* is.

2. Beside the group of twelve apostles plus Paul, the New Testament also refers to a second body of people who exercised an apostolic ministry (Acts 14:14; Rom. 16:7; 1 Cor. 15:5 – 8; Gal. 1:18 – 19).

in God in the midst of a seemingly impossible situation. *Healing* involves restoring people's physical, spiritual, or emotional wholeness through the Spirit's power rather than through medical intervention. *Miraculous powers* provide for those in need, remove hindrances to spreading the gospel, and show God's mercy and judgment. *Prophecy* brings the message that God now has for people. *Discernment* enables us to know whether something has its origins with the Holy Spirit, a human spirit, or an evil spirit. The gift of *tongues* involves prayer in an unlearned language. If it comes as a message for people, it needs to be accompanied by the gift of *interpretation* so that people may understand what is said.

The manifestational gifts are one portion of the somewhat larger category of all the various expressions of the Holy Spirit's power, presence, and activity. The burst of inspiration in which one understands the meaning of Scripture is a manifestation of the Spirit at work. When John Wesley's heart was "strangely warmed" and John Calvin was "vastly delighted,"[3] they were experiencing manifestations of the Holy Spirit through their emotional beings. Today the manifestations that cause the most controversy are those that involve our whole emotional and physical beings, for instance, when a person is overcome with "holy laughter" or starts to shake or falls on the floor. These are not specific gifts of the Spirit but are noticeable expressions of his presence.

A Miscellany of Gifts — 1 Corinthians 12:27 – 31

In 1 Corinthians 12:27 – 31 we encounter an intermingling of gifts from the other three lists. The only apparent newcomer is *administration*, which should not be confused with the Western idea of an office clerk but instead be thought of as a "helmsman" role, similar to the gift of leadership.[4] This diversity of manifestations, ministries, and gifts of the Holy Spirit is the reality that we encounter within a congregation that welcomes the Holy Spirit, for all of them are needed in the church and given by the Lord.

What Is the Purpose of These Gifts and Manifestations?

The power of the Holy Spirit is given in order that the church may bear witness to Jesus Christ and play an integral role in extending the gospel globally (Acts 1:8). The author of Hebrews writes: "This salvation, which was first

---

3. John Calvin, *Institutes of the Christian Religion*, ed. John. T. McNeill (Philadelphia: Westminster, 1960), 1.13.17.
4. Greek *kubernesis* refers to the art of piloting or steering a boat.

announced by the Lord, was confirmed to us by those who heard him. God also testified to it by signs, wonders and various miracles, and gifts of the Holy Spirit distributed according to his will" (2:3–4). To the proclamation by Jesus and by human witnesses is added this supernatural testimony, as experienced by the church in the book of Acts.[5] Peter explained, "Jesus of Nazareth was a man accredited by God to you by miracles, wonders and signs, which God did among you through him" (Acts 2:22), and Paul could affirm, "My message and my preaching were not with wise and persuasive words, but with a demonstration of the Spirit's power, so that your faith might not rest on men's wisdom, but on God's power" (1 Cor. 2:4–5).

During an Upward Challenge[6] at the Community of the Cross, fifty young people had been learning about the gifts of the Holy Spirit through teaching and small group prayer exercises and in the context of worship. On Friday afternoon of the weeklong program, they went on a mission trip to the nearby town of Asheville where a major folk festival was taking place. Before setting out, these young people formed groups of three and spent time asking the Holy Spirit where they were to go and to whom they should speak. Some received clear guidance that they were to stay at the camp and pray for those going out. Others were given images of who they were to witness to or were simply assured that if they followed the prompting of the Holy Spirit, they would know what to do.

That evening the teams returned with great excitement. Many had amazing experiences of receiving guidance, and as they acted on it, they had found themselves in deep engagement with people at the festival, often touching their hearts and seeing lives change. One group received the guidance that they were simply to go to specific people, look them in the eye, and say, "I just want you to know that Jesus Christ loves you!" At each prompting of the Spirit, the effect was remarkable; most just seemed thankful, but one young woman accepted Jesus Christ as Lord and Savior right there.

Another group, all girls, had been drawn to pay attention to a white-haired old man wandering the streets looking lost and confused. They reported, "The Holy Spirit told us just to go up to him. As we were moving toward him, the Lord gave a word of knowledge that his wife and daughter

---

5. As well as the miraculous events of Acts 2:43–47; 3:6–7; and 5:12–16, we have the anointed evangelistic proclamation in Acts 2:1–41 and 4:4, and the divine guidance in Acts 10–11 and 13:1–3.

6. Upward Challenge is a youth-equipping program placed in the camping context, sponsored by PRMI. The purpose of these weeklong events is to bring young people into a deeper relationship with Jesus Christ and pray for them to be filled with the Holy Spirit and to grow in cooperating with the Holy Spirit in ministry.

had just been killed in a car accident." The girls were hesitant but came up to the man and asked if he was okay. "No, not really," he replied. Then one girl ventured, "Sir, you seem to be grieving. Have you lost your wife and daughter?" The man broke down weeping, for that is exactly what had happened a few days before. They had always been together at the festival, but now he was wandering the streets alone. The girls gathered around him and prayed, and when asked how they had known, they were able to tell him that Jesus Christ who knows our hurts had sent them to comfort him.

The fundamental purpose of the gifts and manifestations of the Spirit is to enable Jesus' church to engage in evangelism and express the mercy and love of the Father. They are given for the common good, building up the body of Christ and inspiring worship so that the church may do all that Jesus calls it to do.

A Church Learning to Welcome What the Holy Spirit Is Doing

For the past twenty years, Montreat Presbyterian Church has been a living laboratory for testing most of the concepts in this book. At all levels of the church's life, from the prayer meetings to session meetings, from personal prayer ministry to public worship and preaching, the gifts and manifestations of the Holy Spirit are welcomed and are an integral part of the dance of cooperation. The church has an active healing prayer ministry with a variety of expressions. Teams of people are ready to pray when needed in the context of worship; other teams are ready to join the pastor in praying for particular cases, such as deliverance and inner healing, and a monthly healing prayer service is held.

But it has not always been like this, and several factors have enabled the transition. To begin with, the first and second foundations were in place: the pastor and many in the congregation were born again and had been baptized with the Holy Spirit. A good number already had some experience with the gifts and manifestations of the Holy Spirit, although these were largely in the realm of private experience and not integrated into the public life of the congregation. This gap between what one has experienced in a small prayer meeting or in personal prayer and what happens in the public life of the congregation is not unusual. There is, for instance, a notable difference between personally praying in tongues and expressing that gift publicly in a healing service. Many of us in the church, including the pastor and myself (Brad), had been praying for years that the Holy Spirit would empower every aspect of the life of the congregation. Ultimately this is a sovereign work of God and not something that we can manipulate into being. We could only pray for God to work and ensure we were ready to respond when he acted.

The opportunity came when I was teaching a Sunday school class about Jesus' healing ministry. There were about twenty people in the class, mostly young married couples with children, all eager to explore this topic. As I explained about the breadth of healing ministry, ranging from spiritual healing to deliverance, I became aware that the Holy Spirit was moving over the group. However, I had no specific guidance, so I simply continued teaching. As I spoke about how Jesus often had to cast out demons, Dana, a first-time visitor to our church, started crying and shaking all over. At that point, I didn't know whether the shaking was due to the work of the Holy Spirit, was caused by an evil spirit, or both. My role was to welcome what was happening by not shutting it down, to discern what was going on and to continue cooperating with the Holy Spirit.

The whole group was aware that something was happening. Some seemed fearful, but most were just curious and understood that something spiritual was taking place that was directly related to what I had been teaching. It was important that I remained in my role of overall leadership — to abandon that position of authority could have opened the door for confusion or demonic interference — so I asked Portia White, our pastor's wife, to go and pray with Dana. Portia was the only other person in the room who had any previous experience in prayer ministry, and while she prayed I explained to the group that the Holy Spirit was working, that perhaps deep wounds in Dana had been touched, or perhaps an evil spirit was interfering. At that point, it was time for people to collect their children or go to the 11:00 service, so I asked everyone to pray for Dana, Portia, and myself as we tried to discern what was happening and then cooperated with the Holy Spirit. This simple explanation calmed people's fears and also invited them to participate in the dance.

Later that day Portia and I continued this ministry. Dana was joined by her husband and several close friends, and we saw her experience deliverance from evil spirits and receive deep inner healing from some hurts that were caused long ago. Her husband was also caught up in this wonderful working of the Holy Spirit, and he too confessed some specific sins and experienced deliverance.

Word spread around the church, and the next Sunday my class was overflowing with people all eager to know what was happening. We spent the whole session "debriefing" the ministry and clarifying what had happened in the class. Dana explained what had been happening inside of her as well. Richard White, the pastor, joined us and told about the ministry that had taken place in their home later that day. This debriefing session gave us the opportunity to clear up questions and misunderstandings and to do some teaching on how the Holy Spirit works in inner healing and deliverance. We explained how Dana's emotional reactions were not simply the Holy Spirit moving her nor demons harassing her. Rather, they were the consequences of the Holy Spirit bringing into the light some deep hurts, which, like pockets of infection, were filled with anguish that had started to be expressed. In the Sunday school class, with the love of Jesus Christ filling us and the Holy Spirit moving among us, it had become safe to remember these hurts and to express them.

This was the catalytic event that began an ongoing process in the life of the church. Richard and several of the church elders became part of the class in order to bring this move of the Holy Spirit under the oversight of the church's leadership. I continued the class with a growing number of people, and by the time this six-week unit was finished, the entire group had started to be engaged in healing prayer ministry and many had received prayer for themselves. Now we had a group of people in the church who were eager to keep growing in the ministry of the Holy Spirit.

Changes also started to occur in the church's worship services. After preaching Richard would invite those who wanted to receive prayer for anything to come up front where the elders would be waiting to pray with them. People started to ask about having a regular healing service. The elders discovered how little they knew about prayer ministry, and with a growing number of requests for prayer, they saw that more people needed to become involved and asked PRMI to provide further training and equipping. It was a significant growth point in the church's history, and several factors combined to enable us to enter the dance of cooperation. The Spirit chose to move in sovereign grace in Dana's life; the leadership was ready to welcome the gifts and manifestations of the Holy Spirit rather than quenching them; and people were present who knew how to give leadership in this kind of situation. Instead of being divisive and hurtful (as happened in the church I visited in Canada), this became a ministry opportunity that brought great glory to Jesus Christ and growth to his church. The wonderful fruit of all this has been that Dana's family joined the church, and they all have been very active church members who are gifted at loving and discipling others into faith.

Cultivating a Congregation That Welcomes the Gifts and Manifestations of the Spirit

1. The Need for Leaders Who Are Ready to Cooperate with the Spirit

The task of leaders is "to prepare God's people for works of service" (Eph. 4:12), and this assumes that they themselves are suitably prepared. The leadership team I (Brad) encountered in Canada had no understanding of how to engage with what the Holy Spirit was doing, and neither did they appear willing to learn. Their own lack of readiness hindered the church from joining the dance of cooperation.

When I (Paul) finished my theological training, I visited a United Reformed Church in Warrington (UK) to explore whether I should serve as their minister. This was a congregation that was already experiencing the gifts and manifestations of the Spirit, and although I shared their theology, I lacked any personal experience of leadership in that kind of context. We happily agreed that it would not be right for me to become minister of that church. In the years that followed, I myself have had to learn and become better prepared for leadership in cooperation with the Holy Spirit. As I have grown — in particular through participation in the Dunamis equipping events — I have found myself better able to lead others into active participation in this dance with the Spirit.

Leaders need to develop both *an attitude of readiness* in their own hearts, and *a practical readiness* for taking action when the Spirit leads. Both were present in Montreat Presbyterian Church and provided the open door that welcomed the Holy Spirit to work in power, first in the Sunday school class and then in the whole congregation.

2. The Need for Practical Teaching

In Plymstock I (Paul) have sought first of all to "normalize" the persons and work of the whole Trinity. By speaking of Father, Son, and Holy Spirit rather than the less personal term *God*, and by "drip feeding" stories and testimonies of how the Spirit's gifts have been encountered, people have been learning to see the work of the Holy Spirit as normal (as, indeed, they should!). An extended sermon series gave the opportunity to deal with each of the gifts in turn, and a couple of one-day retreats provided the chance to teach about gifts, first based on Romans 12 and then from 1 Corinthians 12. An introductory training day about personal prayer ministry helped with the move from teaching into practice, and more extensive, in-depth training has been provided by participation in the Dunamis Project equipping events and by training courses run by a local Methodist church. This has been a gradual evolution over many years as we transformed the culture and ethos of the congregation, but there have also been some key periods of transition as opportunities have arisen and as the Spirit has drawn leaders and others into this work.

At Montreat the development took place more quickly. As the demand for healing ministry grew, Richard became overwhelmed by the task and needed a team of people who could work alongside him in prayer ministry. A growing number of people were eager to discover more about the Spirit's gifts, and therefore the elders arranged for some training events. The teaching was delivered primarily by Cindy, and Richard took part in each session by giving a summary, answering questions, applying the teaching to our church, and sharing in ministry. This was intentional as we wanted people to look to their pastor for guidance and prayer, rather than looking to me (Brad) and thus having potential for division within the congregation. A good number of people attended this short course, including most of the elders. Consequently, we gained not only a core team to provide prayer ministry, but also leaders who welcomed the gifts and manifestations of the Holy Spirit and had a firsthand understanding of how to welcome and encourage their expression in the congregation.

In both of these examples, we have focused mainly on the manifestational gifts of the Spirit. We believe that, regardless of their theoretical teaching, most churches gladly welcome a significant number of spiritual gifts already. Few would question the place of gifts of generosity, teaching, mercy, leadership, serving, or encouragement, but this is only a small selection of the full range of the Spirit's gifts. They can be a valuable starting point but must not become the limit of what people understand or expect.

3. The Need to Create Opportunities to Express the Gifts

As people learn to express the gifts of the Holy Spirit, we need contexts where they may be put to use. The gifts are not diplomas of spiritual excellence to be hung on a wall—they are tools for ministry, and they must be used for *doing* ministry if we are to continue to grow in them. Congregational worship and other gatherings of the church are a prime context, for they provide a safe environment of love and discernment[7] where people

---

7. This is the context indicated in 1 Cor. 13:1–7 and 14:29.

can exercise spiritual gifts, knowing that a "safety net" is in place to deal with genuine mistakes and abuse of the gifts. The Corinthian congregation is told: "What should you do then, brothers and sisters? When you come together, each one has a song, has a lesson, has a revelation, has a tongue, has an interpretation. Let all these things be done for the strengthening of the church" (1 Cor. 14:26 NET).

As Montreat Presbyterian Church provided opportunities for prayer following the sermons, and as they initiated healing services, they created a context in which people had increasing freedom to make use of a variety of spiritual gifts. These made the worship services a place where Jesus Christ could be wonderfully and freely at work. Through being involved in prayer ministry teams or serving as intercessors, people grow in their experience, understanding, and usefulness.

I (Paul) was encouraged recently as two members from Plymstock provided intercessory prayer cover at a local training event. At various points during the day, they received visions, words of knowledge, and prophecy that related to the prayer that was happening in various groups around the room. As they shared these with the groups, they themselves were growing in confidence and insight, and the trainees were helped and encouraged as they discovered that the Lord had spoken the same guidance to someone else.

The other main context for the practice of the gifts of the Holy Spirit and the welcoming of his manifestations is that of public witness and outreach. Peter and John were traveling to the place of worship when they met a man who was born lame. They publicly exercised gifts of faith and healing through the power of the Holy Spirit, and later, when they were questioned about the healing, the Spirit manifested his power by equipping them for evangelistic proclamation (Acts 3–4).

For today's church, if mission trips and ministries of compassion are to accomplish their purpose of witnessing to Jesus Christ and advancing his kingdom, they must include occasions when the Holy Spirit is welcomed to show forth spiritual gifts and manifestations of power. Without these times, people will experience our good works but will not experience the transforming power of the gospel.

Recognizing the Time to Act

When this sixth dynamic of welcoming the gifts of the Holy Spirit into the congregation is nurtured, the dance of cooperation is already beginning and ministry will start unfolding in a new depth and breadth. The reason is that now the "power tools" are available for real kingdom work to take place. Often this is the point when congregations start to grow in depth of fellowship and in numbers. They also may start to experience a deeper level of spiritual warfare, for Satan will try to prevent this growth in usefulness in the kingdom. We will return to this topic later, but first we must address the last of the Seven Dynamics: responding to kairos moments of opportunity.

Chapter 15

Dynamic 7: Seeing and Responding to *Kairos* Moments

Jesus healed the lame man at the Beautiful Gate through Peter's obedience as he discerned this moment of opportunity and stepped out in faith. The man was healed, which created an opportunity for a powerful proclamation of the gospel that led to many coming to faith (Acts 3–4). Kairos moments are occasions of pregnant opportunity as God prepares to act and seeks human cooperation — perhaps an instant for ministry or a new season in church life. We need to learn to recognize and respond to these moments and also to cultivate them in the schedules and life of the church.

Sometimes it is "that" time. The time is ripe and "something" needs to happen. One Sunday morning at Montreat Presbyterian Church, we were listening to news about our youth group's recent mission trip to Bolivia. The youth director, Shawn, read some of their letters describing their profound experiences of Jesus, and as he did so an intense silence and stillness descended on the congregation. We experienced an intense presence of God as he moved in our midst, beckoning us into a fresh engagement with himself. People were deeply moved and began weeping, sensing the presence of God. Shawn wept as he struggled to read, and then, feeling awkward, he just sat down. The moment was pregnant with opportunity.

I (Brad) sensed words forming in my heart, "Now call them into a deeper love and commitment to following me!" I knew this was the Holy Spirit's word to speak into this moment, but I had no authority or permission to speak. Our pastor, Richard, was leading, and he appeared delighted by the presence of God but perplexed about what to do next. It was time to speak the word from God.

But at that moment an elder stood to give the announcements, and as he delivered a catalog of details, the expectant sense of God's presence faded. A door had opened to deeper engagement with God, but we had not known what to do. Now it had closed, and we were left with the melancholy awareness that there had indeed been something more. The service continued, but the transcendent dimension was no longer there.

Later I met with Richard and Shawn, and we all expressed the same awareness that God had been about to visit us, but we had missed the moment. Richard had sensed the same words about calling people into a deeper love and commitment but had not known what to do and had been afraid to step into the moment. Many of us in leadership will have experienced something similar. What we missed was a "kairos moment."

Chronos Time and Kairos Time

Chronos is the time that passes with the ticking of a clock, the steady passage of minutes and hours and days. It measures intervals and delays, whether long or short. It is the kind of time Jesus spoke about when he said, "Don't you know me, Philip, even after I have been among you such a long time?" (John 14:9). *Kairos* is the awaited epoch, the point of crisis. It speaks of the season for harvest, the appointed time, the right time, the time of God's arrival (Matt. 21:34; 26:18; Luke 19:44; John 7:6; Rom. 9:9). It is sensed rather than measured, like the time to push when a child is about to be born. This is the type of time announced by Jesus: "'The time has come,' he said. 'The kingdom of God is near. Repent and believe the good news!'" (Mark 1:15).

Kairos moments are the time of invitation when the Holy Spirit is moving and ready to act. They carry a sense of "now" and of holy presence, of readiness and of God waiting for us to take our next step in the dance of dynamic cooperation. Richard and I (Brad) missed that opportunity when Shawn was speaking, and we do not know what work the Spirit would have done had we actually followed his lead. But I do know what the Spirit did on a different occasion when I felt the leading of the Holy Spirit and obeyed.

This was my first inkling of the dynamic of kairos moments and cooperation with the Holy Spirit. It came in 1978 during a Presbyterian Charismatic Communion conference. One evening about two thousand people stood in exalting, Spirit-led praise of Jesus Christ when a deepening silence fell on the group. We were awed, overcome by the weightiness of God's glory and waiting for something to happen. The leadership team stood on the platform in silent expectation, waiting but receiving no guidance.

Suddenly words came to mind: "Bow down before me; bow down before me, for I am the mighty King." I struggled inwardly, believing the Lord was speaking to me, yet fearful of being wrong and looking a fool. The words grew hot. I finally took the risk and spoke. At the first word, "bow," the whole assembly fell instantly to their knees and the room was filled with tears and prayers of recommitment to Jesus Christ. One of the leaders spoke, sharing the vision the Holy Spirit was giving him. He saw Jesus weeping for those with physical or emotional hurts. We then entered an amazing period in which the Holy Spirit moved over the group in wave after wave, bringing healing and other manifestations of power and love.

The Holy Spirit needed these words in order to do his work. The dance continued because of the connection between the word from God and the Spirit of God, and we believe this is a fundamental spiritual principle underlying this seventh dynamic of seeing and responding to kairos moments.

The Spirit Waits for the Word to Be Spoken

In the beginning the Spirit of God hovered, brooding over the surface of chaos, waiting for the creative word. Like an eagle that stirs up its nest, fluttering over its young and spreading its wings wide,[1] the Holy Spirit was stirring. John Milton's early lines of *Paradise Lost* capture the imagery well:

> Thou from the first
> Wast present, and with mighty wings outspread
> Dove-like satst brooding over the vast Abyss
> And mad'st it pregnant.[2]

Yet nothing happened until the Father spoke the words "Let there be light" (Gen. 1:3). Only as the word from God and the Spirit of God come together do we see reality transformed. The two belong together. When the word was not spoken, as happened at Montreat, the Spirit was hindered from leading us deeper into the Father's purposes. But at the conference, we saw a wholly different development precisely because the word was spoken and the Holy Spirit was able to work among us. The word has power only with the presence and activity of the Spirit, and the Spirit acts in accordance with the word.[3]

---

1. Deuteronomy 32:11, referring to an eagle, uses the same Hebrew word as Genesis 1:2 in the description of the Spirit.

2. John Milton, *Paradise Lost and Other Poems*, mentor ed., annotated by Edward Le Comte (New York: New American Library, 1961), bk. 1, ll. 19–22.

3. We use the expression "word of God" as follows: The "Word of God" refers to Scripture and the revelation of doctrine (John 1:1ff.), whereas the "word of God" (or "word from God") refers to guidance or direction or a word spoken in a specific situation, such as the Holy Spirit's leading Philip to the chariot (Acts 8:26–40).

At the time of creation, God himself spoke the word—there simply was no one else to speak it! But now, having created human beings in his image and called us to be coworkers, he speaks (or sometimes enacts) his word through the prophetic participation of men and women. This is our role in the dance of cooperation with the Holy Spirit.

When Jesus raised Lazarus (John 11:1–44), the Holy Spirit was already present, having fallen upon Jesus at his baptism. Jesus' initial delay gives us a clue that he was conscious of the Father's timing, setting aside chronos time and alert to the kairos moment. He stood before the tomb, lifting his eyes to heaven in prayer, and then spoke the words, "Lazarus, come out!" (John 11:43). Just as on the eve of creation, the intent of the word of God connects with the hovering Spirit of God and an amazing miracle took place: the dead man came out. By speaking the word into the kairos moment, Jesus was acting in the role of a prophet.

In the dramatic encounter between Moses and the king of Egypt, this prophetic role is made clear in a repeated pattern: the Lord spoke to Moses, Moses acted in obedience (usually by speaking, sometimes by symbolic deed), and then the power of God worked a miracle. The entire account is a kairos moment in the history of Israel as the Lord liberated his people, yet each episode has its own kairos moment too.

> The Lord said to Moses, "Tell Aaron, 'Take your staff and stretch out your hand over the waters of Egypt—over the streams and canals, over the ponds and all the reservoirs'—and they will turn to blood. Blood will be everywhere in Egypt, even in the wooden buckets and stone jars."
>
> Moses and Aaron did just as the Lord had commanded. He raised his staff in the presence of Pharaoh and his officials and struck the water of the Nile, and all the water was changed into blood. (Ex. 7:19–20)

What terror filled Moses as he teetered on the edge of this kairos moment? He stood before Pharaoh, the most powerful man on earth, with only the word of God that had been spoken in the depths of his own heart. Like all of us, he was made in the image of God, a free and responsible person, a friend, not a slave or puppet. He could have aborted the dance and left the future stillborn in the Father's heart. But Moses obeyed! He struck the water, and God continued the dance.

God's part was to speak to Moses. Moses' role was to listen and obey. This dynamic is implicit in every great miracle of the Bible and of our present day. For Christians there can be no other basis for moving in spiritual power than this simple dynamic of listening and, in obedience, speaking or acting the word in the moment of the Spirit's moving. It is behind every act of God, including drawing each of us to faith in Jesus Christ and being born again. For instance, I (Paul) have already described in chapter 2 how the kairos moment for Deborah's conversion came as I spoke to her son. Seeing tears begin to trickle down her face, I realized that the Holy Spirit was stirring her heart and recognized my invitation to join the dance of cooperation. As a step of obedience, I said, "It's time for you as well, isn't it?" She quietly nodded, and I had the privilege of leading them both in a prayer of commitment to Christ.

Here we find a paradox. It is the Holy Spirit who first gives us the word that needs to be spoken—the initiative is wholly his. But the Spirit then waits for the word to be spoken—the choice to cooperate is wholly ours. And if we do speak the word, giving our "Amen" to his invitation, then the next step depends wholly on him. And so the dance of cooperation continues, God's purposes unfolding before us as we stay in step with the Spirit.

Perhaps the most common occurrence of this is in prophetic preaching. Preaching functions in a variety of ways, sometimes teaching, at other times encouraging, exhorting, persuading, or consoling. But it can also be the context in which the preacher, speaking under the inspiration of the Holy Spirit, obediently declares God's words into the kairos moment. Such a word is creative and prophetic, opening up a dynamic interaction between the hearer and the Spirit. Yet this is clearly not the only context in which we encounter kairos moments, and on each occasion we will be called to respond in different ways, according to what God intends to accomplish.

Recognizing and Responding to Kairos Moments

Kairos Moments in Meetings

I (Paul) have heard plenty of derogatory comments about committees. Let's face it: God loved the world so much that he *didn't* send a committee! Yet the Holy Spirit is pleased to show up when Jesus' followers meet together, and that includes the times when we gather to deal with apparently mundane "business" matters.

When 150 members of the regional South Western Synod of the United Reformed Church met for a day to discuss organizational changes, few of us expected the Holy Spirit to take an interest. During the lunch break, a newcomer handed a note to the moderator describing a prophetic picture, just one piece of "feedback" among the day's proceedings. But as he summarized the discussions, the moderator chose to read the note out loud, and at that instant a profound stillness descended upon the whole group. Everyone seemed touched by the word. It was a kairos moment in a committee meeting! Time paused as I watched to see how the moderator would lead us, and he appeared momentarily unsure of what to do. It so happened that I was seated nearby, right in his line of sight, and I signaled with my hands that we should pray. I had no authority in the meeting, but thankfully he heeded my suggestion and paused to lead us in prayer before continuing with other business. Perhaps we should have moved into corporate prayer or he should have invited people to speak out any other visions, pictures, or prophecy. Or maybe the reading of the note was sufficient, a simple reminder of Jesus' presence and purposes. For me it was a timely reminder that committee meetings are not boring when the Spirit has a voice.

More recently, as we prayed during an elders' meeting at Plymstock, we acknowledged that Jesus had done whatever he saw the Father doing, and asked for grace that we might do the same. I then experienced a dawning realization that nine of our members were taking part in another church's training course for healing ministry and that we had spoken in the past about developing opportunities for prayer ministry in this congregation. What was the Father doing, if not providing the resources we needed? As we finished praying, I described what had happened, and seeing this as a kairos moment, we then dealt with this issue as a priority before tackling any other item on the agenda. Practical plans were made for involving these people in Sunday morning prayer ministry in the short term and for commissioning them and initiating a prayer ministry team once the training was finished.

Kairos Moments in a Global Crisis

On September 11, 2001, I (Brad) woke up early with a deep foreboding. I had a strong sense of the Spirit brooding, a kairos calling into intercessory prayer. I had no idea of details, so I simply lay in bed praying in tongues for protection against impending outbreak of evil. An hour and a half later I watched on TV as an airplane crashed into the World Trade Tower where my brother was due at a meeting that morning, and then heard that my sister (who worked in the Pentagon) could not be reached on her mobile phone. All day long I could not stop praying in the Spirit for God to constrain Satan, sometimes getting the nudge to pray in very specific ways, such as asking God to confuse the plans and communications of the enemy or binding evil spirits of hatred and rage.

In the evening I had a strong compulsion from the Holy Spirit to go up to our church to pray. I went expecting to be alone and was amazed to find the sanctuary packed with people. No announcements had been given; the Holy Spirit had just called people to prayer. I have since met with many people in America, Canada, and Great Britain who received a similar calling. They, too, were drawn into intercession before the attacks actually happened and were then led to their churches to offer corporate prayers of intercession to hold back the evil and to pray for repentance. The Holy Spirit was moving in a global kairos moment, calling people to prayer.

As I have spoken about this prayer mobilized by the Holy Spirit, a surprising number of elderly people have shared similar stories from the Second World War. At key moments of crisis, such as Germany's invasion of Poland, the battle of Dunkirk, and the eve of D-Day, they were called to urgent prayer and led to go to their churches for corporate prayer and confession. Only afterward did they learn that the invasions were under way. But the Holy Spirit had known what was happening and had called thousands of intercessors into this great contest, pushing back and destroying the demonic stronghold of Nazism.

Kairos Moments in a Traditional Service

At a morning worship service at San Mateo Presbyterian Church in California, I (Brad) became aware of the moving of the Holy Spirit as the choir led in worship. We were in the second verse of the traditional hymn "Holy, Holy, Holy," and the words took on a special sweetness as the people sang with intensity and conviction. I recognized it was a kairos moment. I have experienced this many times in traditional worship, though usually we just stick to our program and keep going until the last verse and then stop. This worship leader, however, was listening to the Holy Spirit as well as the lovely music, and he knew that God was calling him to obedience. Instead of finishing the song, he led the choir to return and dwell on the particular verse. This was the word from God, spoken into the kairos moment by repeating the verse. In that moment the Spirit had fallen upon the congregation, and we were caught up in the presence of God Almighty. People were weeping. Some stood with tears in their eyes and their hands uplifted in praise; others knelt on the floor.

Such moments of profound depth in worship and encounters with God were common in that congregation, and both the leadership and the people had learned what to do with kairos moments. The dance of cooperation was a dynamic activity, not confined to their worship services but woven into the very fabric of the church's whole life of worship, evangelism, and ministries of compassion.

Kairos—A Terrible Responsibility!

Kairos is a sobering concept. In that moment when the Spirit invites us to join the dance, there is no backup partner. The people present at that moment are the ones he is dancing with, and if they miss a step—either by not listening or by not obeying—part of the dance simply does not happen.

This is not popular thinking. We tend to declare that nobody is indispensable and that the Father's sovereign will is inexorably fulfilled, and within his ultimate design that is certainly true. But in each moment of history, there is another piece in the picture: Almighty God constrains himself to work in partnership with us. What if Peter had not visited Cornelius or paused to heal the man at the temple steps? Philip could have stayed away from the Ethiopian, and Paul could have avoided Macedonia. Imagine if Mary had rejected her pregnancy or John had refused to baptize Jesus. We are repeatedly faced with the terrible reality that our choice to cooperate in God's kairos moment truly matters. While it is a huge risk for us to listen and to obey, it is also a great risk for God! He takes extraordinary chances with us.

Each kairos moment missed is a tragic blocking of God's plans and purposes. This may be as simple as an individual in a prayer session not receiving the comfort God intended or a congregation not going deep in worship. It may also mean that a nation is not reached, as Archer Torrey once described:

> A young worker from the United States received a clear vision that he was to go to China and witness to Chairman Mao Tse-tung. Encouraged and funded by his church, he traveled to Hong Kong to wait for his visa into mainland China, and there he met a retired pastor. The pastor told the young man how, in a dream, a voice had told him that the visa would be given the next day—a sign to confirm that the dream was authentic—and that he was not to go to mainland China, because within a year thousands of Western missionaries would be allowed into Communist China. He was not to meet with Chairman Mao, as that would hinder this door opening. The young man listened to the word of the distinguished retired pastor, disobeyed the guidance of the Holy Spirit, and returned home. The doors did not open, and there were more years of communist oppression.
>
> Reportedly, Mao Tse-tung had developed a passionate interest in Christianity around this time, and the alarmed government isolated him from any Western visitors. It is reported that the last Western visitor to see him was Henry Kissinger, and all Mao Tse-tung had wanted to talk

about was religion. He died not long after this. It is very possible that God was opening the door and that Mao would have been able to hear the gospel from a working man.

A kairos moment was missed, and God had no backup dance partner. Not only was the gospel blocked from going to this Chinese leader, but the young man and the congregation that was supporting him were all taken out of the dance.[4]

The idea that God doesn't always have a backup plan is profoundly sobering. Let it sink into our hearts and inspire us to obedience! Let us know that we are truly responsible, that our actions truly matter. Either we participate in God's eternal work or we obstruct it. Salvation, healing, and liberty have come through Jesus Christ, but whether the world receives this salvation depends on us who have been called to participate with God in the fulfillment of his purposes. Most of us have a whole history of missed kairos moments. These should call us to repentance rather than despair. We must learn to discern these moments and to listen and obey. God is merciful and determined to accomplish his purposes, so often he will give us multiple opportunities. If we fail to obey, however, they seem to stop, and God chooses someone else more prone to obedience for the dance.

Cultivating the Seventh Dynamic in the Congregation

We have described a variety of examples to help readers better recognize kairos moments. Such opportunities come from the Lord, and we cannot manufacture them by willpower or contrivance. But we can ask for them, be listening to the Holy Spirit, and be ready to obey. We can also prepare ourselves and our congregations for recognizing and responding to whatever kairos moments do arise. To consider how we may do this, let us return to the opportunity that was missed at Montreat.

Teach on Kairos Moments and Provide Discernment

Richard and I (Brad) were deeply disturbed about not acting on the kairos moment that had occurred in the Montreat service, and we spent our prayer time debriefing the events. As we reflected on the flow of the

---

4. For a fuller description of this, see the Dunamis Project Manual, *In the Spirit's Power: Cooperating with the Holy Spirit to do the Work of Jesus Christ* (Black Mountain, NC: PRMI, 2006), 87.

service, Richard became more clearly aware of what a kairos moment was. Leaders and congregations need to be taught about this particular dynamic. Once it has been named and explained, many people can think back to such moments of opportunity and can perceive the consequences of either missing them or acting on them.

The process of discernment is also an important learning opportunity, as the leader and a few others reflect together on the service. When I do this I always ask, "Did I miss a moment of opportunity? Was the Holy Spirit moving or speaking to someone?" As we have learned to see and respond to kairos moments, we have found these observations helpful:

1. *We will have an internal awareness of the presence of the Holy Spirit.* This may be a stirring or a stillness, a quickening or a sense of expectation. It may be a sense of sweetness, heaviness, or something like the lull before a thunderstorm. For some, there may be an awareness that is hard to articulate, as if time is being touched with eternity. There may be no "feeling" at all, but simply a deep knowing that "Now I, the Lord, am going to work!" And others may have a mental image of and awareness of the moving of the Holy Spirit.

2. *Others will be aware of and confirm the Spirit's presence and activity.* Often there will be subtle but noticeable signs that the Holy Spirit is present and moving, just as we see wind moving leaves. We therefore need to keep our eyes open, both physically and spiritually, and observe what is happening.

3. *Alongside this awareness of the Spirit's presence and movement, someone will receive the word from the Holy Spirit that gives the next steps in the dance that we are called to take.* This is the "word" from God that is to be acted out.

4. *When we respond to this kairos moment through the risk of obedience, significant incidences will occur.*

5. *The gift of kairos moments is given to those who are willing to act upon them.* When we lose the will or the faith to act, the opportunities dwindle and God allows us to become spiritually blind to them.

Commit to Obedience and Grant Others the Right to Discern and Obey the Moment

Richard and I were both aware of the kairos moment in the Montreat service and had both received the guidance of what to do: "Call them to a deeper love and commitment to me!" But several obstacles stopped us from obeying. For Richard there was the nagging pressure of not letting the service last longer than an hour lest people be offended. There was also the inertia of habit, the security of sticking to the preplanned service schedule, and the fear of not knowing what to do next.

For me there was the constraint of having no authority or permission to act. At the Presbyterian Charismatic Communion Conference, where I called out, "Bow down before me," we all had explicit permission to speak out whatever guidance the Holy Spirit might give. But in the traditional Reformed service at Montreat, no one, not even the pastor, had the permission to be led by the Holy Spirit outside the accepted order.

At the church in Corinth people had this permission, having been told: "When you come together, each one has a song, has a lesson, has a revelation, has a tongue, has an interpretation. Let all these things be done for the strengthening of the church" (1 Cor. 14:26 NET). If our congregations are to develop this dynamic of seeing and responding to kairos moments, then permission must be given for them to be led by the Holy Spirit. This is not license to disrupt the worship or to usurp the authority of those in leadership. But it is liberty to follow the leading of the Spirit.

Pray for God to Advance His Kingdom

Kairos moments cannot be contrived or faked; they can, however, be prayed for and welcomed. Through intercessory prayer that invites God's engagement, we discover the Holy Spirit bringing kairos moments in which we are invited to take the next steps in the dance. We do need to be careful! Kairos moments can be so exciting that we are tempted to seek them as an end in themselves. Our prayer is not for exciting events for our spiritual entertainment, but for God to work among us and involve us in advancing his kingdom.

When the first disciples came under persecution, they prayed together: "'And now, Lord, pay attention to their threats, and grant to your servants to speak your message with great courage, while you extend your hand to heal, and to bring about miraculous signs and wonders through the name of your holy servant Jesus.' When they had prayed, the place where they were assembled together was shaken, and they were all filled with the Holy Spirit" (Acts 4:29–31 NET). This was the experience of the kairos moment, and their obedient response was that they began to speak the word of God courageously. They continued in the dance, and the results were wonderful: "The group of those who believed were of one heart and mind, and no one said that any of his possessions was his own, but everything was held in common. With great power the apostles were giving testimony to the resurrection of the Lord Jesus, and great grace was on them all" (Acts 4:32–33 NET).

These Seven Dynamics weave together into a fluid, interrelated whole, and through them we share in the wonder of advancing the kingdom of God. But lurking in the shadows lies an enemy who, from the beginning, has sought to undermine and pervert the purposes of God. Paul warns that "everyone who wants to live a godly life in Christ Jesus will be persecuted" (2 Tim. 3:12), and many of us are familiar with the struggle against the world, the flesh, and the devil. Before looking at the synergy that occurs when these Seven Dynamics work together, we turn our attention to the obstacles that inhibit the dance in step with the Spirit.

Chapter 16

Obstacles to the Dance

Even when we know what we should do, we find ourselves prone to fail. Sometimes through simple sinfulness, but also through the diversions of the devil, the dance can go awry as someone other than the Holy Spirit begins to take the lead. Leaders need to be alert to these obstacles so that they may be avoided or removed.

We have been on a long journey exploring the factors involved in growing the church in the power of the Holy Spirit. We began with the Two Foundations — leaders and congregations who embody the reality of the kingdom of God. With these in place, we then examined in more detail the Seven Dynamics, identifying the "dance steps" of cooperating with the Holy Spirit. A synergy happens as these dynamics interconnect, and we will return to this in the final chapter. But before we do so, we must face the unpalatable reality that the dance easily can go wrong. In this chapter, therefore, we will pause to identify some of the major stumbling blocks that form obstacles in the dance of cooperation with the Holy Spirit.

The Galatian Christians had to wake up to an uncomfortable fact: they had been bewitched. Somehow their focus had shifted. They had begun with faith in the crucified Christ, and consequently the Holy Spirit had been poured out and miracles had taken place among them. They had been thoroughly engaged in dynamic cooperation with the Spirit, proclaiming the gospel of Jesus and embodying the reality of the kingdom of God. And then they began to drift off course, with a growing emphasis on their own religious good works instead of maintaining a straightforward trust. This disastrous shift meant that their religion was no longer about what God did; it was about what they could do. So Paul posed a pointed question: "Are you so foolish? After beginning with the Spirit, are you now trying to attain your goal by human effort?" (Gal. 3:3).[1]

Before we are too quick to condemn the Galatians, we should remember that we, too, are not yet perfect. Paul himself was very forthright about this: "I have the desire to do what is good, but I cannot carry it out.... When I want to do good, evil is right there with me" (Rom. 7:18, 21). The process of sanctification has begun but will not be finished until either we die or Christ returns. In Galatia, or Plymouth, or Montreat—or anywhere that Christians are seeking to live out their faith in cooperation with the Holy Spirit—we find that our sinful human nature causes an ongoing struggle. We truly want to stay in step with the Spirit, but sin trips us up. We may begin with the Spirit, but in a variety of ways, we can easily find ourselves relying on human effort instead.

When Humans Take Over from the Spirit

Churches are shaped by their leaders, a fact that we acknowledged when considering Jesus' four requirements for leadership. Their impact is, to some extent, due to the *position* or status they have been given within the church or organization. Others have significant influence because of their *personalities*. Whether helping or hindering, these are men and women whose opinions and preferences sway the decision-making process, shape the culture, and alter the atmosphere.

I (Cindy) saw this dynamic at work in my husband's church. Steve served a Hungarian Reformed Church in central New Jersey for seventeen years. When he arrived almost everyone in the church was Hungarian or married to a Hungarian. He was their first American pastor and the first pastor who spoke English without a Hungarian accent. There was no mission outreach, no reaching out to the community (except fund-raising dinners), no adult education, and little education for children. Within the first few years, the church started opening its doors to the community. Within ten years the church doubled in size, education for adults and children was flourishing, and the church was involved in several mission projects. A few years later, a Spirit-led contemporary worship service was added. Things were going really well.

---

1. In this passage Paul is primarily dealing with the fact that salvation is through faith in Christ and not through the human effort of obeying Old Testament laws (Gal. 3:10–11). This faith enables us to receive the gift of the Holy Spirit (3:2, 14), for faith, Jesus, salvation, and the Spirit belong together. To concentrate on human effort means abandoning the work of Jesus and the Spirit.

Steve provided leadership, but none of this growth and openness to the Holy Spirit would have happened without the support of key leaders and in particular a woman named Helen. She was born in Hungary and immigrated to the United States as a child. She grew up in the church and was a ruling elder when we arrived. She loved Jesus and had a passion to see her church serving him in the community. She was able to bring others along through all the changes and served as a bridge to the "old guard" who were not happy with the new people or with new things happening. But when Helen died very suddenly, her diplomatic work ended. Within a short time, the "old guard" started complaining about the changes and eventually drove out the new people. They ended the Spirit-led service, and mission and education ground to a halt. The progress of fifteen years was dismantled within two years. Watching the church fall apart was heartbreaking. Clearly one strong personality in a church can make a huge difference — opening the door for the Spirit to work or closing the door and blocking the way.

The situation of a few influential members diverting the dance away from the Holy Spirit is extremely common. These are not necessarily bad people, though they might be self-centered. They may well be born again but have such inner hurts or such a need to control that they effectively block the working of the Holy Spirit. Such people have destroyed many thriving congregations and have been the bane of those seeking to center the church in Jesus Christ. This person may be the pastor, the founding pastor, an old respected Sunday school teacher, or the matriarch or patriarch of one of the leading families. In the hearts of such people a shift has been made away from being led by the Holy Spirit to attempting, instead, to do things in their own power, strength, and will. This, in turn, influences the entire congregation, for a little yeast works through the whole batch of dough (1 Cor. 5:6).

We have little control over other people, but the same shift can easily take place within our own hearts. We therefore need to be watchful lest we ourselves become the ones who are obstacles to the dance of cooperation.

The Danger of Depending on People

We are called into this dance alongside others. Jesus sent his disciples out in pairs, and New Testament leadership takes place in teams as elders work together to oversee their churches. God intends for us to have a genuine partnership in the gospel as we labor alongside coworkers whom we love and trust and who share the same vision. Yet danger lurks. It is easy to stop depending on the Holy Spirit's leadership and, instead, to start depending on one another. As this happens, a coworker takes the place of the Holy Spirit, and the dance of cooperation falters.

I (Brad) have struggled with this temptation throughout my leadership. I am severely dyslexic, cannot spell, can barely write, never know what time it is, and have a terrible time keeping up with appointments. I therefore have to be very dependent on others who have gifts that compensate for my weaknesses. Frankly, this is a good thing, because it keeps me humble and dependent on Jesus Christ! But I must constantly guard my heart against the temptation of shifting my focus away from Jesus and onto them. This is a subtle yet very real problem.

One day while in prayer with Richard White, I confessed this tendency to replace Jesus with one of my coworkers. He responded, "Well you are not the only one who struggles with that tendency. You had better hear my confession too! I realized that I was depending too much on my efficient church secretary to be the one to direct my cooperating with the Holy Spirit. At first she was just very helpful in helping me discern which counseling appointments I should take or what visitation I should do. She was older and more experienced than me, and gradually I started to depend on her instead of the Holy Spirit to guide me in these decisions. I have to honor her administrative gifts and her wisdom but not let her replace the Holy Spirit. The struggle is within me; I am the problem!"

For me (Paul) this temptation has surfaced in the very process of learning to cooperate with the Spirit. It was far easier for me to look to Cindy or Brad for guidance in the middle of leading a Dunamis Project event. After all, they had more experience and better insight. Thankfully they were aware of the dangers, and most of the time they would step out of the way so that I simply *had* to take the risks of leadership and learn to discern. But sometimes we all got this wrong: I was too anxious to lean on them, and they were too eager to be involved, so they took the Holy Spirit's place in my own leadership.

This is a constant struggle for all three of us, and one that will always beset those who are dancing together as a team in cooperation with the work of the Holy Spirit.

The Danger of Depending on Programs

Why reinvent the wheel? There are all kinds of programs and resources available to the church, many of them refined by years of experience and insight. Nicky Gumbel's Alpha course for evangelism, Neil Anderson's Freedom in Christ Ministries, Rick Warren's Purpose Driven series for developing discipleship, and myriad materials for vacation Bible schools and holiday clubs have all proved to be invaluable tools in the church's task. The Dunamis Project and Ignite programs from Presbyterian Reformed Ministries International have helped individuals and churches to come alive in the power of the Holy Spirit and grow in their discipleship.

All these programs and methods have a place in Jesus' church. God has used them greatly for his glory, and sometimes the Spirit will have called a church to make use of a specific resource. But the danger is that we begin to depend on the program instead of the Holy Spirit. That may happen from the very beginning as our church adopts a particular program or approach because we are excited by its impact in other congregations. We may become so familiar with a program that we pay no attention when the Lord wants us to move on to something fresh. Or we may simply settle down into running the program itself, neglecting the ongoing call to prayerfulness. In short, the program takes center stage, and we shift from being led by the Holy Spirit to working by human effort.

In 2008 we ran our first conference on "Growing the Church in the Power of the Holy Spirit" at the Community of the Cross, and we taught the principles outlined in this book. Richard White described how the Holy Spirit had led his church to implement the concept of team ministry at Montreat Presbyterian Church, a story we described in chapter 3. Richard was excited about the shift that had taken place in his congregation, and when he finished, several pastors in the meeting all immediately said, "Yes, that is what I need to do in my congregation." What followed was a very excited, animated discussion about what steps were needed to implement this team model of leadership.

In the midst of this lively conversation, Paul blew the whistle on us: "Hey everyone! Look at what we are doing! We are teaching on the dynamic of cooperating with the Holy Spirit. Shouldn't we first check with the Holy Spirit to see if that is what he is actually leading us to do in our churches? Aren't we just taking what worked at Montreat Church and making it into a method for all of our churches?" We all laughed at ourselves and said, "Yes, we are!" So we shifted our conversation away from a program of leadership and onto the person of the Holy Spirit, asking how we could help the leaders in our congregations learn to listen to what the Spirit is saying to our churches. In that way each congregation could deal with the Lord's unique agenda for them, rather than simply emulating the activities of another church.

The danger of depending on programs or methods rather than the Holy Spirit is strong and persistent. If it continues unchecked, we will end up merely enjoying nice programs rather than dancing in step with the Holy Spirit.

The Danger of Spiritual Pride

God's will is good, pleasing, and perfect (Rom. 12:2). So if we are engaged in leadership because it is the Lord's will for our lives, then it will be satisfying work. It may not always be enjoyable, and we may often experience the dissatisfaction that accompanies imperfection, for we have not yet arrived at our destination. But certainly in my own life I (Brad) have found that spiritual leadership — guided and empowered by the Holy Spirit — is an immensely satisfying and exciting adventure. It also means that I often have the privilege of seeing God working in kairos moments in the midst of my ministry.

But leadership also has its temptations. I repeatedly face the danger of spiritual pride, of wanting to be the one who is in control of what is happening, of being the choreographer rather than a dancer. This has happened to me again and again when I have been at the center of what God is doing at a Dunamis equipping event or through a mission outreach team. Every pastor or church leader who stands in the center of God's working faces similar temptations. This danger of egoism is especially dangerous for those who are greatly gifted and anointed for ministry.

I have seen this pride surfacing when I start thinking about what I want to do or start being concerned about my reputation or my legacy. Pride is the source of the fear that leads me to want to make things happen even when I know the Spirit is not moving. It shows when I am not willing to wait for the Holy Spirit to give guidance and I simply invent something to go into the kairos moment, knowing deep in my heart that it came, not from the Lord, but from me. I know that the temptation is strong when the Spirit's anointing is shifting to someone else yet I am unwilling to step back and let that person cooperate with the Holy Spirit. It is at this last point that many anointed leaders have fallen. They started in the Spirit but ended in human effort because they refused to step aside when the Holy Spirit was drawing others into the dance. I must confess that usually my friends and coworkers become aware of these signs in me before I realize it myself.

In 2003 Paul was directing his first Dunamis event in England. I did a lot of the teaching, assisted by Cindy and Paul. On the final evening, we had scheduled time to pray for the infilling with the Holy Spirit. It is the part of Dunamis I love more than anything, and over the years I have witnessed the Spirit work powerfully through me, falling upon people with wonderful manifestations. I find it exhilarating, and I love it!

But this time I was getting some very uncomfortable guidance: I was to step aside. I was not to do the teaching on how to receive, nor was I to pray for people. Instead, Cindy was to do the teaching, and Paul was to lay hands on the leadership team. Then his team was to lay hands on the rest of the people. I did not like the guidance! It was a major struggle for me, because I loved these people, and I wanted to minister to them. I know that I also wanted their love and approval, looking to me as the one through whom they were baptized with the Holy Spirit.

I went for a long walk by myself, arguing with God about this guidance, and when I rejoined the leadership team to pray together before the meeting, it was obvious that the Spirit's anointing was upon them and not me at all. Cindy was ready to teach, and Paul was obviously stepping up to the role of an anointed leader. But I jumped right in and suggested, "Well, I can just do the teaching on how to receive and then lay hands on the group. I hope you will all join me in that." There was an awkward silence, and then Ruth Sermon, one of the intercessors who has an irritating tendency of hearing from God, said very tentatively, "As I was praying, I think the Holy Spirit may have been giving me a vision. I saw a farmer sowing a field with seeds, and then he just went home. The rain and the sunlight came, and the seeds came up."

Immediately the meaning was clear to me: I had sown the seeds; now it was time to let them grow by getting out of the way. I felt awkward, but as I shared this interpretation, both Cindy and Paul said, "Yes, that is right. We really love you! We affirm your leadership, but it is now our turn to move into ministry." So that evening Cindy, clearly anointed, taught about the baptism with the Holy Spirit and then handed the meeting over to Paul and affirmed that he with the team would be praying for people. All the while I was sitting in the back, feeling alone and perfectly miserable. The dance was going on just fine without me! Finally, I just sulked out and took a long walk. Several hours later the team gathered for a debriefing, thrilled with what the Lord had done in and through them. There had been a great outpouring of the Holy Spirit. The team had been launched into power ministry, and we spent a wonderful time debriefing how the Holy Spirit had worked so well. He had not needed me present to direct the evening in order to work.

The Danger of Spiritual Impatience

God's promises become reality. The Bible tells us, "The revelation awaits an appointed time; it speaks of the end and will not prove false. Though it linger, wait for it; it will certainly come and will not delay" (Hab. 2:3). Like an airplane pilot who is told by the controller to stay in a holding pattern until further instructions are given, sometimes we simply have to wait. There will be times when we have taken the steps that the Spirit has shown us and then we wait for guidance for the next step. But heaven seems silent: no kairos moment is given, no word of knowledge, no vision, no guidance — nothing. In times such as this, we are called to linger, to wait, for "those who wait for the Lord's help find renewed strength; they rise up as if they had eagles' wings" (Isa. 40:31 NET). We are told to enter the Holy Spirit's "holding pattern" and thus be enabled to work in the Lord's strength and time frame.

It is during this time of being in the holding pattern and waiting on the Lord that we face the dangers of impatience. We are tempted to step out of the dance led by the Holy Spirit and move into our own human efforts. We create our own plans, we create our own vision statement, and we may even fabricate "guidance" from the Lord. We set out under our own steam and find that it soon runs out. Burnout and exhaustion blight our ministries, and we begin to drift away from God's plans and purposes. This may "merely" lead to ineffective ministry. But if we persist like this, we may end up stepping out of the dance completely and departing from biblical faith.

I (Brad) battled with the temptation of impatience in the summer of 2008 as funds for a construction project ran dry. Overcome by impatience, I tried to resolve the situation in my own wisdom and strength. We were building our first accommodation unit at the Community of the Cross, using a workforce of willing volunteers and an excellent contractor. Money had been donated, more had been pledged, and we were eager to save costs by moving out of rented accommodations in town. But with $50,000 worth of work still to be done, the money ran out! Gifts that we thought were on the way never materialized, and our general funds were so low that we were struggling to meet the payroll.

This was a crisis! The packed program of events during the summer made a later move seem impossible, any delay meant paying more "unnecessary" rent, and there would be additional costs if heavy machinery had to be removed and brought back later. But PRMI has a policy of not spending money that we do not have, and so, reluctantly, we instructed the contractors to stop work. My heart was in turmoil as I watched workmen packing up their tools and construction equipment being driven away. I was driven into a swirling vortex of desperate prayer, overwhelming doubts, and severe impatience.

Several PRMI board members suggested that we should consider a loan, so I visited the bank. We could borrow the money to finish the building, pay less in interest than we were currently paying in rent and utilities, and repay the loan anytime without penalty. It all made very good business sense.

And it was all done without consulting the Lord. I had shifted away from trusting Jesus and his timing to trusting myself and the bank to get things started right away.

My wife, Laura, was horrified. She felt uneasy about PRMI borrowing money, and a verse from Scripture came to her mind: "The borrower is servant to the lender" (Prov. 22:7). Jesus is to be our Master, not the bank. When I shared the proposal with the PRMI staff, most were as impatient as I was to get into the building. But Cindy had the word, "Starting in the Spirit, are you now going to end with human effort?" and she pointed out that just before the money ran out, we had sent out a prayer letter asking for people to pray for the provision needed. She asked, "Should we not just wait on the Lord? Wouldn't a loan be depending on us instead of on Jesus?"

Her words put the brakes on my impatience and sent me back into prayer, seeking the Lord's guidance. The Holy Spirit annoyingly said, "You are not to make the decision alone. Submit it back to the PRMI board." I was irritated by facing another delay and was afraid that the board would fall into micromanagement. But after prayer and discernment, each board member contacted us with the same guidance: "In terms of good business practice, it makes sense to borrow the money and finish the building and stop paying rent. But the Holy Spirit is saying no. Ask people to pray about this, and trust the Lord."

As soon as we made this decision, a series of remarkable events took place, ensuring that the Lord, rather than PRMI, received credit for the building. One good friend offered to match gifts of up to $15,000. Someone else donated $15,000 before we had even mentioned the first pledge. And within a few weeks, the funds had been donated to complete the buildings, sewer system, and electricity.

Now, be careful not to learn the wrong lesson from this experience. I do not think it is wrong for a congregation to borrow money to complete a building project. There are times when that is completely appropriate and good stewardship that may be led by the Holy Spirit. The struggle was about me being so impatient that I was seriously tempted to step out of the dance of cooperating with the Holy Spirit and begin directing the dance myself. If we had solved this situation with our own counsel, we never would have seen the miracle of provision. We would have seen our own cleverness, but Jesus' goodness would have been obscured. Instead, we are able to say, "Look what God did!" The result is that we stayed in the dance with the Holy Spirit, and Jesus is getting all the glory.

I am surely not the only church leader who has been tempted to run ahead of God! The greater the responsibilities and opportunities for advancing God's kingdom, the greater our need to cultivate a leadership style that is led by the Holy Spirit and is willing to wait patiently for his guidance. This means that we must be submitted radically to following Jesus Christ and putting him first. We must be submitted to others who can help us in this task. And we must ruthlessly build into our busy schedules times of waiting on the Lord in prayer. Without these steps, we will press ahead of the Lord and sabotage his plans.

When the Devil Cuts in on the Dance

In dancing, "cutting in" happens when someone steps in to take the place of a dance partner. Montreat Presbyterian Church had organized a formal ballroom dance for the young women who were graduating from high school, and my wife, Laura, and I (Brad) were enjoying it very much. We noticed our daughter, Elizabeth, dancing with a fine young man, and Laura said, "Why, I think we should just cut in! You need to dance with our daughter, and I will dance with that handsome young man." So we danced over to where they were, and I signaled my intention to Elizabeth, who was delighted to dance with her daddy. Without missing a step, we made the change, and with a kiss and a whispered "I love you," I danced off with Elizabeth.

We could do this because we were there at the dance, we knew the steps, and we were also loved and trusted as part of the group. An intruder with obvious hostile intentions would not have succeeded. Indeed, he probably would have been blocked at the door and not welcomed in.

From the account of Eden, the experiences of Job, the teachings and works of Jesus, and the writings of Paul, Peter, and John, it is obvious that we have a spiritual enemy (Gen. 3:1–14; Job 1:1–2:7; Matt. 4:1–11; Mark 3:22–26; 2 Cor. 2:11; 1 Peter 5:8; 1 John 3:8). Satan will try any devious means possible to divert the church away from the Father's purposes, and oftentimes subversion is more successful that outright assault. "Satan himself masquerades as an angel of light" (2 Cor. 11:14), and we need to be diligent "in order that Satan might not outwit us. For we are not unaware of his schemes" (2:11). For the Devil to "cut in" on our dance of cooperation with the Holy Spirit, he must first find a way in through the people who are loved and trusted as part of the body of Christ. Having gained a foothold, he may then build a stronghold, a base from which he can work, leading believers into steps that were not ordered by God.

A Deceptive Generosity

In the early church, we see a clear example of the Devil trying to cut into the dance through two members of the fellowship, Ananias and his wife, Sapphira (Acts 5:1–11). We know little about them, but on the surface they probably seemed like really nice, wonderful people. In their own minds, their course of action may have seemed innocuous. They had freedom to give as much or as little as they wished, but they wanted others to regard them as being especially generous people. They appeared to be an admirable couple; their deception was completely hidden from the eyes of the people. Who would have suspected that they were simply pretending to be more generous than they truly were?

But Peter was given spiritual insight and exposed their deception. Rather than the fruit of the Spirit's work, Satan had filled their hearts and caused them to lie. Superficially they appeared to be cooperating with the gracious material provision that was being orchestrated by the Holy Spirit, but a shift had taken place within them. Satan had obtained a foothold and was now misleading them, working to create a stronghold of deception. What a different story it would have been if Ananias, rather than Barnabas,[2] had become influential within the church! Human sin is responsible for more than just causing us to trip up and get out of step with the Spirit. It also gives a foothold for another spirit, the Devil, to deceptively cut in on the dance.

Dancing with the Wrong Partner

As participants in the dance of cooperation, we must be alert to the Devil cutting in on our own dance with the Spirit before looking outward to observe it happening with others. There are several times in my (Brad's) own life where the Devil has cut in and started to direct me in the dance, but it is too embarrassing to give more than one example.

The foothold that Satan had in my own life was some deep hurt and wounding in my own heart that had not been fully healed. Some ten years previously one of my coworkers had been called to another ministry, but I had not forgiven the man for leaving. This foothold was entirely my fault, for the call was truly from the Lord and has contributed greatly to the advancement of the kingdom of God. But I still resented him for leaving and was left with a great insecurity about trusting coworkers in general. Satan had room to start to play on my insecurity.

---

2. Barnabas showed similar (but genuine) generosity and was instrumental in persuading the apostles to welcome the newly converted Paul and in restoring Mark's ministry.

Sometime later I had another coworker whom I trusted, and we worked very well together. But he began to experience some personal struggles, and in retrospect I believe he became less and less led by the Holy Spirit and was making choices that were inconsistent with our ministry vision. At the time, I experienced my own struggles about what to do about my coworker's problems, and although I knew I had to raise questions, I was really not sure what to say. Also, a subtle shift was taking place as I became more and more isolated from our leadership team.

The fact is I made a series of very bad decisions as I tried to keep this coworker happy rather than correcting him. Although his choices were causing problems for the whole team, I was afraid that if I made the needed course correction, I would lose this person as a friend and coworker. Being in leadership can be lonely, and sometimes the need for friendship can be so deep that one fails to notice when one's friend is no longer a friend of Jesus. I was blinded to this reality, and as a consequence, one area of PRMI's ministry ceased to be consistent with our own vision and was out of step with the leading of the Holy Spirit.

This would have continued with disastrous consequences, except for the intervention of another coworker. With words of knowledge given by the Spirit, she revealed my true motives to me and exposed how I had deceived myself and let Satan lead the dance. As she did so, the lights went on, and I realized that the Enemy, rather than Jesus, had been directing the dance. This humbling and terrible realization drove me to repentance, and mercifully the stronghold Satan had spent so much time building was dismantled and we all got back into the dance. I myself received prayer ministry for inner healing, including forgiveness and release of my feelings regarding the first coworker. I also had to resubmit myself to the oversight, love, and friendship of the board of directors and my other coworkers.

Staying on with Our Partner

It is tragic that human sinfulness can genuinely affect our ability to remain in step with the Spirit. Similarly, it is sobering to realize that Satan exploits human brokenness and sin, gaining a foothold by whatever means possible in order to derail the purposes of God. No wonder Peter warns us, "Be self-controlled and alert. Your enemy the devil prowls around like a roaring lion looking for someone to devour" (1 Peter 5:8).

We have included this chapter because these dangers we have discussed are genuine threats for anyone who seeks to participate in the great dance of cooperation with the Holy Spirit, and to be forewarned is to be forearmed so that we may stand firm in this battle (Eph. 6:11–13). But we wish to conclude the book by turning our attention to the wonderful synergy that happens as these Seven Dynamics interconnect. After all, when we remain with our proper partner, the dance can be exhilarating, creative, and powerful.

Chapter 17

The Synergy of the Dance

The Seven Dynamics have a synergy, an impact quickened by the Holy Spirit that is greater than the sum of all the parts. In this synergy people experience the very real presence of Jesus Christ working in and through his church in such a way that it truly is the body of Christ. As the church grows in practical understanding and experience of the Holy Spirit, the Spirit in turn grows the church so that it becomes an agent, vanguard, and expression of the kingdom of God on earth.

In the classroom one may dissect an eye, cutting it open to identify the various parts and learn the way in which each contributes to the whole. The iris adjusts to control how much light enters; muscles adjust the lens in order to focus light onto the retina; the retina senses the light and converts it to nerve impulses that are then carried by the optic nerve to the brain. None of the parts is intended to operate alone, and the true power of the eye is seen when all the parts combine. It is a wondrous organ that provides a dynamically changing view of the world around us. Through it we appreciate beauty and majesty, navigate pathways, observe data, and relate to people through visual clues.

In the preceding chapters of this book, we have treated the Seven Dynamics in a similar manner, "dissecting" the whole in order to clarify the contribution made by each part. We have surveyed the component steps that we can take in that great dance of cooperation with the Father, Son, and Holy Spirit. We have also given numerous case studies of how these dynamic steps of divine-human partnership have taken place in practice. These have come mostly from local church life or from events associated with the Dunamis Project, and we have described them in a way that highlights a particular dynamic, but in reality all seven Dynamics were operating in each story. As with the eye, all these distinctive facets belong together, and when they interconnect, we discover a wonderful synergy in which the church truly becomes a living expression of Jesus' sovereign presence.

These Seven Dynamics are not the curriculum for a particular church program, nor are they material for a particular style of congregational worship. A vast wealth of program and worship resources is available to the church, catering to a wide range of theological and cultural contexts and styles. But these dynamics address a more fundamental issue. They take us deeper. They put us more closely in touch with the heart, vision, and intentions of Jesus. They are the practicalities of seeking, discerning, and then acting on the guidance of the Holy Spirit, drawing us into active cooperation with the work that Jesus is doing. Thus they enable us to keep in step with the Spirit by engaging in the particular actions, ministry, program, or worship that he desires. These Seven Dynamics are the spiritual disciplines of allowing the Lord to direct the life of his people and his church.

In order that these dynamics can be integrated into the church's life, key biblical foundations must first be in place. Leaders have a formative influence within a church and therefore need to be people who themselves embody the reality of the kingdom of God. The four characteristics that we identified are *integration* into the body of Christ by being born again; *information*, which includes both "head" knowledge of the Bible and doctrine and "heart" knowledge of Jesus through a living relationship; *transformation* by the sanctifying work of the Holy Spirit within, creating Christlike character; and *empowerment* by being baptized with the Holy Spirit. A full balance of all these areas is essential, and therefore we need to acknowledge and redress the shortcomings in our own particular situation. The second foundation is that churches need to be growing to fullness in Christ, which includes the same four factors we have mentioned in connection with leaders.

With these Two Foundations in place, the church is able to learn the dance steps of cooperating with the Holy Spirit, whose purpose is growing congregations that are effective in advancing the kingdom of God in the world today. Through these dynamics, churches are able to experience Jesus as Prophet, Priest, and King. As Prophet Jesus speaks the Word of God in power and authority. As Priest he brings forgiveness, healing, cleansing, and reconciliation to his people. As King he advances the kingdom of God, calling men, women, and children to enter it, and overturns the kingdom of Satan. He is seen to be really present in the midst of his church.

Knowing the Real Presence of Jesus

The "real presence" of Jesus is a phrase usually associated with the Roman Catholic Church's teaching about the transformation of bread and wine used in communion. But the phrase cannot be narrowly restricted to this one area, for Jesus promised his presence as people gather in his name (Matt. 18:20) and as his church engages in its mission (28:20). As the body of Christ, the church should know his real presence throughout its life, and when these Seven Dynamics are integrated into the church's life, this presence becomes an experiential reality. We see and hear the evidence of Jesus at work in our midst.

Certainly this is what Paul anticipated as he wrote to the Corinthian church about what went on as they gathered to worship. Genuinely prophetic messages would demonstrate the very real presence of Jesus:

> But if an unbeliever or someone who does not understand comes in while everybody is prophesying, he will be convinced by all that he is a sinner and will be judged by all, and the secrets of his heart will be laid bare. So he will fall down and worship God, exclaiming, "God is really among you!"
>
> What then shall we say, brothers? When you come together, everyone has a hymn, or a word of instruction, a revelation, a tongue or an interpretation. All of these must be done for the strengthening of the church. (1 Cor. 14:24–26)

The church in Corinth certainly displayed some unhelpful excesses in the way they conducted themselves, but they also truly engaged in the dynamic of cooperation with the Holy Spirit. This enabled the church to be built up and enabled people—including visitors—to be aware that Father, Son, and Holy Spirit were truly present and at work.

I (Brad) experienced this happening on one occasion that was not a worship gathering but a wine and cheese party. Jesus himself supplied the wine for a wedding celebration, so I was very happy to experience his presence at this party too! I was the keynote speaker at a renewal conference in a growing congregation in northern California. During the conference I stayed at the home of a couple who had hosted a prayer meeting for more than twenty years.

They had started this home prayer meeting after they were baptized with the Holy Spirit, and with the full support of the pastor, this prayer group had been the beginning place of nurturing the Seven Dynamics for the whole congregation. The synergy of the dance was seen in the many programs the church ran. It was seen in the packed-out worship service where we experienced the holy presence of Jesus, in the growing number of people coming to that church, in the mission trips they undertook, in the service they gave to the homeless, and in the deep fellowship they shared in one another's homes. The presence of God the Father, Son, and Holy Spirit in that congregation was almost tangible.

But what struck me the most was what I found at the wine and cheese party on Saturday night. At this party were the church leaders as well as many members of the home prayer group. I was a little skeptical about the California culture in wine country, because it did not feel at all "churchy," and I wondered whether these classy-looking people could really be Christians. But all my doubts about their authenticity quickly dissolved as I caught snippets of conversation as I moved from group to group. "I wonder what Jesus is going to say to us in the service." "I am so amazed and thankful for what Jesus did in the life of my non-Christian friend I brought to the last prayer meeting. She had never experienced such love before and was just blown away when the Holy Spirit spoke right into her life." "May I offer you an excellent cabernet? It comes from the vineyard not far from here." "Thanks. Here's to you Jesus! I praise you that you are the resurrection and the life!" "Yes! Lord, I love you! Here's to you! Thank you for setting me free!" "I have been reading our Sunday school lesson, and the Holy Spirit has really been speaking to me. What did you learn from that passage?"

I was astonished! These people were truly excited, not about their nice church or its programs, but about what God was doing in their midst. They talked about Jesus as if he was truly real and present. And in that congregation he certainly is a real working, speaking, healing, and delivering Person.

In the midst of that party there was a kairos moment of opportunity, and I encountered Jesus there as well. I was being introduced to one group as the new executive director of PRMI. I was in the middle of explaining the purpose of our ministry when suddenly one of the people said, "Hold on just a moment! I think the Holy Spirit is moving!" At that moment, I was aware of his manifest presence, and one of the women said, "Yes, I think I may be getting a word of prophecy for you in your work." She spoke out the word, and it was right on track, connecting with an issue that I had been struggling with but had not mentioned to anyone.

"Yes!" I said, "that is right on!"

"May we pray for you?" someone offered, and immediately they put down their wine glasses and all laid hands on me and prayed. For the next thirty minutes, through them dancing in step with the Holy Spirit, Jesus ministered to me and spoke to me in the deep places in my soul. It was the most exhilarating wine and cheese party I had ever attended! And it turned out that Jesus Christ and God the Father, through the Holy Spirit, were at the party as well and dancing with the people.

When a congregation is moving in the Seven Dynamics and is caught up in the dance led by the Holy Spirit, every aspect of its life is affected. Every gathering place becomes holy ground. Whenever and wherever the church gathers, the believers know the real presence of Jesus.

But the conversations, prophecy, and prayer at the wine and cheese party are only a sample of what happens as the church learns to cooperate with the Holy Spirit. In the early chapters of Acts, we see six areas of activity that characterized this Spirit-led, Spirit-equipped community of Jesus' people. These areas of activity gave expression to the kingdom of God, making it objectively real in people's experience.

Expressing the Reality of the Kingdom of God

The kingdom of God is the central theme of Scripture. This kingdom—the exercise of divine government[1]—is seen from the delegated, representative dominion entrusted to our first parents in Eden, via the Jewish nation called to live under the rule of Yahweh, right through the ministry and message of Jesus, and on to the climactic vision of the new Jerusalem in the book of Revelation. As Jesus began his ministry, he announced, "The time has come.... The kingdom of God is near. Repent and believe the good news!" (Mark 1:15). His parables painted pictures of the kingdom, his miracles demonstrated the reality of that kingdom, and changed lives bore witness to it. Demons were evicted, sinners were reoriented, sick bodies were restored, hungry people were fed, and men, women, and children chose to follow him. Jesus was (and still is!) reigning as King.

The early church continued Jesus' ministry, guided and enabled by the Holy Spirit. The reign of God was evident in their lives, just as it had been in Jesus' own life, and showed itself in six areas of activity. Each of these could easily be explored in much more detail, but our purpose here is simply to highlight how the Spirit directed the church so that it expressed God's government. These are not merely programs that were voted for by a board. They are areas of work that the Spirit led them to engage in that fulfill Jesus' vision and purpose for his church.

1. *Empowered preaching and teaching of the Word of God.* Peter was anointed by the Spirit to proclaim the message about Jesus on the day of Pentecost; in Solomon's Colonnade, having healed a lame beggar; and on several other

---

1. R. T. France writes, "I have offered the phrase 'divine government' as another way of avoiding the unfortunately territorial or institutional implications of 'kingdom,' while retaining its dynamic focus." R. T. France, *Divine Government* (London: SPCK, 1990), 13.

specific occasions in the book of Acts. Stephen (Acts 6:10; 7:2–60), Philip (Acts 8:5–12), Paul (e.g., Acts 9:17–22; 13:16–52; 14:1), and Apollos (Acts 18:24–28) did the same. With opportunities, insights, and words supplied by the Holy Spirit, the message of God was declared faithfully and powerfully, impacting lives and enriching people's understanding.

2. *Spirit-led corporate worship, prayer, and fellowship.* The Spirit created a true community, drawing people together in homes and in the temple for praise, prayer, and meals. They participated in the corporate worship, not only with their songs, but also by exercising a variety of spiritual gifts. They met frequently and shared their material resources, growing in their relationship with the risen Christ and with each other.

3. *Ministries of prayer, compassion, and healing that meet human need.* Peter and John were involved with the healing of a lame beggar. Crowds brought people who were sick or tormented by evil spirits, and all of them were healed. Deacons distributed food daily to needy widows, and the believers redistributed their finances for the benefit of the whole community.

4. *Governance and management of the fellowship and the ministries.* The apostles oversaw the life of the fellowship, taking practical steps to ensure that the daily distribution of food was managed in an appropriate manner by people who were known to be full of the Holy Spirit and wisdom. Elders were appointed to give leadership to local congregations, and unity of understanding and practice were promoted through the decision made at the Jerusalem council (Acts 15:1–29).

5. *Turning converts into disciples of Jesus Christ for life and work in the kingdom of God.* New believers were welcomed into the community, and their faith was nurtured by the apostles' teaching and by participation in the worship and witness. They were taught to obey everything Jesus had commanded, and they were educated, encouraged, and corrected through letters and personal visits.

6. *Evangelism that extends the kingdom of God and routs Satan.* The gospel message was proclaimed to crowds, presented in chariots, and discussed at riversides. Signs, wonders, and miracles gave supporting evidence to the news about the life-changing, death-trumping power of God. People emigrated from the dominion of darkness into the kingdom of the Son of God.

The kingdom of God that Jesus spoke about became observable reality in the lives of these early Christians. They not only experienced the presence of Jesus, but also evidenced the reign of Jesus. These activities all happened because the church was growing in its understanding and experience of the power of the Holy Spirit. And because of this, the Holy Spirit was actively growing the church. People entered the kingdom of God by being born again. They did the work of the kingdom by acting as coworkers with God here on earth. And thus God's original intentions for humankind were being restored and the work of Jesus was being continued through the agency of the Holy Spirit.

When we ask, "What *did* Jesus do?" we look backward and ensure that faith is rooted in scriptural revelation. When we ask, "What *would* Jesus do?" we look at our choices and ensure that our actions are compatible with the teaching and example of Jesus. But we also need to ask, "What *is* Jesus doing?" as we look around us and listen to the Holy Spirit so that we may join in with his activity. Jesus did only what he saw the Father doing. We are called to do the same!

Many Personal Stories

We have told many personal stories in the chapters of this book, illustrating ways in which we have endeavored to discern and cooperate with the activity of the Spirit. These are risky stories, for they might simply sound impressive. We would rather omit them than give the appearance of boasting, but they can (and should) be a source of encouragement and inspiration for readers to discover more about living in cooperation with the Holy Spirit. It may sound like a cliché, but the three of us have plenty of experience of getting it wrong, failing to appreciate what the Spirit was doing, or striving in our own wisdom and strength. Many of these could be summed up briefly by saying, "Well, we missed it that time."

We have featured two churches, Montreat Presbyterian Church and Plymstock United Church, most often, because these are the local church contexts with which we are most familiar. We wish they were perfect, but the reality is that any growing church is going to have a range of maturity and experience within it. There are newcomers who know little of these dynamics, longstanding members who have yet to appreciate what they are all about, and others who have begun to dance in step with the Spirit. The situation is simultaneously thrilling and frustrating. We are delighted by the growth and progress that have been made, and frustrated because there is so much yet to be learned. But that's just the way it is.

As the church grows in its understanding and experience of the Holy Spirit's power, learning to participate in the dance of cooperation, the Holy Spirit grows the church. This is the way Jesus intended it to be. It's what he said in his final conversation before ascending to his Father's throne (Acts 1:4–8).

"He gave them this command:"

Are we prepared to obey it?

"Wait for the gift my Father promised, which you have heard me speak about."

Do we believe Jesus' teaching?

"You will be baptized with the Holy Spirit."

Have we received this baptism?

"You will receive power when the Holy Spirit comes on you;"

Are we operating in that power?

"And you will be my witnesses ... to the ends of the earth."

About the Authors

Dr. Zeb Bradford Long (DMin, Union Theological Seminary, Richmond, VA), an ordained PCUSA minister, is Executive Director of Presbyterian-Reformed Ministries International (PRMI), a mission organization working for spiritual renewal and church growth around the world. Brad served as a Presbyterian missionary in Korea and Taiwan for ten years before coming to PRMI. He has written extensively about the person and work of the Holy Spirit and how to cooperate with the Holy Spirit in missions and ministry today. Brad and his wife live in Black Mountain, NC.

Paul Keith Stokes (MA, Cambridge University) was ordained in 1992 by the United Reformed Church in the United Kingdom. Paul is minister of Plymstock United Church and is an Evangelism and Renewal Advocate for the Group for Evangelism And Renewal (GEAR). He became involved with the PRMI Dunamis Project in November 2001, served as Track Director for six years from 2003, and in 2005 was appointed as one of three national directors for the newly formed Dunamis Fellowship in Britain and Ireland. Paul has two children and lives in Plymouth, Devon, England.

Cynthia R. P. Strickler (MDiv, Princeton Theological Seminary) was ordained by the PCUSA in 1986. She is the Director of the Dunamis Fellowship International, the international leadership team of PRMI. The Fellowship's purpose is to mobilize, equip, and deploy Holy Spirit-empowered witnesses for Jesus Christ around the world. Before joining the ministry staff of PRMI, Cindy worked as a hospital chaplain and a certified ACPE supervisor in central New Jersey. She and her husband live in Lenoir, NC.

Share Your Thoughts

With the Author: Your comments will be forwarded to the author when you send them to *zauthor@zondervan.com*.

With Zondervan: Submit your review of this book by writing to *zreview@zondervan.com*.

Free Online Resources at
www.zondervan.com

Zondervan AuthorTracker: Be notified whenever your favorite authors publish new books, go on tour, or post an update about what's happening in their lives.

Daily Bible Verses and Devotions: Enrich your life with daily Bible verses or devotions that help you start every morning focused on God.

Free Email Publications: Sign up for newsletters on fiction, Christian living, church ministry, parenting, and more.

Zondervan Bible Search: Find and compare Bible passages in a variety of translations at www.zondervanbiblesearch.com.

Other Benefits: Register yourself to receive online benefits like coupons and special offers, or to participate in research.